The Morphology of Tourism

Morphological research studies the physical form of landscapes, including how landscape structures function and operate, the adaptability of forms, and how functions and forms change over time. Applying the methods and models of morphology to tourism, this innovative book explores some of the complex relationships between tourism and morphological changes in urban and rural destinations across the globe.

Tourism-related impacts on the physical environment and sociocultural values surrounding a given destination reflect the need for both theoretical and empirical approaches to strengthen our understanding of the ways in which tourism functions. This study examines key sectors and locations such as coastal tourism, urban tourism, and waterfront redevelopment, which are increasingly important in terms of their influence on sociocultural and morphological transformation. It advocates that awareness of the critical link between temporospatial impacts and morphological progresses is necessary to accommodate changes within a pattern of evolutionary growth.

International in scope, employing case studies from Asia, Australasia, the US, and Europe, this book makes a new contribution to the literature and will be of interest to students and researchers of tourism planning, urban design, geography, environmental studies and landscape architecture.

Philip Feifan Xie is Professor of the Tourism, Hospitality and Event Management program at Bowling Green State University, Ohio, USA. His areas of specialization include cultural and heritage tourism, tourism analysis, and event management.

Kai Gu is Associate Professor of the School of Architecture and Planning, University of Auckland, New Zealand. His areas of specialization are in urban morphology and urban design.

New Directions in Tourism Analysis
Series Editor: Dimitri Ioannides, E-TOUR,
Mid Sweden University, Sweden

Although tourism is becoming increasingly popular both as a taught subject and as an area for empirical investigation, the theoretical underpinnings of many approaches have tended to be eclectic and somewhat underdeveloped. However, recent developments indicate that the field of tourism studies is beginning to develop in a more theoretically informed manner, but this has not yet been matched by current publications.

The aim of this series is to fill this gap with high-quality monographs or edited collections that seek to develop tourism analysis at both theoretical and substantive levels using approaches which are broadly derived from allied social science disciplines such as Sociology, Social Anthropology, Human and Social Geography, and Cultural Studies. As tourism studies covers a wide range of activities and subfields, certain areas such as Hospitality Management and Business, which are already well provided for, would be excluded. The series will therefore fill a gap in the current overall pattern of publication.

Suggested themes to be covered by the series, either singly or in combination, include consumption, cultural change, development, gender, globalisation, political economy, social theory, and sustainability.

44 **Being and Dwelling through Tourism**
   An Anthropological Perspective
   Catherine Palmer

45 **Resort Spatiality**
   Reimagining Sites of Mass Tourism
   Zelmarie Cantillon

46 **The Morphology of Tourism**
   Planning for Impact in Tourist Destinations
   Philip Feifan Xie and Kai Gu

For more information about this series, please visit www.routledge.com/New-Directions-in-Tourism-Analysis/book-series/ASHSER1207

The Morphology of Tourism

Planning for Impact in
Tourist Destinations

Philip Feifan Xie
and Kai Gu

Routledge
Taylor & Francis Group

LONDON AND NEW YORK

First published 2019
by Routledge
2 Park Square, Milton Park, Abingdon, Oxon OX14 4RN

and by Routledge
605 Third Avenue, New York, NY 10017

First issued in paperback 2021

Routledge is an imprint of the Taylor & Francis Group, an informa business

Publisher's Note
The publisher has gone to great lengths to ensure the quality of this reprint but points out that some imperfections in the original copies may be apparent.

British Library Cataloguing-in-Publication Data
A catalogue record for this book is available from the British Library

Library of Congress Cataloging-in-Publication Data
A catalog record has been requested for this book

Typeset in Sabon
by codeMantra

ISBN 13: 978-1-03-224173-9 (pbk)
ISBN 13: 978-1-4724-7878-8 (hbk)

DOI: 10.4324/9781315555461

Contents

List of figures   vii
List of tables   ix
Preface   xi

Introduction   1
The production of space 1
Urban morphology and tourism 4
The emergence of morphological thinking in tourism 7
Problems of the tourism-morphology nexus 10
The book's structure and themes 11

1 **The historical development of urban morphology**   17
Introduction 17
Relevant theories in urban morphology 19
Summary 37

2 **A conceptual framework for the morphology of tourism**   42
Green spaces, genius loci and non-lieux 42
The history of tourism morphology 47
Elements of urban tissue for tourism 56
Toward an integrated approach to the morphology of tourism 64
Summary 67

3 **Morphological changes and the evolution of coastal resorts**   69
Introduction 69
BRM and conceptual framework 70
Methodology 75
Morphological analysis 76
Research implications 86
Summary 88

4 **Destination morphology in an ancient Chinese city** 90
Introduction 90
Urban morphology in China 92
Research setting 95
Methodology 104
Stages of tourism development 105
Summary 112

5 **Morphological processes and impacts of tourism** 115
Introduction 115
Waterfront redevelopment and impacts of tourism 117
*The morphological process of the waterfronts in
    Auckland and Wellington 119*
Methodology 124
*The impact of governance structures on
    morphological changes 125*
*Morphological processes in Auckland and
    Wellington waterfronts 129*
The impact of tourism on morphological changes 132
Summary 135

6 **Urban fringe belts and the tourist-historic city** 139
Introduction 139
The historic city of como 142
Methodology 145
Streets, plots and buildings in Como 146
The three fringe belts of Como 148
Evolving trajectories of tourism development 152
Summary 155

Conclusions 158
Summary of the chapters 160
Conjoining habitus, parallax, and the longue durée *166*
Critical considerations for the morphology of tourism 168

References 173
Index 199

List of figures

1.1   Basic elements of the ground plan   22
1.2   The Traditions of Landscape Research and Urban Morphology   38
2.1   The Cheonggyecheon Stream in Seoul, Korea for Changing
      the Natural Context   59
2.2   Fatehpur Sikri (the City of Victory) in the Northeast of India   60
2.3   Conceptual Framework of the Morphology of Tourism   66
3.1   Conceptual Framework for Denarau Island, Fiji   75
3.2   Cartographic Representation of the Morphological
      Elements of Denarau Island from 1977 to 2007   78
4.1   An Aerial View of Pingyao   95
4.2   Morphological Frames and Fixation Lines in Pingyao   97
4.3   Morphological Hierarchy of Streets in Pingyao   99
4.4   Plot Types in Pingyao   101
4.5   Changes of Ownership Boundaries and Building Block-
      Plans in Pingyao's Courtyards   103
4.6   Evolutionary Morphology in Pingyao   111
5.1a The Waterfront Areas Adjacent to the CBDs in Auckland   120
5.1b The Waterfront Areas Adjacent to the CBDs in Wellington   121
5.2   The Formative Processes of the Waterfront Areas in
      Auckland and Wellington   122
5.3   Principal Plan Units in the Waterfront in Auckland
      and Wellington   123
6.1   The Main Built-Up Areas and Topography of Como   144
6.2   Fringe Belt Evolution and Land Use in Como   149
6.3   The Three Fringe Belts   151

List of tables

1.1 The Existing Morphological Analysis 39
3.1 The Development of Resort Morphology Research 75
3.2 The Morphological Changes in Denarau Island, Fiji 79
5.1 Key Urban Planning and Design Documents Prepared for
     Auckland's Waterfront Redevelopment 126
5.2 Key urban Planning and Design Documents Prepared for
     Wellington's Waterfront Redevelopment 127
5.3 Characteristics of Streets, Plots and Buildings of the Plan
     Units in Auckland's Waterfront Area 130
5.4 Characteristics of Streets, Plots and Buildings of the Plan
     Units in Wellington's Waterfront Area 131

Preface

The impetus for this book was responding to a number of theoretical gaps in the fields of urban morphology and tourism studies. The former primarily focuses on the physical form of landscapes, including how landscape structures operate, the adaptability of structural forms, the dominant functions of a given structure, and how functions and forms change over time. Urban morphology has long been utilized in a wide range of disciplines, ranging from geography, archaeology, history, and ecology, to urban planning and landscape architecture. Its methodologies and theoretical concerns facilitate multisite explorations of urban form while providing a context for a gamut of seemingly disparate literature. However, only a few, if any, attempts have been made to apply the methods and models of urban morphology to tourism. *The Morphology of Tourism* is perhaps the first book-length study addressing the morphology of tourist destinations. Our aim is to facilitate a better understanding of the relationship between tourism, the physical environment, and changing sociocultural values; as well as the flow of people, capital, goods, and ideas that form the core of tourism development. The key centers on the impact studies distributed in space and time at various locations.

This book would never have taken shape as it did without two reasons. First, our long-standing interest in the morphology of tourism is kindled by a familiarity with and curiosity about vacationscapes, which was solidified by the completion of a PhD degree in urban and regional planning. Both authors graduated at the University of Waterloo, Canada, and our experiences have fed the curiosity about planning and urban design. Particularly, Dr. Kai Gu was former Secretary-General of the International Seminar on Urban Form who has been active in the study of urban morphology. Second, our interests in morphology are based on our experiences visiting and living in a number of radically changing cities worldwide. In recent decades, economic prosperity has precipitated the redevelopment of urban areas, and many cities are building futuristic skylines of gleaming metal and glass towers at breakneck speed. While these cities benefit from their regeneration, some are increasingly becoming places for tourists rather than for inhabitants. As part of this process, a growing number of tourist destinations have been stripped of their sense of place and are in danger of entering a state of "placelessness." For example, both authors have visited major metropolises like Hong Kong and Macau, where burgeoning numbers of jewelry shops and pharmacies selling milk powders mainly target tourists from Mainland China, filling the already overcrowded streets. As a result, the changing morphology of streets, spaces, and buildings has led to a dramatic rise in rental prices and a marginalization of local businesses, affecting the livelihood of local people. There is a lack of balance between tourism development and protection of a city's history, personality, and sense of community.

It is evident that the socioeconomic milieu in which research and practice are undertaken is a crucial factor in understanding spatial arrangements. Urban morphology goes hand in glove with tourism development. However, this is not to suggest that the direction of the relationship is or should be unidirectional. In the fertile interrelationship of research and practice, understanding gained from the experience of tourism activities can contribute to the advancement of morphological theory. Tourism is not only a means of creating new urban forms but also a means of understanding them. Hence, morphology and tourism can become mutually supportive. There is a strong need to broaden the scope of morphological research in tourism, which can be accomplished by further combining a realm of research as a geographic subdiscipline in its own right and by embracing this study area within a number of other disciplines such as urban and regional planning.

The book is comprehensive in nature and provides a good foundation for examining the nature of tourism morphology. It attempts to (1) show the causal relationships between morphology and tourism using different models, particularly the historico-geographical approach, in order to contextualize changes within a pattern of evolutionary growth; (2) demonstrate how tourism morphology can be theorized from historical, cultural, social, and economic perspectives; (3) present case studies that compare decision-making and regional planning processes between multiple countries in Asia, Australasia, and Europe; and (4) make suggestions about the future of morphology research and development in tourism.

The main goal of this book is to provide systematic analyses of the tourism–morphology nexus. By tracing the historical development and current state of tourism and morphological changes, it pays close attention to key sectors, such as coastal tourism, urban tourism, and waterfront redevelopment, which influence the morphological change of origin–destination flows. We will substantiate the choices in terms of compelling reasons for case studies work here, consisting of the current diversification of urban forms. We believe this study, and the field it outlines, will be useful for planners, marketers, and practitioners, and serve as a scholarly text for tourism researchers, geographers, and urban planners interested in enhancing their understanding of the morphogenetic process and forms of tourist destinations. It should be of interest to tourism industry and policymakers who wish to enhance their cognizance of the management of morphological transformation.

We are grateful for the intellectual support and friendship of urban morphology researchers such as Dr. Jeremy Whitehand, Professor Emeritus of the University of Birmingham, who is one of the world leaders in this field. He not only provided invaluable assistance in our research but also continues to challenge, test, and refine our understanding of the morphology of tourism. We are indebted to Adrienne Hill at Bowling Green State University in the US, who did an outstanding job copyediting the manuscript and made many helpful suggestions for improving both the writing and the content.

Finally, we express our appreciation for the continuing support and assistance of Ms. Carlotta Fanton, the Editorial Assistant at Taylor & Francis/ Routledge. Her generous support and involvement, with whom we are proud to be associated, has placed Routledge as the world's leading publisher of scholarly tourism texts.

Introduction

The production of space

The rubrics of architecture, emphasizing *firmitas, utilitas,* and *venustas,* reflect a complicated system for the built fabric of cities. In this system, urban materiality is inextricably intertwined with space usage. Both are influenced by the cultures that inhabit a given space, and urban form reshapes culture in turn. Changing landscapes have functioned for different purposes over periods of time. For example, former fortifications, such as walls and fortresses, have become major tourist attractions; coastlines and waterfronts originally reserved for the shipbuilding industry have been set apart distinction for the purpose of leisure, and transportation infrastructure, such as railways and highways, has been appropriated for a range of recreational activities. Concomitantly, aspects of urban form contribute to socially dividing the city into precincts now turns into a draw for tourists to gaze the gentrifying neighborhoods. Whether cultural landscapes progress gradually over time or result from extensive urban planning, they demonstrate and influence the city's multitude of identities, industries, and economies at varying points in its history.

The word "architecture" is widely used to describe what urban morphology refers to as the form and diversity of urban spaces (Kropf 2009, 2017). The rediscovery of place through temporospatial analysis becomes a norm in contemporary society. Lefebvre's seminal book, *The Production of Space,* proposes the existence of a "differential space" in urban environments, where planning was not considered a subject in its own right until the rise of medieval towns and the subsequent establishment of "urban systems" in Europe. His conceptual triad for space encompasses spatial practice, representation of space and representational space. Lefebvre (1992: 46) further suggests that the impact of industrialization has morphed in the mode of production where "the shift from one mode to another must entail the production of a new space." In a similar vein, Foucault (1982: 187), through the study of Heidegger's "nearness" of both time and place, proposes a "space of domination," in which isomorphic forms illustrate institutional regimes in the built fabric. Space has a morphogenesis, including socioeconomic and environmental impacts, and is an ever-changing historical entity (Mugavin 1999).

Spatial development has been an integral part of the urban planning and landscape architecture fields since the Enlightenment and Industrial Revolution, during which many European cities were remade into symbols of the nation-state (Vale 1992). The ensuing movements, from the City Beautiful in the late 1800s, to the Garden City in the early 1900s, to contemporary New Urbanism, reshape identity, experience, and behavior in urban settings (Smith 2002, Lew 2017). For example, DeJean (2014) documents that the Parisian model for urban space was in fact invented in early seventeenth century, when the first full design for the French capital was implemented. During this period, Paris became the first city to tear down its fortifications. A large-scale urban plan was created and executed, with organized streets and boulevards, modern bridges, sidewalks, and public parks. Venues opened for urban entertainment of all kinds, from opera and ballet to recreational shopping. Therefore, a great city should be more than a collection of major buildings or monuments. It is worthy of a visit because of contemporary architecture, economic life, cultural activities, and the range of entertainments that made it vibrant.

From an architect-urbanist perspective, an urban reality, in the form of chaos, constantly produces new types of spaces, which become fundamental to the everyday practices of a society (Castello 2010, Certeau 2011). A space is not a background object, but a specific social production, supporting usages that are themselves specific (Depaule 1995). As time passes, space becomes more mobile and dynamic, bearing the mark of temporal flows (Grosz 2001, Gehl 2011). Similarly, the concept of *fabrique urbaine* (Noizet 2009) posits a socio-spatial urban development model, in which the practices and representations of the residents may be analyzed as a series of historical moments, or "social temporalities." Then the spatial structure of the town, especially the aggregation of plots into street blocks, can be precisely described, but with its own temporalities. The link between social history and urban morphology illustrates that social temporalities are not conscious steps in the process of the development of the urban fabric. Instead, there is a dialectical interaction between these two orders of facts.

In a sense, a space perceived as a territory frames chaos provisionally and in the process produces qualities (Grosz 2008). However, the space increasingly becomes heterogeneous at higher spatial levels, containing a variegated mix of commercialization (Prideaux and Singer 2005). Over time, such spaces can become popular tourist destinations. The spatial values, perceptions, memories and traditions become a landscape with a new meaning. Tourist cities are palimpsest which have changed over time and demonstrated evidence of these changes. Particularly, a city represents a layering of multiple activities and cultures that unfold within the same place over time. Each layer constitutes the base for the next layer that gets added, and consequently, built elements can be sustained through time and leave their own distinct imprints in space.

The cultural geography tradition has begun to draw on an actor–network theory in thinking about the complexity and richness of space (Oliveira 2016). For example, Thrift (2003: 95) argues that space is not a common sense external background to human and social action; rather, it is "the outcome of a series of highly problematic temporary settlements that divide and connect things up into different kinds of collectives which are slowly provided with the means which render them durable and sustainable." One of his proposed dimensions includes the place space, which not only offers certain kinds of interaction, but also provides cues to memory and behavior. Place is involved with embodiment and continuous transformation. In such a case, morphology may be understood as the form and function of a place, as well as the shifting relationship between form and function over time. The interplay of time and space determines the characteristics of morphology. Stanilov (2010) considers the reciprocal benefits of connecting urban modeling more closely with morphology and argues that combining land-use dynamics with building typology gained from morphological analysis is critical in understanding of how cities grow and change. He also envisages recreational activities for strengthening the sense of place in the management of the built environment beyond its role in conservation.

Despite the growing importance of spatial-temporal development, only a small body of literature addresses the possible link between spatial changes and tourist activities. Logan and Molotch (1987) initially propose a theory of "urban fortunes," which assumes that a growth machine can be fueled by a select group of players via a process of continuous spatial development and reinvestment. This theory implies that the emergence of urban centers through spatial development produces wealth, which, if appropriately reinvested, can lead to additional upward mobility. The emerging tourism space is a type of urban fortune, which transforms both rural and urban landscapes and creates an assortment of identities (Makowska-Iskierka 2013). Similarly, Clark (2004) coins the term "entertainment machine," emphasizing the role of the entertainment and tourism industry in attracting large numbers of visitors and causing the local economy to flourish. In recent decades, the development of cultural and entertainment activity has become a kind of a new urban development factor. The green space has gradually morphed into a "city of leisure" and exerted potential impact on spatial organization. As a result, the city yields a variety of images of "third places," places where individuals spend most of their time after regular home and work (Oldenburg 1989). Clark argues that even in a former industrial power like the city of Chicago in the US, entertainment has become a leading industry, in which city officials define as including tourism, conventions, restaurants, hotels, and related economic activities. An entertainment machine arises when "workers in the elite sectors of the postindustrial city make 'quality of life' demands, and in their consumption practices can experience their own urban location as if tourists, emphasizing aesthetic concerns." These practices impact considerations about the proper nature of "amenities" on urban growth. The city is an "entertainment machine" whose fortunes are increasingly constituted by flows, mobilities, and connections, as well as the product of performativity leveraging culture to enhance its economic well-being. From the notion of "spaces of flows" (Castells 1989) to "a sociology of fluids" (Urry 2007), spatialized encounters activate processes of cultural negotiation and new identity formation, which underpin the symbolic relevance of the city. As the entertainment components of cities are actively and strategically produced through political and economic activity, they become the work of many urban actors.

Urban morphology and tourism

Morphology comes from the Greek root word *morph*, meaning "shape." Urban morphology originated from morphogenetic studies reveals the physical and spatial structure of cities (Moudon 1994). It studies all physical elements of the cities, including streets, squares, buildings, and plots of land; and its theoretical concerns include the relationship between form and function, how structures operate, and how features of the urban landscape adapt and change over time (Pearce 1978, Liu and Wall 2009). It began to take shape at the end of nineteenth century as a field of study concerned with landscape (Whitehand 2007). Urban morphology is characterized by a number of different perspectives, but some of its most important roots are in the work of German-speaking geographers. Arguably, the father of urban morphology was the geographer Otto Schlüter, who envisaged the city as part of the wider landscape (*landschaft*) (Schlüter 1899). Particularly under his influence, the urban landscape (*stadtlandschaft*) came to occupy a central place within human geography in the first three decades of the twentieth century. This early period of urban morphology within geography had a marked influence on how the field developed in the course of the twentieth century. From its very beginning, urban morphology was, in keeping with its origins in geography, inherently about distinguishing, characterizing, and explaining urban landscapes.

Historically, there are at least two schools of urban morphology: the British school advocated by M.R.G Conzen, and the Italian school, founded by the architects Muratori and Caniggia. Both schools concern themselves with "a study of the city as human habitat" (Moudon 1997: 3), and they define the city as "the accumulation and the integration of many individuals and small groups, themselves governed by cultural traditions and shaped by social and economic forces over time." The field stresses the concrete outcomes of socioeconomic forces and analyzes the prism of its physical form. It reflects a dominant function in a specific setting, such as commerce, residence, recreation, or industry (Pearce 1978). In recent decades, urban morphology has become increasingly interdisciplinary, deriving from more traditional fields of knowledge, such as archaeology, architecture, history, geography, landscape architecture, urban planning, and urban design. A number of generalizations with respect to morphology and the functional structure of towns and cities are apparent in the field of urban geography. Only a few, if any, attempts have been made to apply these models in the context of tourism and resource management planning (Xie and Gu 2011).

The enthusiasm for the morphological approach that has developed in the past decades is inextricably tied to the increasing interest in cultural heritage and the political project of urban revitalization. Urban morphological features often form the focal point of tourism promotion, and some are important tourist attractions. The space of tourism impacts land use, recreational buildings, and the development of spatial patterns. Thus, urban morphology can be utilized as a tool to make analytical assessments and to find answers for the preceding questions (Edwards et al. 2008). Generally, recreational land use begins with minor modifications to the natural landscape, with small-scale tourism development, the success of which initiates further development and extensions until the landscape has been completely transformed. This leads to concerns about environmental, social, economic, and cultural degradation, as the decline and failure of tourism infrastructure begin. Similarly, the growing rural transformation development forces traditional villages to reshape themselves. It is accompanied with the land-use change, especially the changes of arable and residential land (Long and Li 2012).

Tourism is traditionally viewed as less important to cities than activities such as manufacturing or finance; however, it has increasingly become a global priority and has changed the way the cities operate, look, and feel. Tourism development benefits local land markets, elevating property values by increasing demand for centrally located sites and by creating positive externalities for space adjacent to tourist sites (Fainstein et al. 2003). Tourism impacts on the multidimensional urban space are of great importance nowadays. "Tourist-historic cities" (Ashworth and Tunbridge 1990) and "cultural-creative city" serve to improve pedestrian access in the city centers, develop tertiary services, and retail settings, along with the necessary refurbishment of streets and historical buildings.

The significance of tourism can be understood via a developmental perspective encompassing four interlocking themes (Spirou 2011: 2). First, postwar urban restructuring forced cities to search for alternative means of economic development. Rapidly evolving elements of globalization led cities to embrace a variety of entrepreneurial strategies, which, in turn, helped position tourism as a viable industry, one that came to be quickly viewed as capable of generating positive economic benefits. Second, the emergence of tourism as a fiscal growth strategy reorganized the physical landscape of cities. The massive development of infrastructure changed the built environment in ways not seen since the early period of city building. Third, the remaking of the urban core through tourism altered the culture of cities, and drew greater number of people from all walks of life. Fourth, some of the implications associated with the rise of tourism included controversial social and economic benefits, the diversion of valuable resources, and difficulty sustaining an identity for both visitors and residents in the long run.

By the end of the twentieth century, most world cities have focused on tourism as a source of revenue (Hoffman et al. 2003). The economic and cultural production of cities through tourism becomes instrumental in late capitalism (Rabbiosi 2015). It is an intensely geographic phenomenon involving the pursuit of the embodied experience of other places, both as individuals and in groups, and at scales from the local to the increasingly global. Tourism appears in diverse forms, such as entertainment places, shopping malls, historical settings, museums, and hybrid complexes, directly impacting the urban form. Gotham (2002: 1753) opines that tourism is "something involving people traveling to locations that are consumed as spaces of consumption, instead of the circulation of commodities among people." Urban commodification and the construction of tourist spaces are omnipresent in major cities that Berdet (2013: 155) defines as *fantasmagories du capital postmodernes* (postmodern phantasmagorias of capital).

Tourism research explores subjects such as the patterns of and processes behind the distribution of tourist phenomena, the evolution of land use, the influence of landscapes, and the nature of attractions offered by different destinations. The consequence of travel also brings about urban fragmentation, referring to the morphological differentiation of pieces of urban land and their dispersal within urban space (Carsjens and van Lier 2002, Wei and Zhang 2012). Every city and town has its own physical distinctiveness, and their spatial implications are uneven encompassing a mix of physical geography, place morphology, and infrastructure. For example, Urry and Larsen (2011: 40) document that tourism has reshaped the landscape of Blackpool in the UK due to "land ownership patterns and scenic attractiveness." A landscape should be understood as something that is "shaped" and "produced," and which is contingent on human or natural "processes and agents" (Andrews and Roberts 2012). "Touristic cultures" eventually emerge as the localized morphology and produce new meaning for both residents and visitors. For this reason, Rothman (1998: 10–11) claims that tourism is a "devil's bargain" because it triggers "a contest for the soul of a place." The mix of tourism and other sectors explain why some regions become popular destinations while others do not, and it accounts for variations across urban forms in different places in terms of their planning and marketing strategies.

Tourism also displays a dual effect on the urban landscapes of cities and towns. On the one hand, "vacationscape" (Gunn 1972) is created through multiple forces that work together, simultaneously becoming "places of cloning" (Castello 2010: xvii). Ringer (1998) proposes that tourism is constantly place-centered and constructed by means that both establish and falsify local reality. The tourism landscape has increasingly become locally constructed, and destination communities both adapt to and modify tourism in such a way that is no longer easily divorced from the cultural mainstream. On the other hand, tourism forms the intervening variables that require newly designed morphological structures. They cannot be easily copied and, once built, will bring individuality and distinctiveness to their adjacent built environment. In North America, the rise of the "creative class" conceptualized by Florida (2002) has had a considerable influence on cultural distinctiveness as tourism is nurtured as a way to foster the competitive edge of cities and towns. It has an intimate relationship to morphology where the built form of the tourist destination becomes a complex representation of social, political, technological, and economic forces. Davis (2001: 127) notes that "histories, cultures, power relations, aesthetics and economics all combine at a place to create a context." Knudsen et al. (2008) further argue that the locus of study for tourism is and should be the landscape, or tourism landscape, stemming from the humanistic tradition in geography and the end result of a process of social construction that has played out over a number of decades, and perhaps centuries and millennia (Minca and Oakes 2006).

The emergence of morphological thinking in tourism

The concepts of morphology and evolution in resort destinations were first introduced by Gilbert (Butler 2011), who addressed a prevalent phenomenon in seaside resort development in the UK. These were later separated and evolved in different directions, which, after some time intertwined together as evolutionary models between the 1970s and the 1990s (Brent 1997). In the generic model, Barrett identified several common features of resort morphology, such as the significance of the seafront to the structure and location of the commercial core, "distinct zonation" of visitor accommodation and residential areas, and an extension of settlement parallel to the coast (Pigram 1977: 525, Getz 1993: 584). Barrett's model identifies a zone of frontal amenities that encompasses tourists and touristic activities and facilities, and observes that with distance from the central beachfront, tourism-related activities decrease, creating a "concentric pattern" of architectural and the phenomenological recreational patterns (Jeans 1990, Smith 1992a,b, Meyer-Arendt 1993). This pattern of development where the intensity decreases with distance is reflected in the market value of the land. In North America, Wolfe's pioneering work on tourism geography in the 1950s examined the historical evolution of the resort area of Wasaga Beach, Ontario, Canada. This study also expands the scope and depth of the scholarly research on recreation migration, tourism flows, urban development, and demand systems.

In contrast, Stansfield and Rickert (1970) focus specifically on retail activities in resort towns, and develop a concept of the Recreational Business District (RBD) through studies of the New Jersey seashore as well as

Niagara Falls. The concept of RBD explores the characteristics of the specialized frontal trading zone, which is based on a recreational attraction, rather than upon proximity to residential areas or transportation routes. Building on this research, Lavery's study (1971) of Western Europe presents a schematic diagram of a typical coastal resort, consisting of a mixture of tourism-based land use and buildings (Pigram 1977: 527, Getz 1993: 584–585). In this model, features such as larger hotels occupy prime frontal locations, while both land value and tourist-oriented functions gradually change with distance away from the seafront. By classifying resorts into eight types and associating them with certain landscape characteristics and features, Lavery emphasizes the spatial and functional separation of the RBD from the Central Business District in urban redevelopment. Similarly, Meyer-Arendt (1990) applies the RBD in Gulf of Mexico seaside resorts and suggests that incipient RBDs evolved at seaside termini of railroads, highways, and footpaths. Construction of casinos and beach hotels at these sites was followed by nearby clustering of secondary and tertiary recreational enterprises. Lateral expansion of coastal roads eventually led to RBD elongation and resulted in redevelopment of older resort landscapes.

However, these morphological claims present disadvantages at present. For example, urban morphology, as initially outlined by the Chicago School Sociologist, Ernest Burgess, asserts that the centralized locational tendencies of manufacturing are theoretically obsolete in contemporary society. Another problem is that the first line of development often consists of high-rise structures, forming visual and physical barriers between the inner residential zones and the coast. The vehicle path creates a further barrier for the pedestrians by disrupting their flow to the coast. The linear development pattern itself is often displeasing and degrading, both aesthetically and environmentally. The vicissitudes of tourism activities add another layer of problems to the study of urban form.

In the meantime, the evolutionary method of morphological analysis has gained attention on tourism development at various stages (Pearce 1978, Smith 1991, Getz 1993). It starts with the evolution of the pilgrimage site and the steady accumulation of hotels and other facilities for tourists. Gradually, it spreads to the evolution of recreational land use as well as the changing morphology in spas. For example, in Thailand, the initial stage of tourism development involves the construction of low-budget simple visitor dwellings, which are later upgraded as visitor numbers increase, and then procured by developers who construct hotels to meet increasing tourist demands (Nordstrom 2000). Ultimately, morphological changes lead to the expansion of physical buildings and infrastructure. In China, Xi et al. (2015) observes that a core-periphery pattern emerges for rural tourism in selected villages, in which villages show higher degrees of land-use intensity in the areas closest to the core scenic spot. Spatial morphology indicates the touristification of traditional villages in different stages of tourism development, forwarding a model in which selected villages show the characteristics of "modern town," "semi-urbanization," and "traditional village," respectively, corresponding to three land development types: "intensive reconstruction type," "enclave extension type," and "in situ utilization type." The spatial evolution patterns of these villages showcase the spatial characteristics of the touristification of traditional villages in different stages, and also have great representative value for tourism planning in rural China.

The rapid development exerts an influence on communities through heavy concentration of tourist and ancillary facilities in a core urban area. A well-defined Tourist Business District has evolved with imprints on urban morphology (Jim 2000). Hotels and the travel industry have direct environmental impacts. At the same time, the drastic landscape modifications and the resulting effects raise governmental and public concerns with regard to sustainable development and management. Russo (2002) shows that, with reference to Venice, day trippers have little available time and thus tend to cluster around principal landmarks, which ultimately aggravates the carrying capacity of the tourist city and forms the vicious circle. Kadar (2013) utilizes geographically referenced photography of Vienna, Austria, and Prague, Czech Republic, to build graphs of spatial distribution of tourist attractions and routes. Both cities demonstrate that tourist morphological structure causes congestion, overcrowding, and monofunctional usage of the city center. Furthermore, rapid urban growth over the past decades without adequate governance and planning regimes has facilitated an accelerating process of socio-spatial polarization, in which resorts and hotels are increasingly self-segregating and fortified enclaves, providing segregated high-amenity communities for tourist consumption, isolated from the environmental and social problems of poorer areas.

Correspondingly, tourism creates distinctive relationships between tourists and the host spaces, places, and people they visit, which has significant implications for destination development and resource use. It brings to communities and the protection they require while the holiday tourists can truly benefit from recreation and the exploration of places that the communities invite them to engage in. Tourism as a complex economic activity has multiple linkages to a wide range of other economic sectors and yields positive multiplier effects and a potential to act as a catalyst for economic development. On the other hand, negative impacts as the sectoral, environmental, spatial, and sociocultural imbalances derived from the rapid and unplanned expansion. It takes greater account effects on the landscape as well as on the physical surrounding and natural environment (Sarrion-Gavilan et al. 2015). For example, the changing landscape of Hong Kong, a former British colony, has experienced rising rent buoyed by an influx of mainland Chinese tourists, forcing traditional stores to shut down. The main streets have shifted to luxury watch and jewelry shops or pharmacy stores to cater to tourists' needs. For many locals, these changes are yet another sign that Hong Kong's local culture is eroding. There is a sense that the city is becoming less "Hong Kong" and more mainland

Chinese in character, and that the lines between both are blurring. Tourism impact reconfigures everyday life, and transforms the ephemeral into static, ahistorical displays that appeal to tourists. Therefore, analysis of the morphology of destinations helps us to better understand the evolution of tourist destinations, and of the flow of people, capital, goods, and ideas that are at the core of tourism.

Problems of the tourism-morphology nexus

Changes to characteristics of the urban landscape as a result of morphological processes have been investigated in recent years (Feliciotti et al. 2017). Among scholarly disciplines, architecture, geography, and planning have provided the most contribution to the study of urban morphology (Oliveira 2016). The morphology of tourism is both a key modern phenomenon and a substantial urban form, yet its importance has generally gone unrecognized by academics and practitioners. While some attempts have been made in the past to advance the study of tourism's role in urban morphology, they have been sporadic and disconnected. There is a continuing paucity of interactions between urban morphology and tourism.

One of the major concerns is treating urban form largely in terms of separate components and physical structures, rather than as an integrated entity including tourism. While its prominence has been given to interdisciplinarity, at the same time, unexplored gaps have come into existence as new specialisms have developed. Within the interdisciplinary field of urban morphology and tourism, the net result has been less integrated bodies of knowledge than those explored by our predecessors. The opening up of gaps requiring exploration has occurred both within and between relevant disciplines. New specialties in terms of tourism impacts and touristification have continued to multiply. However, a lack of awareness of relevant work in the morphology of tourism is compounded by a lack of interest in examining buildings and landscapes from the perspective of tourism researchers, as well as in the perceived benefits of employing the methodologies of urban morphology.

More problematic is the fact that scarcely any of the linkage is to historico-geographical and architectural morphology in the context of tourism. Research that builds on the historical development of urban form, for example, connecting to morphological periods or the typological process, continues to be rare at the borders with tourism studies. Complex urban morphological processes involve multidimensional spatial and temporal semantics. However, due to scare partial data sets available on history, urban morphologists mainly rely on a series of "synchronic cuts" (Camacho-Hubner and Golay 2007) through urban evolution as a basis for heuristic abduction of relevant diachronic processes. In addition, most work on aspects of urban form treats the city as primarily a physical object here and now rather than as a historical, culturally laden phenomenon, characterized in part by the touristification of destinations. The morphology of tourism is viewed to build on selective readings of history and a reimagining of the past that serve present political and economic ends. In turn, this interpretation of morphology lacks the form and spatial configuration of tourist destinations and fails to relate to the visual and psychological characteristics of when and how these developments took place.

Most importantly, the definitions of morphology in tourism are seldom clear, singularly interpreted, unanimously accepted by scholars and practitioners, or stable over time. The oft-noted difficulty of finding an acceptable definition and academic ground with which to describe morphological studies is no different from the experiences of those engaged in human geography. Nonetheless, just because something is hard to describe does not mean it is impossible or that it is unimportant. In this book, the definition of the morphology of tourism serves to explain the form, as well as the agents and processes responsible for the transformation and diversity of a tourist destination. It is noted that the morphology of tourism is evolutionary and fluid in nature. Very often, a new pattern of "eclectic excesses," "integrated resort" or the "smart city" showcasing entertainment offerings, green spaces, recreational waterfront, and shopping activities surfaces to replace conventional "concentric zones" proposed in the early 1970s. Tourist destinations, characterized by theme parks and shopping malls, quickly become the new city squares for social interaction. Examples include the changing landscape of Las Vegas in the US, largely due to its integrated concept of entertainment, gaming, and hotels located in the well-known Strip area (Fainstein and Judd 1999). The newly built CityCenter, inspired by similar urban structures such as the Guggenheim Museum Bilbao (Franklin 2016), the Pompidou Center in Paris, and the Sony Center in Berlin, indicates a new phase of tourism development. In the UK, a tangle of railway lines has been transformed along many city centers and Dickensian industrial architecture turned into one of the coolest corners of the cities. Tourism ultimately engenders "fantasy cities" (Hannigan 1998), whose natural and built environments are fabricated to accommodate "placemaking" and "placemarketing" (Hannigan 2007: 959).

The book's structure and themes

The focus of this book is encapsulated in the phrase "the morphology of tourism." It will explore some of the complex and changing relationships between tourism and morphological changes in urban and rural destinations across the globe. The premise that informs this book is that morphological analysis showcases the form, use, and effects of tourism on the landscape. Tourism-related impacts on the physical environment and the changing sociocultural values surrounding a given destination reflect the need for both theoretical and empirical approaches to strengthen our understanding of the ways in which tourism functions. More precisely, we wish to engage with the diverse means by which tourism impacts and is impacted by other ordering attempts, and thus how tourism and morphology co-constitute each other and reshape urban forms. In order to develop these approaches, we are guided by research questions such as: How does the morphology of a destination change over time alongside tourism development and cultural expectations? How are elements of the built environment repurposed for tourism? What can planners do to promote morphological sensitivity while developing tourist landscapes? And why do neighborhoods develop within urban spaces to cater to tourists' needs? To begin answering these questions, there is a strong need to broaden the scope of morphological research in tourism. This can be accomplished not only by further combining tourism and urban morphology research as a geographic subdiscipline in its own right, but also by embracing this study area within a number of other disciplines, such as urban and regional planning. In essence, this book attempts to contextualize tourism and morphology by problematizing the interrelations between function, urban form, and development, and by situating a discussion of these relationships within the wider discourse of social and cultural geographies.

Within the contours of the book, it assumes that tourism is an essential function of contemporary urban contexts; therefore, it argues that morphology is a process of placemaking, which is the result of social construction reliant on relations, practices, and mobilities (Sheller and Urry 2006, Lew 2017). Franklin and Crang (2001: 8) argue that because of increased mobilities and the resulting changes in the experience of space, tourism is "at least part of the way we now perceive the world around us, wherever we are and whatever we do." Tourism morphology further legitimizes the impact studies distributed in space and time. We are experiencing a time of diversity and expansion, as well as an era of adjustment and change. Tourism is essentially place-based, involving the production of destination identity at different scales (Dredge and Jenkins 2003). It endeavors to include a broad cross section of morphological changes and tourism attractions of every scale from around the world, to show not only the diversity of destinations available, but also the issues associated with developing them for tourism for the long term. Through the exploration of the morphology-tourism nexus, we hope to demonstrate the intellectual value of tourism planning and marketing, and concurrently, convince researchers of the virtues of such an approach for a number of other recreation and geographic fields.

This book does not provide exhaustive coverage of all sectors comprising the travel and tourism industry. Instead, it pays close attention to certain key sectors and locations, such as coastal tourism, urban tourism, and waterfront redevelopment, which are increasingly important in terms of their influence on the morphological change of origin-destination flows. It aims to serve as a scholarly text for geographers, tourism researchers, and urban planners interested in enhancing their understanding of the morphological changes and forms of tourist destinations. The format provides a blend of readability and scholarship that presents tourism morphology across a wealth of cross-cultural and global examples. It should be of interest to the tourism industry and policymakers who may wish to enhance their cognizance of the administration of morphological transformation.

Throughout this book, we examine various morphological forms and their concomitant tourism themes, links, subtexts, and connotations; bringing together research from a range of disciplines including planning, sociology, and anthropology; and considering them through a set of tourist destinations. This provides a number of synergies with tourism studies, which has moved from a singular quantitative field to incorporate more research into how tourism influences urban forms. The text's geographic coverage indicates its principal emphasis on landscape transformation, proceeding a variety of impact studies. In addition, the text has included a wide range of countries, such as China, New Zealand, Italy, and Fiji, to illustrate the significance of this field.

This book comprises seven chapters. Chapter 1 reviews the work of schools of thought on urban form and its loose association with tourism. Drawing on the holistic nature of urban form studies, a range of social science disciplinary views are presented. These schools of thought, developed over decades, have generated lively debates among researchers of the built landscape, including geographers, architects, planners, sociologists, and others. It identifies an array of problems, concepts, and theories of the relationship between the social and environmental transformation. This chapter provides an overview of fundamental morphological definitions, along with an introduction to some of the major themes in contemporary tourism research, which are further developed in subsequent chapters of this book. Chapter 2 proposes a conceptual framework to form the basis for analyzing the multifarious spatial practices, social interactions, and cultural performances which constitute the morphology of tourism. The aim is to use different perspectives to analyze the impact of tourism in urban destinations. The investigation of the rise and importance of morphology tourism is structured around the relationship between socioeconomic impacts, forms and functions, and specific locations. This framework potentially broadens generalizability vis-à-vis academic understanding of urban form impacted by tourism, as well as in areas beyond this domain.

Chapter 3 focuses on how spatial patterns of coastal tourism have evolved over time, as their primary sources of investment have shifted from regional governments to global corporations. The inherent character of the coastal area makes its tourism distinctive, and the resultant product is often a resort with a unique morphology (Wong 1998). The chapter analyzes coastal morphological changes on Denarau Island in Fiji from physical, environmental, and social perspectives. It shows that morphological changes on Denarau Island do not follow the traditional Beach Resort Model due to the influence of the master plan implemented by Territorial Local Authority, which played a major role in preventing unexpected expansion.

The case study examines the coastal morphology linkage from the differing viewpoints of insiders, who actively participate in developing Denarau Island, and outsiders, who happen to be local residents left from the island. The findings suggest that coastal tourism development in Fiji began with international hotel expansion. As demand for tourism development in the area rose, rapid urbanization caused adverse environmental effects and, in turn, impacted local communities. Extensive recreational development followed in the form of new construction and conversion, permanently altering the coastline of Fiji. The study indicates a need for legislative reform to require a spatial plan suitable for tourism developments, conservation, and resource management in order to avoid decline in coastal resorts and sustain coastal resources. It also confirms the importance of sharing common goals and having sufficient communication and coordination between key players for effective collaboration.

Chapter 4 offers an extended discussion of spatial morphology in a walled city. The sites of fortifications are often the records of the expansions of city cores with mainly public and residential buildings, commercial facilities, and public spaces. The transformation of the wall results in the creation of an urban landscape, showing inner fringe belts forming boundary zones between historically and morphologically distinct housing areas. The city of Pingyao, Shanxi Province in China, illustrates the significance of architectural heritage; particularly, the distinctive feature of the city wall is the reification of identity. It traces three stages of intramural and extramural changes under governmental policies as tourism becomes a means of economic growth. Urban tourism has profound impact on the transformation of the *danwei* units and preservation of historic buildings. The use of the city wall as a historical landmark promotes a sense of place and authenticity. This chapter presents a variety of tourism policies embraced by local policymakers aiming to bring about economic growth. It closes by suggesting that the integration of spatial morphology with tourism planning will foster a better understanding of the complex interplay of urban form and function.

Chapter 5 explores a range of major themes in the morphology of tourism, including the changing morphology of the commercial waterfront in Auckland and Wellington, New Zealand. It seeks to examine the wider impacts and implications of hosting special events, such as the America's Cup and the Rugby World Cup held in Auckland, which provide an impetus for the redevelopment of an underutilized waterfront area. At a time when many cities are struggling to address the effects of deindustrialization and urban decline, tourism has become a significant economic development strategy. By using an evolutionary analysis of the spatial structure of the waterfront landscape, this chapter demonstrates that government development agencies and event tourism have been key agents of change in influencing its redevelopment at different phases. The waterfront looked to convert to tourism and leisure destinations and invested millions in that transformation. The findings illustrate the role of government in the context of economic restructuring and the embrace of tourism as a significant element in waterfront planning. This study proposes to establish a systematic understanding of morphological changes in order to create a sound base for waterfront landscape management and tourism planning.

Chapter 6 turns to applied morphology with an overview of the different roles of planning for tourism as a means of spatial redevelopment. The urban fringe-belt concept is introduced to provide a specific frame of reference for depicting, explaining, and comparing the physical structure and historical development of urban landscapes. The city of Como in Italy possesses well-preserved historic urban environments that are representative of their respective tourism traditions. Tourism in Como is a situated phenomenon, given its proximity to Lake Como. The pattern of the fringe belts in Como have resulted from their divergent dynamics of historico-geographical developments and evolving trajectories from an industrial city to a tourist one, especially during the period after the mid-nineteenth century. The examination of fringe-belt character and change highlights important issues of urban transformation, which are pertinent to tourism management.

The study of morphology plays a major role in elucidating urban forms as embodiments of cultural values, and in communicating the speed of change to interdisciplinary fields. The recent morphological change caused by investments in tourism and entertainment services requires the adoption of a better understanding of urban forms that are timely and comprehensive. Tourism relates to both the intrinsic importance of urbanization and the basis it provides for landscape conservation. Though the study of morphology is particularly an aid to learning about the past and how urban forms can be maintained and adapted within existing destinations, the effects of tourism on the spatial-morphological level need a careful study. The concluding chapter strives to fill that void and in the process by providing feedback for academics and practitioners. A reconstituted urban environment, with amenities and considerable investments in leisure-oriented infrastructure, proves to have additional effects on physical landscape. Tourism fuels the restructuring of cities along lines of recreation, and provides a source of experience from which the creation of new landscapes can benefit. At the same time, tourism development brings about a set of new issues, such as gentrification and displacement, uneven development, and questions about the role of governments in assisting the development of tourism businesses. The morphology of tourism demonstrates that economic development helps breathe new life into once distressed and dilapidated cities, while simultaneously generating new forms of social inequalities. Research on historical development and future roles of tourism landscapes has a niche place in maintaining and enhancing this consciousness.

The morphology of tourism serves as a process affecting urban areas, which poses many opportunities and problems for the development, management, and functioning of such destinations. This book serves to provide a clear understanding of the impacts of tourism morphology in different localities, some of the general similarities and differences in relation to the process of tourism, and the systems developed to exploit and manage it in different tourist environments. Its aim is to raise awareness of the international significance of the morphology of tourism and to develop a more integrated approach towards the study of this specific field. It is hoped that through this book, the morphology of tourism will develop into an established, interdisciplinary research field. This subject not only continues to deepen its internal theoretical understandings, but also reaches out to other fields and regions that have received limited attention within tourism studies. It is also necessary for the morphology of tourism to grapple with a number of problematic tendencies within the field and the wider readership, including the systematic study of tourism impacts on landscape over periods of time.

1 The historical development of urban morphology

Introduction

The concept of morphology has its origins in early Western philosophy and can be dated back to the Hellenistic period of Greek civilization. Ancient Hellenistic thinkers believed that there is an inherent order in the cosmos, which the human intellect is capable of understanding (Bowen 1981). Two aspects of thinking constitute the basis of the morphological tradition: the concept of wholeness and the idea of evolution. The former was later developed into empiricism by Francis Bacon and John Locke, who argued that analytical methods begin with particulars or simple elements. Therefore, the concept of wholeness refers to components from each element to form the whole. However, with a growing emphasis on the progressive development of human knowledge, evolutionary ideas have gained prominence since the second half of the eighteenth century introduced theories of biological evolution proposed by Jean-Baptiste Robinet. A group of philosophers in Germany, including Johann Wolfgang von Goethe and Lorenz Oken, expressed a strong interest in the morphology of plants and animals, as well as the common features of their structure. Similar to bioscience, the core principles of morphology are the notions of a formative/transformative process and the relative positions of the parts making up the whole form as it grows and changes.

Over the past decades, morphology has gradually become an extension of traditional philosophical thoughts and the subsequent rise of empiricism in geography, which emphasizes the importance of explaining and identifying structural elements and their developmental sequences. An underlying assumption is that this analytical process is used to recapture the inherent order and maintain the integrity of wholeness, as every city constitutes a set of elements of urban form ranging from streets, street blocks, plots, and buildings. Therefore, urban morphology is an explanatory theory in the context of the physical form of the city, the progressive constitution of the urban fabric, and the analysis of the reciprocal relationships between the constitutive elements of the urban fabric defining particular combinations of spatial features (Allain 2004). In this theory, cities are seen as a composite of cultural, anthropogenic, and geographical objects interacting with each other and being able to be "read" in the depth of history and at a given scale (Camacho-Hubner and Golay 2007).

Urban morphology can be divided into four broad approaches (Kropf 2017), each focusing on slightly different aspects of urban form: (1) The typo-morphological approach originates from the fields of architecture and urbanism. It refers to process typology, which seeks to inform architectural and urban proposals with a critical understanding of the built environment as a context for development. The typo-morphological approach examines the detailed structure and the historical process of its formation. (2) The configurational approach focuses on the geometric and topological attributes of built form with the aim of understanding the interrelationships between different attributes and measures, the ways in which different spatial configurations affect the use of urban environments and buildings, and the predication for future performance. (3) The historico-geographical approach seeks to explain the geographical structure, patterns, and character of human settlements through a systematic analysis of their constituent elements and the development through time. One of this approach's principal methods is a detailed analysis of the chronological sequence of town plans with the systematic distinction of a hierarchy of plan element complexes, including street, plot, and building patterns. (4) Finally, the spatial analytical approach conceptualizes human activity as a set of spatial interactions. Central to this approach is the view that cities are complex adaptive systems involving a dynamic, iterative, and reciprocal relationship between social and economic interactions and the physical form of settlements.

All the four approaches tie to the relevant theories used in the context of urban morphology. In addition, there are three important associated methods available for the study of urban form that are not explicitly morphological but complement the above approaches: (1) townscape analysis, (2) city image analysis, and (3) overlay analysis and geographic information systems (GIS). They incorporate the perception of the built environment as directly experienced from the ground. It is argued that there are more streams of research that are primarily concerned the study of urban form.

The aim of this chapter is not to summarize all existing theories in the literature, but rather to introduce some key ones that point towards a potential connection between morphology and tourism with the inferred links and framework further developed throughout the book. The sectional thinking that lies at the root of restricted views of urban landscape phenomena has affected the various disciplines and professions differently. Urban morphology has expanded to a wide variety of issues and concerns, namely, environmental, sociocultural, and economic impacts on the changing urban form. These theories are closely associated with tourism as travels influence the social fabric and local residents. The characteristics of urban morphology, namely, urban tissues as well as aforementioned approaches, have distilled the development of tourist attractions. Therefore, an integrated analytical framework is needed to better understand the complex of urban morphology. The relevant theories are broadly divided into town plan analysis, political economy analysis, environment–behavior studies, architectural approaches, the ecosystem theory, neo-rationalism, and space morphology studies. The following sections detail each study area and its unique characteristics in order to review and clarify the relationships among these relevant theories.

Relevant theories in urban morphology

Town plan analysis

The morphological idea was introduced to geography by Carl Ritter (1779–1859) for the study of the forms and structure of the landscape, which was considered to have an organic quality (Sauer 1925). In an essay on *Deutsche Stadtanlagen* (the layout of German towns), published in 1894, Johannes Fritz used town plans to compare the physical forms of urban areas. It is evident that empirical field-based research underpinned his plan analysis (Larkham and Conzen 2014). Fritz delimited the different layouts (street layouts in particular) of which the city of Rostock was comprised. Though crude, it exemplifies the beginning of a potentially important research activity that is often referred to today as *morphological regionalization*: the recognition of the way in which urban landscapes are structured into unitary areas (Whitehand 2014a). Recognizing such unitary areas is not only part of the activity of discovering how urban landscapes are composed but also fundamental to the planning and design of what should happen to those landscapes in the future (Whitehand 2014b).

The research of morphology started to take shape as an organized field of knowledge at the end of the nineteenth century. Some of its most important roots were in the work of German-speaking geographers, such as the geographer Otto Schlüter, who proposed the city as part of the wider *landschaft* (landscape). He had published two papers: a programmatic statement about settlement geography in general and *kulturlandschaft* (cultural landscape) in particular (Schlüter 1899), and a second paper about the ground plan of towns. He drew heavily on an earlier paper by Johannes Fritz's *Deutsche stadtanlagen* and reproduced from that paper a number of simple maps of the layout of German towns. Though they were merely descriptive in nature, essentially diagrams of street patterns delimited on the distinct physical parts into which the historical cores of the towns could be divided, they emphasized the interdependence in geography of form, function, and development, with a particular focus on *stadtlandschaft* (urban landscape) as distinct from the rural landscape. These were early examples of tracing the historical development of urban form that was in the next century to become a primary feature of urban morphology. Enriched by the contributions of architects (e.g., Siedler 1914) and historians (e.g., Hamm 1932), this approach was later referred to as morphogenetic.

A key feature of the morphogenetic approach from its early days was the mapping of the various physical forms within urban areas. The geographer Hassinger (1916a,b) probably pioneered the practice of plotting the map in color. He followed Fritz's interest in street plans by mapping buildings according to their architectural periods. Hassinger (1916b) detailed the historical architectural styles in the city of Vienna based on Walter Geisler's major work in inner Danzig (Gdansk), culminating in comprehensive classifications of the sites, ground plans, and building types of German towns (Geisler 1918). These early works recognize that a city is an extremely complex object, and their maps reflect a hierarchical view of the city, structured according to a set of fundamental physical elements (Oliveira 2016).

It is noted that morphology has critical links with several disciplines including the Berkeley school of cultural geography established by Carl Sauer (Whitehand 2007). In terms of literature, there was considerable scrutiny of aspects of urban morphology within German-language publications. The most succinct review of the field in its early years is a 1930 paper on the state of urban geography by Hans Dörries. The monograph on Vienna by Bobek and Lichtenberger (1966) is also a prominent example. In more recent decades, Vance's (1990) book entitled *The Continuing City* introduces the morphology in Western civilization, while Remy Allain's (2004) *Morphologie Urbaine* is notable in French. Both books propose that the characteristics of urban structure include morphogenetic method, cartographic representation, and terminological precision.

Kropf (2009, 2011) rephrases morphology as urban tissues to illuminate the character of a city. Urban tissue is defined as an organic whole that can be seen according to different levels of resolution, each corresponding to different elements of urban form. The higher the level of resolution, the greater the detail of what is shown and the greater the specificity of morphological description. At a very low level, urban tissue encompasses only the visible streets, while, at a high level of resolution, it might include a number of details, such as the construction materials of an open space or building. Kropf's argument is that urban form should pay attention to the internal transformations of urban tissue and the combinations of urban tissue in the process of polymorphogenetic accretion.

Town plan analysis has been mainly developed by the Anglo-German geographical school associated with M. R. G. Conzen. The application of this analysis to the urban landscape originates with Schlüter's (1899) papers, published in the late nineteenth century, which call for the detailed description of the visible and tangible forms on the ground and their genetic and functional explanations in terms of the actions of man in the course of history and in the context of nature. From the beginning, Schlüter envisaged the development of an explanatory morphology that is fully aware of the interdependence in geography of the three traits of form, function, and development (Whitehand 2007).

In assessing the key factors at the intra-urban scale, the historical expressiveness of urban landscapes merits particular attention. Its importance and how it might be approached within urban planning were initially addressed by Conzen. In a University of Berlin dissertation, Conzen (1932) mapped the building types in 12 towns in an area to the west and north of Berlin. Different colors denoted different types of buildings, while differing color depths indicated the number of each building's storeys. Later, Conzen (1958, 1962) used a similar approach to produce his better-known maps of the English port town of Whitby. In his map of the building types, priority is given to historical periods, which he conceptualizes as morphological periods marked by a unity of physical forms. Conzen (1966: 56–61) observed the difficulty that British society was having in the cultural crises of the early postwar decades, and decided to "keep its sense of continuity and its capacity to see things interconnected," a problem reflected in uncertainty in the grasp of long-term values. He repeatedly stressed the importance of a physical environment of the fullest possible historical expressiveness in enabling the individual to put down roots in an area, demonstrating the historical dimension of human experience and thereby stimulating comparison in a more informed way of reasoning. He further argued that "the state of the cultural landscape and in particular the preservation or neglect of its historicity reflects closely the average cultural consciousness of that society and thus indirectly the long-term efficiency of its education system." It was Conzen who put forward a tripartite division of urban form into (1) the town plan, or ground plan (comprising the sites, streets, plots, and block plans of the buildings); (2) building fabric (the three-dimensional form); and (3) land and building utilization (Conzen 1960: 4). He expounded the tripartite division for giving high priority to historicity and went on to set out a method whereby it could be incorporated into urban planning.

The most famous proponent of town plan analysis is Conzen's book (1960) entitled *Alnwick, Northumberland: A Study in Town-Plan Analysis*, which ultimately led to the development of the Conzenian School in the UK. In his book, Conzen subdivided the town of Alnwick for analytical purposes into streets and their arrangement in a street system, plots and their aggregation into street blocks, and buildings, or more precisely their block plans (Whitehand and Larkham 1992). The constructs Conzen applied to describe these subdivisions, such as "plan units," "morphological periods," "morphological regions," "morphological frames," "plot redevelopment cycles," and "fringe belts," are still in use in the study of urban morphology (see Figure 1.1). Conzen's contribution to a historico-geographical approach on urban form can be summarized in five major points: (1) the establishment of a basic framework of principles for urban morphology; (2) the adoption for the first time in English-language geographical literature of a thoroughgoing evolutionary approach; (3) the recognition of the individual plot as the fundamental unit of analysis; (4) the use of detailed cartographic analysis, especially employing large-scale plans in conjunction with field surveys and documentary evidence; and (5) the conceptualization of developments in the townscape (Whitehand 1981).

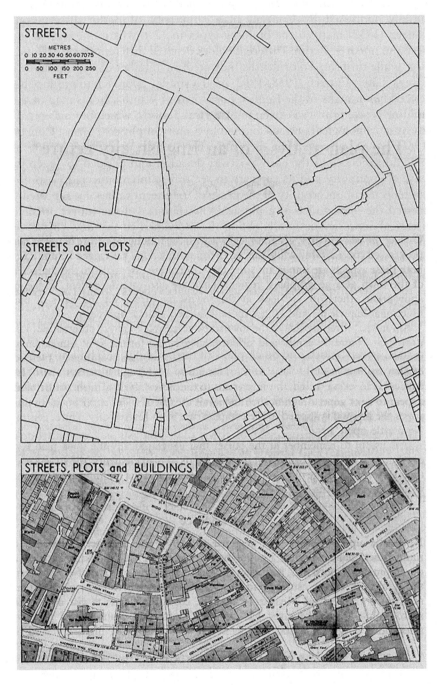

Figure 1.1 Basic Elements of the Ground Plan. (Source: Whitehand 1981)

One of the concepts raised by Conzen was the burgage cycle, in which the progressive built occupation of the back of the plot culminates in a significant reduction of open space, resulting in the need to release this space and in a period of urban fallow, which, in turn, precedes a new development cycle (Oliveira 2016). Burgage is a medieval land term used in England, which means a town (borough) rental property owned by a king or lord. Conzen deftly utilized the burgage cycle in the case study of Alnwick, but this phenomenon quickly gained attention from other urban morphologists, who applied it to additional contexts. These can be subjected to metrological analysis, which affords an important means of reconstructing the histories of plot boundaries (Lafrenz 1988). For example, by analyzing measurements of plot widths in the English town of Ludlow, Slater (1990) was able to detect regularities, speculate about the intentions of the medieval surveyor when the town was laid out, and infer the original plot widths and how they were subsequently subdivided, while Oliveira (2016) observed that the city of Porto in Portugal carries a similar developmental cycle. The burgage cycle conceptualizes a process of plot occupation and construction of working-class housing in the back of the bourgeois building facing the streets, without changing the plot structure. A period of "urban fallow" prior to the initiation of a redevelopment cycle is a particular variant of a more general phenomenon of building repletion where plots are subject to increasing pressure, often associated with changed functional requirements, in a growing urban area.

Perhaps the most significant ideas are the concepts of the plan unit and the fringe belt, around which a considerable amount of research has subsequently been constructed. Conzen (1960, in Whitehand 1981: 14) defines a plan unit as "examination of the town plan shows that the three element complexes of streets, plots and buildings enter into individualized combinations in different areas of the town." Each combination derives uniqueness from its site circumstances and establishes "a measure of morphological homogeneity or unity" in some or all respects over its area. It represents a plan unit, distinct from its neighbors. A basic characteristic of a plan unit is that it exists as a specific component of an urban area. Baker and Slater (1992: 49) explain that

> areas exhibiting a "measure of morphological unity" may be defined at very different scales from the whole intra-mural area down to a minor plot series. Further, in some cases, characteristics which distinguish an area from its neighbors may not be uniformly present throughout that area.

In Baker and Slater's discussion, plan units can vary in size and be assigned sometimes even with a vague boundary around it. To identify and investigate plan units is an important basis of other town plan analysis approaches, such as morphological period, regions, frame, and fringe belts. It is a preliminary step to comprehending a city or town as a complex of wholeness.

The most widely quoted concept in Conzen's town plan analysis is the fringe belt, which is defined as

> the physical manifestations of periods of slow movement or actual standstill in the outward extension of the built-up area and characterized in the initial stages of their development by a variety of extensive uses of land, such as various kinds of institutions, public utilities and country houses, usually with below average accessibility requirements to the main part of the built-up area.
>
> (Conzen 1960)

Regarding the physical forms, Conzen (1966) stresses that the major significance in the formation of a fringe belt is the existence of a fixation line, defined as the site of a strong, often protective linear feature, such as a town wall marking the traditional stationary fringe of an ancient town. In Whitehand's study (1988: 48), the sequence of fringe belt development may be divided into two principal phases. The first phase, fringe belt formation, occurs when land at the fringe of the built-up area is taken up for the first time by urban or quasi-urban land uses. It continues until land under these uses no longer abuts on to rural land, and further development of the fringe belt by the addition of new plots at the actual fringe of the built-up area is thereafter precluded. The second phase, fringe belt modification, commences when the growth undergoes formation and modification phases. The purpose of the fringe belt concept is to explain and describe urban growth and transmission processes, and the value of this tool is to suggest and arrange appropriate new changes in evolutionary consequences. The fringe belt concept has been widely applied, particularly in study of the areas between the urban and suburban, and rural areas which usually are deemed "sensitive" and where more challenges and opportunities are concentrated.

Various directions have emerged in recent decades regarding the implementation of town plan analysis, and its importance to historical preservation and tourism development remains strong. This morphological analysis is widely used as a practical device for establishing guidelines for design control and urban development management (Whitehand 1992). Tourism, as a means of economics, has embodied in the town plan analysis, as a systematic study is required for destination planning and physical transformation for tourists and commercial development. The application of Conzenian school in tourism can be found in Chapters 4 and 6 for the study of ancient cities in China and Italy.

Political economic analysis

Changes in urban form may be explained via theories that emphasize political, economic, and sociocultural elements. In particular, the political economy becomes the driving force for the transformation of urban form. For example, boosterism for tourism development can be found at various levels of government, in order to regenerate local economies and revitalize inner cities. Therefore, a political economic analysis is crucial to understand the magnitude of economic impact as well as landscape changes due to policies set by governments.

In the discipline of geography, there are two distinctive strands of morphological studies that are rooted in the US: first, the Berkeley School, a strand of cultural geography which focuses on rural settlement rather than urban areas, and second, a somewhat eclectic political and economic perspective, which emphasizes land-use studies. Having adopted the concentric zone model of sociologist Ernest Burgess (1925), and the sector model of land economist Homer Hoyt (1939) as well as creating their own multiple nuclei model (Harris and Ullman 1945), the followers of political economic analysis export their ideas abroad in the 1960s. Urban functional structure was formed during that period of time to explore the relationship between socioeconomic theories and the historical development of land-use patterns. Beyond the explanation of the disposition of land-use patterns within the urban functional structure, Christaller's "central place theory" or "locational interdependence school" (1964) dissects the distribution of the cities themselves, making an attempt to see if there is any correlation between their location, spacing, and size. The theory has been utilized in tourism studies since it delineates the direction of tourism development from a core outward to peripheral regions (Ritchie and Crouch 2003). The emergence of a "core-periphery" pattern of spatial evolution shows the impingement of tourism upon landscape (Xi et al. 2015). The most important implication for the central place theory is that more interest is generated in the theoretical explanations of links between urban landscape and neoclassical economics.

Political economic analysis exerted its highest level of influence during the 1960s and 1970s. It links the formation of the built environment with commodity production in general (Wu 1998). Harvey (1985) sketches out principles of epistemological theory, questions of moral and political commitment, ontological paradoxes, and the march of urban progress. He attributes the restless formation and reformation of geographical landscapes to the imperatives and contradictions inherent in capitalism. His theory of "capital circuits" (1978) focuses on the switching of capital in the changing landscape. Ball (1986) further develops Harvey's concept to "the structure of building provision," which argues that the set of social relations is involved in the provision of the built environment form, including the development industry, planning profession, and professional service classes for whom they are built, that cannot be ignored in explanations. In the following studies by Knox (1991, 1992), provision involves an even wider range of actors. For example, by studying the transformation of urban landscapes of the Metropolitan Washington, DC, Knox (1991) proves how sociocultural factors, as well as economic ones, influence the status of master-planned communities, high-tech corridors, mixed-use developments, and gentrified neighborhoods. The insights obtained from political economy analysis can be summarized in two points: first, it demonstrates that the urban landscape links the formation of the built environment with the general process of production and reproduction; second, it reveals the structure of building provision, explains how development is organized and assesses the functions of various social agencies involved in the process.

Tang (2000) traces the general development of urban planning over history based on political economic analysis. Urban planning was seen essentially as an exercise in physical design (Keeble 1952). After the 1960s, a scientific view emerged, calling for planners to systematically analyze the built environment (McLoughlin 1969) and to come up with rational recommendations (Faludi 1973). Since the late 1970s, planners have realized that the role of urban planning is less rational and more complicated than we originally thought. Neo-Marxist urban theories have characterized planning as a facilitator of capital accumulation (Preteceille 1976, McLoughlin 1994) and its theory as an ideology (Harvey 1978). The neo-Ricardian school positions urban planning as the preprocessor of political information in conflicts of capitalist commodity exchange (Roweis 1981). Later, urban planners were seen as mediators of different interests in regeneration (Throgmorton 1992). In the postmodern era, the roles of urban planning have been described as varying from the intersubjective communicative turn (Tewdwr-Jones and Allmendinger 1998), the guidance power (Roweis 1983), the representation in the regime of practice (Fischler 1995), the regulation of distribution of the social product in the global economy (Low 1996), to the consideration of culture diversity (Montgomery 2014).

Ostensibly, the history of planning is replete with examples of the search for the ideal urban form as a cure for the urban ills of the time. Urban forms have permeated utopian or visionary thought as the ideas of architects, social thinkers, and urbanologists have found their way into planning theory and practice (Graham 2017). In the past three decades, diverse concerns and interests have reflected changes in policy making and identity reconstruction such as impact analysis, growth management, social planning, and economic development. The diffusion of planners' competence is, however, more apparent than real (Levy 2017). Nevertheless, the focus of morphology is and always has been on the physical built environment of cities and towns. Hodge (1998: 162) states that a great deal of planning, under the influence of political and economic factors, centers around two issues: (1) the spatial impact of proposals for new development or of changes in existing development on the physical environment and (2) the spatial coordination of the various functions and activities that constitute the physical environment. To illustrate, morphological analysis has become an important tool for planning practices, such as heritage preservation, development management, and design control. Ascher (2007) concludes that planning is principally judged by the appearance of development that has received planning permission. The value of urban form studies is the ability to accommodate changes within a pattern of evolutionary growth.

Environment–behavior studies

In the early 1950s, design professionals, in conjunction with psychologists and other behavioral scientists, began to show a growing interest in the relationships between physical environments and human behavior and experience. A number of designations were employed in these discussions, such as architectural psychology, environmental psychology, man–environment relations, and ecological psychology. In the following two decades or so, not only did this school of thought establish its own small but definable scientific turf, but also the designation "environment psychology" seemed to supplant all others (Proshansky and Altman 1979). Regarding urban morphological concerns, Gehl (2011) and Rapoport (2008) have established a connection between human activities and the changing process of an urban setting. These works focus on the understanding of how people perceive the particular environments and how they behave within them.

One of the salient features of environment–behavior studies is the use of chaos theory to explain the environmental behavior. In simple terms, chaos is order without predictability (Gleick 1987), or chaos is not anarchy or randomness but an "invisible" order. What it implies is a kind of inherent "uncertainty principle"—not just in how we perceive the world but in how the world actually works (Cartwright 1991). To the extent that tourism acts as "non-correspondences" (Hanson and Hillier 1987: 251), that is, functioning more probabilistically and allowing transpatial groups to overcome distances, can permit local disorder and at the same time enable encounters among different social categories. The value of chaos theory lies in its disturbing integration of order and disorder, certainty and uncertainty, and calm and turbulence. Chaos theory has profound implications for planning, which affects the way we approach our subject matter (analysis), the way we choose what to do (plan making), and the way we expect our recommendations to be carried out (implementation). It has an ambiguous message for the planner: on the one hand, chaos theory implies that human behavior may be a good deal more complex than we previously thought, so much so that a complete understanding of some of the things we plan may be beyond all possibilities on the other hand, it suggests that some understanding of highly complex behavior may be found in quite simple models. They extend to both analysis and intervention, to the way in which planners try to understand the world, and to their efforts to change it. Generally, the theory suggests that the world environment may be both easier and more difficult to understand than we tend to believe, as noisy and untidy cities may not be as dysfunctional as we often assume, and that the need for planning that is incremental and adaptive in nature may be more urgent than we tend to think (Cartwright 1991).

Complexity, uncertainty, and chaos theories provide an important understanding of the interactive relations between social construction and the transformation of urban morphology (Syamwil 2012). In addition, environment–behavior studies deal with how people perceive the city and make spatial decisions within it. There are two main preliminary requirements for these analyses: first, a collection of maps, plans, and planning documents related to urban landscape changes; second, the identification of local people's perceptions of urban environmental changes, which can be procured through observation, interviews, and questionnaire surveys. Although the concepts and methods of morphological analysis and environmental behavioral studies examine physical urban form from different dimensions and emphasize "subjective" and "objective" aspects separately, they can complement each other and provide a balanced basis for urban form analysis. Both morphological analysis and environmental behavioral studies are major methodologies that can be set in a political economy analysis context, while the issue of urbanization can be used as a platform to link them together and reach more consistent and rational conclusions.

For instance, Michelson (1970) synthesizes past research findings on human developmental stages, social class, value orientation, and pathology with the study of the urban environment. His findings demonstrate empirically how lifestyle affects preferences for physical settings. By investigating research in this field, he identifies two approaches: "mental congruence," or the way people expect a particular environment to influence their behavior (e.g., people will oppose an urban relocation scheme if they anticipate inadequacy of their new housing), and "experiential congruence," or how well the environment accommodates the needs and behavior of people within it. Michelson concludes that cities must eliminate "planned incongruence" by isolating suspected physical and social factors and testing remedies for each in subsequent studies. He also advocates the creation of a social review board to assess the impact of housing, transportation, and other urban developments on behavior over time.

Christopher Alexander, an architect with behavioral science training, in his book entitled *Notes on the Synthesis of Form* (1964), conceives that design of a given environmental setting should be derived from the functions or goals of the institutional structures in that setting. Studer (1966) echoes the work of Alexander and maintains that needs or goals expressed in terms of patterns of behavior are the correct unit of analysis for designing and programming human-occupied built environments. More recent works by Rapoport (2008) discuss people's reactions to particular environmental contexts and advocate the "invisible in architecture" approach to the built environment. This approach begins with the proposition that design consists of making human and environmental characteristics congruent with each other. That is, the designer must be aware of the full implications for an environment–behavior interaction. Drawing from this construct, they note that many of our current urban problems are the result of "anti-urban and anti-human forces." An evolution produces an environment that should be suited to the lifestyle and cultural needs of the communities. They propose to learn from this to overcome current urban problems and must recognize the complex interface between the built environment and human behavior.

Based on the above fundamental conceptions, Michelson (1975) opines that behavioral research methods can be generally grouped into two broad categories: survey research and observational methods. Survey research includes typical social science research approaches, such as questionnaires, interviews, and mental image surveys, which can play an active role in enriching our understanding of the relationship between various environmental settings and human responses. Observational methods include photographic recording and behavior setting observation. Behavior setting observation can be further isolated into three distinct steps: scouting and mapping, recording and describing, and analysis and reporting (Aas 1975). The questioning–observation dichotomy is related to the "outside-inside" question: The objects of study are behaving persons, and we have the choice of describing them from the outside through an observer or from the inside by asking the behaving persons to give us their descriptions and experiences.

Environment–behavior studies have gone through a significant change in recent decades. The topic of sustainable development advocated by planning communities has created a growing awareness of the critical link between environmental impact, environmental justice, and urban form. Specifically, the introduction of neo-traditional development and transportation demand management facilitates the significance of perceived open space for these studies. Open space is regarded as any land with minimal building structures, existing for the use and enjoyment of the general public. Studies of open space examine its impact on the mental and physical health of urban residents, and attempt to determine the long-term personal and intergenerational effects of living in populous cities that lack open spaces. Recreational use of open spaces becomes an important topic for this study.

Architectural approaches

Architectural approaches encompass typological and contextual studies developed by architects and urban designers, which provide distinctive perspectives for understanding urban form. The typological studies are derived mainly from Italy and France. Indeed, this field of study has developed primarily around the works of the Italian architectural school, closely associated with two urban planners, Gianfranco Caniggia and Saverio Muratori

(Caniggia and Maffei 2001). Later, the Muratorian school is established to conduct an in-depth study of architecture and urban form.

Caniggia's most notable work was on the historic center of Florence, which served as a vehicle for the careful and systematic development of typological processes (Samuels 1990). His techniques are based on a number of fundamental principles, concerned with examining the evolution of the urban fabric in order to determine how building types have been adapted and changed over time. This examination focuses on dwellings, which are seen as "the basic tissue." Caniggia seeks to identify the original, traditional form of structures, which he terms the "first building" types, and hoped to establish a series of principles which determines the way in which these have been adapted and changed (Caniggia and Maffei 2001). The model, in which mutation and adaptation take place, is the "leading type" of Florence's architecture. The underlying assumption is that at any specific time, there is an optimum built structure, the form of which will be determined by current social, economic, and environmental conditions. Viewed in this way, they can be "read" as a series of modifications over time used by designers to ensure that a strict and continuing connection is carefully maintained between each part of the city and its first building. Rossi (1975: 304) affirms that

> if the type is a constant, it can be found in all the areas of architecture. It is therefore also a cultural element and as such can be sought in the different area of architecture, typology thus becomes broadly the analytical moment of architecture and can be characterized even better at the urban level.

From this perspective, typology can best be used to bridge the gap between the urban and the building scale. Generally, typological studies focus on the classification of building types and open spaces in order to describe and explain urban form, and then suggest possible directions for future adaptation and change. Their implications for design practice and townscape management have been implemented broadly (Moudon 1997, Kashef 2008, Kropf 2009).

The essence of architectural context study lies in understanding the natural, cultural, and human characteristics of physical space, and creating a meaningful place that derives from a broader regional context. Its approach is demonstrated thoroughly in the works of Appleyard et al. (1965), Cullen (1961), and Rowe and Koetter (1978). In these works, the most oft-cited concept seems to be the "townscape," originally developed by Cullen (1961). This concept is based on the laws of perception that can be objectively identified by anyone sensitized to them and used to "manipulate the elements of the town so that an impact on emotions is achieved" (Cullen 1961: 9). Through an analysis of "serial vision," "place," and the "content" of built environments, Cullen identifies and compares attempts to "make all new, fine and perfect" towns, with the great variety within "color, texture, scale, character, personality and uniqueness." The last one is particularly valuable and should be promoted in creating a sensory place. His works demonstrate the need to understand and graphically analyze the individual character and sequence of public spaces in the physical environment (Trancik 1986).

The ecosystem theory

In recent years, environmental policy and research circles have advocated various ecosystem approaches (Marcus and Colding 2011, Pickett et al. 2013). The urban ecosystem is seen as being both a system in itself and an important, if not essential element in understanding the transformation of all other ecosystems. The theory developed from these concepts has been widely used in the study of urban morphology in practice. Bowen (1981: 272) initially suggests that the ecosystem theory contrasts with traditional views of knowledge which consider the scientific observer as an individual detached, intellectually at least, from the objects of observation, with knowledge occurring in a kind of linear sequence: object, sensation, reflection, and generalization, leading to knowledge or theory and so to further observation. According to that view, the human mind is separate from the material world, so that thought cannot be regarded as a part of nature. Environmentalism and ecology have been determined to

> emphasize the view that all knowledge occurs not only in society but in the dynamic space-time context of the earth ecosystem; the observer— and the scientist is no exception—thus must be considered always as part of the system being observed, the ideas and actions that issue from such observation are themselves incorporated in the dynamic system, to become part of the future environment.

Since the 1970s, there has been a growing awareness of the need to bring the ecosystem to the development of land and the management of natural resources. The city as system has been a central metaphor for urban morphology. Urban ecology emerges to investigate the urban environment and all its inhabitants as an ecological system. It is essentially a formalized method of determining the role of components within the overall operation of a system (Exline et al. 1982). At the core of the theory is the presumption that each system has coherence or unity, which enables us to distinguish it from other systems and to view it as a complex whole. Ian McHarg (1995), a Scottish landscape architect, and other proponents of the environmental planning movement have brought into focus the evolving philosophy that ecological processes provide an indispensable basis for urban planning and design. The dependence of one life process on another; the interconnected development of the living and physical processes of earth, climate, water, plants, and animals; and the continuous transformation and recycling of living and nonliving materials—these are the elements of the self-perpetuating biosphere that sustains life on earth and which constitute the central determinants of form for all human activities on the land.

Hough (1989), in his book entitled *City Form and Natural Process*, summarizes that the urban analysis and design principles of the ecosystem approach are responsive to urban ecology and can be applied to the opportunities through its inherent resources. The ecosystem approach, in other words, forms the basis for an alternative design language. Within this context lies an economy of means that derives the most benefit from the least effort and energy, diversity as the basis for environmental and social health, an environmental literacy that begins at home and forms the basis for a wider understanding of ecological issues, a goal that stresses an enhancement of the environment as a consequence of change, and the integration of human with natural process as its most fundamental level. A technique that attempts to incorporate the results of human activities into the understanding of urban dynamics is defined as the flows approach. Like all ecosystems, a city can be studied in terms of inputs and outputs of resources, materials, and energy. The emergence of "landscape urbanism" (Waldheim 2016) views the city as an ecological system with quantifiable flows of energy materials and information. The "humanness" of cities as well as minimizing their impact on hinterlands make the city system more sustainable and livable.

The ecosystem approach to managing the urban environment has increasingly gained attention worldwide and been used as a confluence of thinking, at the theoretical level, that a holistic ecological approach to solving problems is needed to deal with today's environmental problems. Rapid urbanization coupled with tourism has brought considerable environmental, social, and economic challenges to cities and societies. The ecosystem approach is used in various scales from global to supra-regional (supra-macro level), national to regional (macro), city to district (mezzo), neighborhood to street (micro), and parcel to building (supra-micro) (Yigitcanlar and Dizdaroglu 2015).

Neo-rationalism

In the late 1960s, a new rationalist movement emerged in architecture, claiming inspiration from both the Enlightenment and early-twentieth-century rationalists. A rationalist approach takes a wider view of the city and its architecture as an integral part of the evolution of society. The research that focuses on the application of historical experience has and is continuing to influence the field of study and practice. The main proponents of various theories include Andres Duany, Elizabeth Plater-Zyberk, and Peter Calthorpe with regard to neo-traditional planning, and Christopher Alexander with regard to a "New Theory of Urban Design."

In particular, neo-rationalist theory and practice, as conceived by Aldo Rossi and Leon Krier, are a reaction against the Modernist Movement. They view the city as an organization of individual building types, each surrounded by space leading to "a culture tragedy to which there has been no precedent in history" (Moughtin 2003).

Rossi's neo-rationalist opus (1984: 86–87), *The Architecture of the City*, points out that cities should be regarded as historical texts containing man-made objects that retain traces of their time. In other words, history is seen as analogous to the skeleton, which bears the imprint of past actions. More importantly, the city is the collective memory of its people, and this memory is contained within urban artifacts. Rossi identifies urban phenomena, which evolved within the city over time, becoming part of its collective memory. The primary concern is that "specific urban elements ... participate in the evolution of a city over time in a permanent way." They represent not only monuments or fixed points in the city but also important events, the definitive characteristics that should "play an effective role in the dynamic of the city." At a more detailed level, urban artifacts are identified which are specific man-made objects within the urban structure, which have retained their original values and functions or may have had to adapt or change. Analysis of the typology of these artifacts is important, particularly that of the individual dwelling, which is both representative of urban form and the precise manifestation of a culture's way of life.

The common features of neo-rationalism are to use the existing traditional city framework as a basis for drawing out stable formal categories, which may be adapted for future use. In this case, a city is regarded "not as a blank site for the construction of solutions to urban problems, but as a species of viable organisms which have already defined the genetic type-solutions available to use and which need not be re-invented but only reapplied" (Gosling and Maitland 1984: 134). Krier and Vidler (1978: 42) propose that the themes of the neo-rationalist movement encompass (1) the physical and social conservation of historic centers as desirable models of collective life; (2) the conception of urban space as the primary organizing element of urban morphology; (3) topological and morphological studies as the basis for a new architectural discipline; (4) the growing awareness that the history of the city delivers precise facts, which permit one to engage an immediate and precise action, in the reconstruction of the street, the square, and the quartier; (5) the transformation of housing zones (dormitory cities) into complex parts of the city, into cities within cities, into quartiers which integrate all the functions of urban life; and (6) the rediscovery of the primary elements of architecture: the column, the wall, and the roof.

Perhaps Krier's approach presents the most comprehensive of rationalist investigations of the city and its elements. He bestows a detailed analysis of the typological and morphological elements of urban space in the book entitled *Urban Space* (1993). In enumerating the basic forms that constitute urban space, he relies heavily on historical data in identifying the range of possibilities and in considering how building sections, elevations, and intersections with other spaces affect the particular space. By analyzing examples of the formations and life of preindustrial communities, Krier (1993: 85) points out that a city is "a text composed by a community and readable by everyone ... all the functions of urban life were contained within a clear order of streets, squares and monuments." He constructs a rational classification of types by arguing "the spatial unity of the historical city has been the result of the interaction throughout the urban fabric of these types." Three particular features emerge as key organizational elements of the traditional city, which can be used to create new places, or be mixed into existing places to create a new synthesis (Lane 1993: 47):

1   The quartier, defined as "a city within a city." The quartier must "integrate all daily functions of urban life (dwelling, work, leisure) within a territory dimensioned on the basis of the comfort of a walking man" (Papadakis 1984: 70). The area of a quartier should not exceed 35 hectares in size and should be articulated into public and domestic places, monuments and urban fabric, classical architecture and vernacular buildings, squares and streets, all based on the preindustrial city.

2   The urban block is the key element in maintaining a cohesive city structure in the preindustrial city, and as such it forms the body of the present-day city. By comparing different urban street patterns in different areas of history, Krier firmly makes the point that the size of the urban block is central to the success of his approach: a block "should be no bigger than that necessary to house a dozen or so families" (Maxwell 1976: 200). These blocks should accommodate the mixed uses of living, work, recreation, and social ritual, all acknowledged as the set patterns of human behavior.

3   Distinct building typologies. Historically, various types of buildings—civic, commercial, industrial, and residential—have constituted the city, creating recognizable and intelligible places. Neo-rationalists suggest that as a replacement for the Modernist Movement's preoccupation with developing experimental models devoid of cultural or historical reference, architecture must be refounded in the intelligence of history. It must take as its concern the understanding, adaptation, and evolution of building types, which express human needs and experience.

Space morphology studies

This theory is concerned with analyzing and explaining the fundamental urban geometric character at a variety of scales. By taking apart and describing the relationships between urban components, the underlying assumptions behind these studies include the existence of spatial elements that create urban form such as rooms and transportation channels, and the need for quantifying the elements and their relationship (Moudon 1994). Space morphology research was launched in the 1950s, particularly in the Centre for Urban Form and Land Use Studies at Cambridge University, founded by Martin and March (1972). Since then, broader concepts of the organization of shapes and forms have defined the discipline, and the use of computer technology has become one of the most remarkable space morphology study developments. For example, Xi et al. (2015) undertake the spatial morphology evolution of three villages in tourism area, China, and suggest that space morphology is a dynamic process representing the methods and purpose of land use, which can be elaborated from three aspects: land-use spatial expansion, land function change, and the resultant landscape alternation.

In space morphology studies, the use of computer applications has surged in popularity (Hillier et al. 2012). Computer modeling in this field can be generalized into three broad areas of interest. The first models the three-dimensional form of urban areas and is particularly concerned with aiding geometrical composition so that proposals for new forms, or for the adaptation of existing forms, can be evaluated both visually and in terms of functional efficiency. The second is primarily concerned with the analysis of physical structures, especially individual structures such as dwelling houses, viewed in two dimensions. Much of the work relating to two-dimensional representation of urban structures can be linked to earlier attempts to develop scientific approaches to architectural geometry. Probably the best known is that of "space syntax," which can be defined as "a set of techniques for the representation, quantification and interpretation of spatial configuration of buildings and settlements" (Hillier 2009: 300). The concern, however, is not primarily with defining spatial representations; rather, it is for sociological and anthropological purposes. It is believed that social relations are actually embodied in or constituted by the spatial organization of buildings and settlement patterns (Steadman 1983: 227). In the third, the accent is upon areas, or land-use parcels, as physical configurations, especially as represented cartographically. For example, Griffiths et al. (2010) combine Conzenian and space syntax approaches in their study of the persistence of suburban centers in Greater London. A more recent notable example is the comparison of four different approaches employed in an area within Porto, Portugal, by Oliveira et al. (2015), which explores the use of morphological region, typological process, spatial configuration, and cells to improve the description, explanation, and prescription of urban form.

Similar to space syntax, there is a growing awareness of using mental maps to identify how people perceive each site and bring forth these elements/path markers, either material or immaterial, that best describe each site's physical structure. Mental map becomes a tool for reading embodied spatial configurations or generating patterns of social relations, which are invisible in plan (Psarra 2012). The mental mapping exercise tends to expose those structures that constitute each area's intangible elements. Visibility graph analysis, a method of analyzing the intervisibility connections within buildings or urban networks, is added to illustrate mental maps' visual integration values (at eye level), the visual distance from all spaces to all others (Hillier 1996). This purpose is to compare the actual visual zones of space with those of the mental one, to identify any overlaps that might arise, and to uncover those elements that affect the perception of each site's image. Where necessary, the drawings of each complex were adjusted to fit the mental maps created by the participants, which were also simplified and scaled for a comparable analysis.

In addition, the significance of space morphology studies is largely reflected in its relationship with urban design (Gosling and Maitland 1985, Jacobs and Appleyard 1987, Southworth 1990). Space morphology studies are form-giving to build environments as a primary activity involving the professions of architecture, landscape architecture, and planning (Schurch 1999). In recent years, GIS, accompanied by remote sensing (RS) and global positioning systems, have been used to explore subjects such as natural and cultural resource management, transportation, and urban planning. These techniques have been transformed and applied to urban design and morphological issues, such as (1) mapping and classifying natural and cultural landscapes (Lilley et al. 2005), (2) analyzing spatial patterns and the interaction of urban elements (Bender et al. 2005), (3) evaluating relationships between spatiotemporal changes in elements and related causal factors using both RS and socioeconomic data (Kalivas et al. 2003, Li and Yeh 2004, Xiao et al. 2006), (4) using GIS in the study of urban historic cartography in the field of urban morphology (Pinho and Oliveira 2009), and (5) applying GIS-based systems to aid in resource management and planning (Tremblay 2005).

The use of GIS in spatial analysis; in collecting, classifying, and managing multi-format data; and in abstracting complex phenomena into spatial connections between data objects has become increasingly central to morphological studies (Jiang and Claramunt 2002, Ye and Van Nes 2014). Based on much of the basic functionality for handling digital maps and the associated data for two-dimensional analysis, GIS provides a rich set of map visualization and analytical tools, as well as map creation and drawing functions. Pinho and Oliveira (2009) argue that the use of GIS enables rigorous representation of the spatial characteristics of urban phenomena, demonstrates the evolution of urban form, and identifies urban expansion areas. Li et al. (2015) employ GIS to map hotels in Hong Kong and investigate the characteristics of the land use, attractions, and transport facilities around hotels. The spatial relationships are analyzed with a set of logistic regression models. The results reveal that commercial land type and the number of attractions around hotels are significantly related to the distribution of upper-grade hotels in Hong Kong. The analysis is important theoretically for analyzing the relationships between hotels and urban structure, and for conceptualizing and identifying tourism functional zones. GIS can also handle other data such as aerial photography, spreadsheet tables, and charts.

Another prominent example of using the new technology for urban morphology is virtual reality (VR) (Gospodini 2001, Thompson et al. 2006). It uses the potential of multiple and layered perspectives through transparency and abstraction, first through the dynamism of drawing and then through the X-ray possibilities of three-dimensional modeling and digital technologies. By utilizing this technology, detailed geometric data on land parcels and buildings are becoming available and can be easily captured. It pursues principles of fragmentation, explosion, and fluidity in the process of conceptualizing buildings and spaces. VR has become a new information age tool which certainly has a profound significance for quantitative urban form research.

Summary

The study of urban morphology has attracted the interest of researchers in a number of disciplines. The traditions of urban morphology and their antecedents in landscape research are summarized in Figure 1.2; *inter alia*, the Berkeley school of cultural geography, established by Carl Sauer, can be traced back directly to German geographical roots. However, its lasting impact lay in rural landscape study rather than urban areas. Parallel to the development of the urban Anglo-German geographical school, associated with M. R. G. Conzen in town plan analysis, has been the Italian architectural school, associated with Gianfranco Caniggia and Saverio Muratori, which developed building typological thinking (Caniggia and Maffei 2001). These two schools came together in 1994 to form key components of the International Seminar on Urban Form (ISUF). Exploring the relationship between these two theoretical frameworks has been part of ISUF's wider interest in developing a body of integrated knowledge of urban form across cultures and disciplines (Moudon 1994, 1997).

The listed studies, combined with seven key approaches, provide a wide range of methodologies to delineate and analyze urban patterns. This polysemy can be found at least in three different approaches leading to the study of morphology of tourism: (1) urban growth and morphologies using classic models and techniques derived from a set of analytic measures of configurations and largely based on the observation of human behavior and people movement in a given urban environment (Hillier 2009); (2) the historico-geographical approach led by Conzen and Whitehand in the UK; and (3) the architectural typo-morphology studies led by Muratori and Caniggia in Italy. Table 1.1 summarizes the key methods used in each approach which outlines important contributions from urban morphologists in the past decades. This brief summary reflects interests in

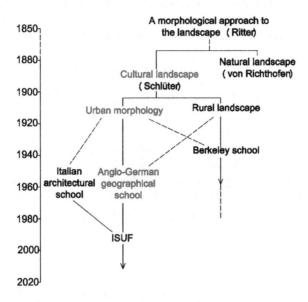

Figure 1.2 The Traditions of Landscape Research and Urban Morphology. (Source: authors)

urban characteristics, including population structure, urban intensity, and labor structure. The existing research tends to build up stronger connections between tourism and the natural environment as a whole, and lay a solid foundation for the study of specific tourist districts and attractions.

Over the course of several decades of separate development, these schools of urban morphology have established varying foundations grounded in their respective disciplines. However, the majority of urban morphological and related literature is, in spite of the revolution in information technology, still limited in its visibility. Consequently, although there has been a widening in the geographical spread of cities investigated, changes in the substance being researched have been somewhat less pronounced. In terms of conceptual roots, both the Muratorian and Conzenian Schools remain resilient and expansive with research adopting these approaches having diffused widely in different cities. There is also some evidence of the diversification and hybridization of schools of thought, but none of them specifically apply to tourism studies.

Morphological analysis relies on the existing physical fabric of the city, maps, and city plans, which range from two-dimensional to three-dimensional objects. The central purpose of such analysis is to interpret urban manifestations and anatomize the inherent information about local authority for planning control purposes, and the architects', owners', and specialists' responsibilities for urban morphological changes (Whitehand 1987). The evolutionary processes of forms identified in various theories are based on the understanding of relationship between physical objects of

Table 1.1 The Existing Morphological Analysis

	Morphological Analysis					Political Economy Analysis	Environment–Behavior Study
	Town Plan Analysis	Architectural Approaches	Ecosystem Theory	Space Morphology Studies	Neo-rationalism		
Key Authors	Conzenian School: Conzen (1960) Larkham (1996) Slater (1990) Whitehand (1981, 1992, 2007)	Muratorian School: Caniggia and Maffei (2001) Contextual studies: Cullen (1961) Roweis (1983)	Bowen (1981) Hough (1989) McHarg (1995)	Hillier and Hanson (1984) Hillier et al. (1987) Moudon (1994) Steadman (1983)	Krier (1993) Lane (1993) Rossi (1984)	Ball (1986) Harvey (1985) Knox (1991, 1992)	Alexander et al. (1987) Gehl (2011) Michelson (1970) Rapoport (2008)
Techniques for analysis	Maps, photographs, urban design plans, buildings and physical urban fabric					Qualitative, quantitative and statistical methods	Social survey, observational study
Implication	Environmental design, design control, urban development management, heritage preservation, site planning, and natural resource management					Urban geography studies	Architecture, urban design, and planning fields

the city and the sum of many different kinds of actions. In urban morphology, these actions are not simply human driven having an influence on the physical shape of objects. They are a way to explain the changes observed in forms in a given context through time (Gauthier and Gilliland 2006, Camacho-Hubner and Golay 2007). Changes are driven by endogenous causes or by the interaction of a form with its environment, such as tourism and commercial development. These actions can be stated as an abstraction of the intrinsic relationship derived from agents of change (Whitehand and Whitehand 1984), which include socioeconomic, cultural, and environmental impacts on the formal reality.

It is particularly disconcerting that some of the gaps between research and practice relate to findings embedded in the literature of urban morphological research long ago. The implications for urban planning of the markedly different degrees of persistence of street systems, building form, and land use in the 1960s have received little consideration in the planning profession (Whitehand 2015, Gu 2018). More widely, it is still not uncommon for planning to focus on land use, with ground plans and building forms receiving comparatively little attention. The problem, of course, is by no means only a matter of narrow vision among architects and urban planners. An undue focus on the particularities of the urban landscape is evident among other fields and professions. The tendency to treat features in the urban landscape such as buildings, streets, and open spaces as individual objects rather than parts of an integrated entity is widespread. Within built environment studies and professions, appreciation of the objects under consideration, though commonly grounded in a functional or formal typology, frequently lacks understanding of, and sympathy with, how they fit together and why these changes occur.

Another problem lies within the realm of heritage conservation. Much of the singling out of urban heritage sites for protection and special treatment has focused in a rather narrow way on landmark monuments and sites of historic significance rather than viewing these as an integral part of a wider historical urban landscape. Heritage sites are often developed for the purpose of tourism, and a process of commercialization is evident in some historical landmarks. The UNESCO World Heritage Centre is currently addressing this very matter through its focus on historic urban landscapes in its Cities Program. However, only belatedly have some of the significant problems of conservation inherent in such a limited perspective been recognized, and they are far from being resolved. The incidence of the problem has also varied geographically and historically. The challenge is to look in more detail at the different approaches to urban morphology, especially at their logic and focus, to better understand if and how they fit together and might more actively complement one another. An integrated approach to the urban landscape is crucial for linking urban morphology to other disciplines, such as tourism, so that the field can advance to the next level.

This chapter provides an overview of urban morphology theories developed over the past decades. It reveals that morphology is not to be interpreted as form but refers to the science of form (Larkham 1996). All the elements defined above continue to provide basic building blocks for creating cities, towns, villages, and rural spaces that people can easily understand, navigate, and appreciate. The spatiotemporal perspectives have existed in all definitions of morphology from the early decades to the present, and the majority of research has been longitudinal and historical. On the other hand, although there is an overlap in several theories and approaches, they lay the foundations for investigating the morphology of tourism. Exploring the relationship among these emphases and further forming an integrated framework promise to be the cutting-edge work of tourism morphology research. Morphological analysis, specifically town plan analysis, architectural approaches, the ecosystem theory, and space morphology studies, deals with more "objective" elements such as maps, urban design plans, and existing buildings, space, and natural environments. All are closely associated with tourism and the use of physical elements for planning tourist destinations. Particularly, environment–behavior studies are concerned more about people's "subjective" intentions and the relationships between human behaviors in the context of social, cultural, and built environments. These contexts reflect the problems and prospects of using tourism resources for commercial purposes, such as the involvement of public participation and the comprehensive tourism planning required to make better use of the sociocultural infrastructure in the community. Finally, political economy analysis focuses on the political and economic impacts on urban form and the functions of social agencies in the development process. This approach has gradually transformed policy towards investment in tourism and leisure services.

2 A conceptual framework for the morphology of tourism

Green spaces, genius loci, and non-lieux

Since classical times, towns and cities have performed tourism and leisure functions, and therefore, such places have a long history for tourist consumption (Page 2011). From its inception, tourism has been associated with geomorphology, in which physical distinctiveness is the focus, for example, the Grand Canyon, Yellowstone National Park, and other natural wonders. It is also closely related to green space, which offers different configurations and levels of access, such as public parks, sports grounds, and the grounds of institutions. Billinge (1996: 450) comments that "perhaps the single newest element in the townscape after the general regulation of the street, was the park, and more specifically the recreation ground ... was essentially a nineteenth century phenomenon and a symbol of civic pride."

Green spaces illustrate the existence of enormous spatial variations in the proportion of the landscapes that have historically been set aside for public and private recreational activities (Fuller and Gaston 2009). The spatial development shows periods of outward expansion of the mainly residential built-up areas and gradually converted them for recreational purposes, notably green spaces, form fringe belts at or a little beyond the urban fringe, which later become embedded within the urban area in subsequent expansion. The zones of mostly low-intensity land use that tend to be created in this way play a significant role in tourism. Not least they give shape and intelligibility to the urban area for comprehending distributions such as those of green spaces (Taylor and Hochuli 2017) and providing a framework that can contribute to redevelopment and conservation.

Postmodernism provides a new path for morphological processes, where the importance of green space is rediscovered and reconstructed for tourism and leisure. The commercialization of space is arguably important for the "movement economy" (Hillier 1996), where the power of movement generates social and economic outcomes in cities, in particular by bringing people in and facilitating encounters. The successful examples include Stanley Park in Vancouver, Canada, Kings Park in Perth, Australia, and

Auckland Domain in New Zealand, where many multiple-use green spaces have been converted into tourism attractions (Hall and Page 2014). Space has shifted as a continuing dynamic including a component of history, power relations, and changing built fabric, which also provides a focal point for community interaction, a context for commercial development, allowing opportunities for meeting tourism needs and provision of visual amenity. The acceleration of mobility and globalization entails a sort of time-space compression that has radical impacts on how people choose to travel and their appreciation of nature, landscape, and other societies. The physical form of cities is understood as a type of embodied knowledge that is activated by human use for leisure purposes (Marcus et al. 2016). Gradually, towns and cities provide the rich context for a diverse range of social, cultural, and economic activities in which the population engages, and where tourism, leisure, and entertainment form major service activities (Minhat and Amin 2012).

Foucault (1977, 1986) declares that "space itself has a history"—that the interstices of built places are derived from social, cultural, and economic contexts. The force of tourism drives the changing landscape and impacts the configuration of almost every assumption, objective, skill, and preference of the society at large. Space has increasingly become mobile and interactive with locals and tourists (Sudradjat 2012). Hadid (2016) proposes that the renovation of London's Leicester Square should turn into "a public room, habitable and submerged beneath the surface, a heart that beats within the city." From this perspective, green space embodies the surrounding environment where

> solid and transparent skyscrapers slicing into the earth could contain accommodation, and water could cascade down these inverted canyons as a cooling mechanism for an overworked heart. Bridges and passages would traverse the voids and solids of the new subterranean fabric, while light slits would remind the visitor of the city's familiar fabric hovering above.

In a similar vein, Judd (1993: 179), in his discussion of tourism in US cities, suggests that

> agglomeration economies apply to tourist districts not principally because concentration lowers or increases the efficiency of business transactions, but because a full panoply of services and businesses is necessary to make the space maximally attractive to consumers of the tourist space.

The tourist space emerges, including tourism infrastructure such as convention centers, sports franchises, shopping malls, casinos, and "carousal zones," and reshapes the urban tissue. Therefore, the morphology of tourism tends to emphasize the systematic description while analyzing a tourist destination as a multilayered place. The identification of isomorphic patterns in tourism focuses on valid spatial codes that integrate sociocultural, economic, and environmental aspects of transformation.

The growing attention to tourism in recent decades is largely attributed to the "cultural turn" and the pursuit of *genius loci*: a "sense of place" or "spatial spirit" (Karimi 2000) developing from the spatial reordering of the world. The concept of the cultural turn is rooted in an ideological paradigm viewing tourism as the dynamic motor of the economy. Tourism is heavily implicated in what Barnes (2001: 558) labels the "new economic geography," which "emphasizes above all the social and especially the cultural character of the economy." Tourists consume goods and services that are in some sense "out of the ordinary," where the viewing of tourist sites and places can generate "a much greater sensitivity to visual elements of landscape or townscape than is normally found in everyday life" (Urry and Larsen 2011: 3).

The thinking and making function of tourism resources are a way of organizing, knowing, and describing the changing world. Buildings, structures, and vacationscapes are creations of a process of reimagining for tourists from all over the world. From a supply-side perspective, the appreciation of vernacular architecture plays a significant role in attracting and structuring the tourist experience (Xie and Sohoni 2010), which both draws people towards a destination and provides the structures that support tourism, such as hotels and shopping malls. Dupont et al. (2016) posit that the "cultural turn" is largely a function of globalization and neoliberalism worldwide. The former draws cities into competing against other urban centers on a global stage, while the latter reflects a powerful dominant discourse and strategy to restructure, rescale, and reorder accumulation and regulation in capitalist societies. Globalization engenders an accelerated shift from manufacturing to informational economies, and from the latter to cultural economies. Hall (2000) and Polyák (2015) further argue that this economic shift influences social attitudes, generates new values, and turns culture into a device to formulate an attractive urban image to mobile capital. In this context, tourist cities are being reconfigured, giving rise to "a 'glocalized' landscape; an emerging urban landscape-collage" (Beriatos and Gospodini 2004: 312) dominated either by tradition, with local spatial references, or by morphogenesis, illustrating a flow of tourists from all over the world.

Meanwhile, the Latin term *genius loci* describes a new esthetic appreciation of landscapes and becomes allied to the "character" of a place (Worskett 1969). Jakle (1987) stresses the individual and subjective nature of place in his discussion of *genius loci* and finds an innate conflict between verbal and visual thinking. He proposes that the best person to experience and express the *genius loci* is not local residents but tourists, as tourism "involves the deliberate searching out of place experience" (8).

Walter (1988) implicitly applies *genius loci* to a study of the "expressive intelligibility" of places, for example, a quality that can only be perceived holistically through the senses, memory, intellect, and imagination. Similar to Tuan (1977)'s view of space as the embodiment of the feelings, images, and thoughts of those who live, work, or otherwise deal with that space, tourism connects spatial change with tourists' perception of *genius loci*. This is especially so when a place's various publics have been steeped in economic, cultural and sociopolitical changes, and where landscape is revitalized for tourism.

Nonetheless, tourism development involves the movement of people through time and space, either between their home and destinations, or within destination areas. Typically, tourism activities have a positive effect on the development of culture and entertainment, thus becoming a progressive formation of experience societies (Rifkin 2011). The desire to understand the spatial interactions of tourists within a destination and the movement of tourists between destinations has played a critical role in the developing investigation of the phenomenon of tourism (McKercher and Lew 2004). In the meantime, the rapid development of culture, entertainment, sports events, and festivals is often used to restructure different urban spheres, as well as to create a positive image of a city. Tourism has entered a new stage of historical and socioeconomic development in which spatial transformations occur constantly. The urban revival is a particular feature of postmodernism, which is exemplified by the redevelopment of open spaces via tourism. The rise of *genius loci* and pursuit of authenticity (Ouf 2001) elucidate the importance of urban regeneration and the impact of tourism on urban form. A wider discussion of the "character" of towns and cities is developed (Jiven and Larkham 2003) in relation to *genius loci*, which arises from the experiences of those using places rather than from deliberate "place-making."

The challenge in how space is developed for tourist consumption is a major concern for urban planners and architects. Nowadays, activities for work, creativity, and leisure may simultaneously occur in *non-lieux*: spaces without clear functional identity. The term "*non-lieu*," or non-place, has been proposed by Marc Augé (2009), who observes three kinds of accelerated transformations that are responsible for what he calls the "supermodernity" of the changing urban form. The first is an "acceleration of history" (26) leading to an excess of events, where economic activities have overwhelmed the original function of the sites. The second is a surplus in the realm of space, in which "the excess of space is correlative with the shrinking of the planet" (31). The last is "figure of excess," a sign of transformation of what he calls "the figure of the ego, the individual" (36). Reterritorialized spaces, in the context of supermodernity, should embody the past within historical and social meanings; concomitantly, "normal" social interaction ought to occur. Augé designates places in which these connections do not happen as "a space which cannot be defined as relational, or historical, or concerned with identity," or "a non-place" (77–78). Non-places are produced by supermodernity and do not integrate with earlier places.

Augé's "non-place" theory posits that the morphology of tourism is a complex process in which development can be easily divorced from any sense of locality. Tourism plays a dual role: on the one hand, it resuscitates local economies, encouraging the redevelopment of existing urban forms, the adaptive reuse of old buildings and the construction of new spaces of consumption. On the other hand, tourism projects are sometimes at odds with the goal of maintaining a connection to the history and culture of local communities. Understanding the spatial implications of such processes requires the use of evolutionary methodologies to understand the complexity and simplify the reality of tourist activities to a more meaningful series of concepts and constructs.

Although tourism geographers play a substantive role in demonstrating how the larger process of cultural transformation manipulates and shapes the contemporary economy, there is much contention and debate over what constitutes "morphology" as "tourism." Dialogue between tourism scholars and urban morphologists is relatively muted. One reason is that morphology is not confined to urban morphology alone, tourism takes place outside conventional urban settings and has distinctive forms and shapes. Another reason for this is that research emphasis has changed over time and, appropriately for urban morphology, over space as well. There is a dearth of appropriate concepts posing the difficulties, especially for tourist cities witnessing the fastest rates of population and labor force growth. No analysis of the morphology of tourism can commence without an understanding of the historical and geographical processes related to its development. By tracing tourism development since its rapid expansion in the early twentieth century, it is possible to examine many changes to the form, function, and format of morphology and its spatial occurrence in these key elements.

This chapter begins with a review of classic theories of morphology, and considers their applicability to tourism development. It starts with the review of historical development of tourism morphology with its multidisciplinary and scalar interpretations. The second part considers elements of urban tissue in the context of tourism planning, as well as the importance of points, lines, and areas for development. The final section proposes a conceptual framework and presents the complex interplay of urban morphology, tourism, and its impact on all levels of societies. It shows the close relationships between the physical form of the urban morphology and tourism activities. It examines how elements of urban morphology, such as the natural context, the street system, the plot system, and the building system, have an impact on tourists' attraction in the environmental, sociocultural, and economic contexts.

The history of tourism morphology

The 1920s–1930s: the green belt concept

The development of morphology as an academic discipline can be dated to the 1920s, when geography was established as a major subject at the university level (Hall and Page 2014). Carl Sauer, a well-known American geographer, was probably the first scholar to address the issue of travel morphology in English literature. His seminal article entitled *The Morphology of Landscape* (1925) describes morphology from the biological perspectives by focusing on the study of organic forms and structures, or the architecture of organism. Through classifying the forms and characterizing their historical structures, ranging from concrete materials to social phenomena, Sauer identifies the complex structures of the cultural landscape and subjects them to compare with different periods as homologies in order to trace developmental stages. He boldly proposes that the process of morphology relates to cultural geography in the following ways: (1) units of organic or quasi-organic quality, for which certain components are necessary, comprise the "form" of a given structure; (2) similarity or functional equivalence of the form in different structures is recognized to render those structures "homologous"; and (3) structural units may be placed in a series according to their developmental status, ranging from an incipient to a final or completed stage. As a result, the morphological method is viewed as a particular form of synthesis, an inductive procedure for identifying the major structural (form) elements in the landscape and arranging them in a developmental sequence (morphogenesis). Morphogenesis has been gaining prominence in social science fields, where the continued synthesis of phenomena by morphological methods has been recognized.

One consequence of geography's development in the 1920s and the rise of an applied focus on geography was the increasing move towards the coastal areas of European countries (Liu and Wall 2009). The changing coastal line in Britain inspired the first scholarly forays into the field of resort morphology, which is defined as the study of the forms, including environment as land uses and the associated functions of a destination area and its development. The coastal areas are viewed as dynamic and interactive over different periods of time. Williams and Shaw (1998) analyze the rise and fall of the English seaside or coastal resort and examine the two principal concerns of the historical geographer: continuity and change in the development, and organization and prospects for the resort. Resort morphology is regarded as a representation of resort evolution, while tourism becomes an integral part of resort town planning rather than a mere adjunct (Smith 1992a).

In the 1930s, the green belt concept was initiated in Britain and quickly spread to many other European cities. The green belt was a band of open space on the city's periphery, created in order to compensate for the lack of open space in the built environment. As part of urban planning, such designations were intended to limit urban sprawl, rather than the characteristics of the land itself and its use (Gant et al. 2011). The green belt concept is used to describe the traditional space set aside for commercial leisure use as well as the urban-rural fringe, or peri-urban zone. McKenzie (1997) defines this kind of fringe as an area extending from the edge of a city's contiguous urban development to the outer edge of the vehicular commuter belt. Typical features include high population growth and commercial development, accommodated by spatially extensive urban-oriented land uses. The encroachment of tourist attractions, such as golf courses, is highly visible along the green belt. The centrifugal forces that draw people away from city are counterbalanced by centripetal forces, such as employment for tourism and diversity of services (Weaver and Lawton 2001). The green belt not only serves as the grounds for the evolution and rise of a chaotic set of conflicting land uses amid pressure for urban growth, but also highlights the major recreational role key sites play in a given locale, although their lack of identity and seemingly anonymous non-place status is juxtaposed (Gant et al. 2011). As with tourism destinations, rapid change in the green belt generates tension, leading Troughton (1981) to describe the exurbs as a zone of competition and conflict. Relevant issues include the loss or fragmentation of farmland, environmental problems caused by the proliferation of septic tanks and wells, road congestion caused by commuting, and the high costs of servicing a dispersed population.

The 1960s–1970s: from townscape to vacationscape

In 1959, Italian urban morphologist, Saverio Muratori, published a book entitled *Studi Per Una Operante Storia Urbana Di Venezia* ("Studies for an Operative History of Cities"), which analyzes eight principal areas of the city of Venice. The investigation is based on a set of fundamental urban concepts, such as type, urban tissue, and organism and operative history. Aldo Rossi's *L'architettura della città* ("The Architecture of the City") came off the press in 1966 and spread the theory of typo-morphology through schools of architecture worldwide. Both books suggest that the rationality of history is through the reconstruction of the process of derivation of both the architectural and urban form. Urban tissue is a part of intellectual history, inasmuch as the idea emerged within the context of debates on architecture and urbanism. Muratori argues that Renaissance Venice was a symbolic synthesis of a continuous and polycentric city. Although the book does not specify the influence of booming tourism in Venice, his work is widely seen as the harbinger of tourism morphology, where the cities as tourist origins have been frequently studied (Pearce 1978, 1979, 1998). This book also marks the start of using distinct architecture combined with history for tourism resources.

Following the rise of the Muratorian School, tourism morphology has gradually received more academic attention in the 1960s and early 1970s, when the urban landscape became the primary theme of geography studies. Kevin Lynch's book (1960) entitled *the Image of the City* examines the look of the city as well as the possibilities of changing it. In Lynch's series of studies (1960, 1972, 1981), his primary contribution is the use of "mental maps" as a means of representing individual perceptions of a place. He proposes a model in which city images, related to physical forms, are classified into five elements: paths (channels along which people move through the city); edges (the boundaries in continuity); districts (areas characterized by common characteristics); nodes (strategic focal points for orientation); and landmarks (external points of orientation). These elements were utilized to check the visual forms of Boston, Jersey City, and Los Angeles. In addition, Lynch takes the notion of "legibility" (also called "imageability") as being synonymous with the "legibility" of a place, that is, "the ease with which its parts can be recognized and can be organized into a coherent pattern" (Lynch 1960: 2). A truly "imageable" environment enables its residents to feel at home in their surroundings. He also emphasizes certain qualities as requisite for a livable city or good urban form including vitality (biological and ecological), access (open space, services, and jobs), control (human space), sense (clarity with which it can be perceived), fit (adaptability), efficiency (cost), and justice (social equity) (Appleyard et al. 1965).

Five elements and certain qualities proposed by Lynch serve as a fertile ground for tourism planning, particularly the described interrelated ways, the form qualities, the sense of the wholeness, and the process of design. In addition, his method of using sketch maps to uncover environmental images has been adapted as a tool in both tourism planning and policy-making. The combination of the residential history, socioeconomic status, information sources, experience, and preferences of a tourist creates a cognitive image, which, in turn, influences the choice of destinations. However, the analysis of sketch maps is an inherently subjective exercise, as the distinction between nodes and landmarks may be unclear without a cross-examination of the map drawer. The typology of map elements also poses a problem for tourists, as the perceived nodes fluctuate to the geographical location as well as the size of nodes varies. Therefore, Lynch (1960: 5) adds that "a distinctive and legible environment not only offers emotional security but also heightens the potential depth and intensity of human experience." There is great need for further qualitative research to work out why mental maps take the form that they do and how quickly they change as the environment changes. Especially, there is a need to investigate whether landmarks for tourists can be transformed into nodes as learning continues and tourists become more familiar with the environment (Jenkins and Walmsley 1993).

Jane Jacobs, one of the best-known critics in urban planning, lashed out at the evils of massive urban renewal and relocation projects in her

1961 book *The Death and Life of Great American Cities* (1961), claiming that these projects have undermined the social fabric and economic vitality of the city. Jacobs' strong interest in understanding how cities actually work, rather than how they ought to look and function, led her to explore the patterns of social behavior found in urban neighborhoods, particularly the uses and social functions of leisure sidewalks, small neighborhood shops, and local parks in New York City's Greenwich Village. Opposing the vast impersonal nature of most city projects, she argues that human scale must be preserved in neighborhoods. In her suggestions to urban designers and planners, Jacobs advocates diversity in neighborhood planning, dense concentrations of people, small blocks, mixed building types, and mixed space to encourage the presence of people on the streets and to create a sense of shared responsibility, tempered by a respect for individual privacy. Her emphasis on surveillance (i.e., eye on the street) as a means of ensuring neighborhood safety was later incorporated into Newman's (1972) work on defensible space. Jacob's theory of urban tissue has served to prompt a reexamination of prejudices, a reconsideration of established habits, and a revision of what the city is and how to act upon it in order to sustain its life (Malfroy 1995).

Published in the same year, the book *Townscape* by Gordon Cullen documents the basic ingredients of township and argues that the art of relationship depends on three fundamental concepts: serial vision, place, and content. Serial vision is strongly related to optics and motion, in which the landscape becomes an open text to interpret. What the book proposes for is that the city is fluid containing specific fabric of towns, such as color, texture, scale, style, character, uniqueness, and authentic experience. The term "townscape" connotes historical expressiveness or historicity in its own *personnalite'* (Conzen 1949: 89). Conzen (1966) further advocates that, when form after form is added to the surface of the earth, the whole cultural landscape should be seen as an "objectivation of the spirit" of a society. Commercial development highlighting the protection of heritage, the monumentalizing of historic centers, and the restoration and maintenance of historic building for the sake of "collective inheritance" becomes an integral part of township planning. The concept of the townscape refers to geographical variations in the composition of town plan, building pattern, and land utilization.

Cullen's concept of the townscape has been widely adapted by tourism scholars who view the tourism development and its concomitant effects as an evolutionary process. Stansfield (1969, 1972) initiates the development of modern seaside resorts in the US and England from parks and recreation perspectives. Clare Gunn's work in *Vacationscape: Designing Tourist Regions* (1972) deftly switches focus from the townscape to the vacationscape in order to illustrate the reality of destinations. The concept of the vacationscape was extended and expanded in his following book entitled *Tourism Planning* (1979). It is probable that Gunn's early experiences traveling with his family in a Model A Ford on the primitive roads of 1929 from Michigan throughout the West piqued his interest in tourism. As he recalls,

> because we were traveling West long before roads were capable of handling the "modern" cars, we had 29 flat tires and wore out a set of brakes. But this and other camping trips enabled us to drink in the wonders of nature.

Gunn's *Vacationscape* was arguably the world's first textbook on tourism (Crompton 2015), as he acknowledges that the focus of tourism is almost exclusively on promotion; however, research, planning, visitor impacts, and relationship of tourism to the built and natural environments are of at least equal importance.

The 1970s witnessed the evolution of the towns and cities where people live, work, and engage in leisure. Eventually, it resulted from the process of urbanization (Pacione 2009). Urbanization, largely driven by a series of interrelated processes of change, is a major force contributing to the development of towns and cities. Many studies started addressing the pattern of land use, infrastructure, Central Business Districts, Recreational Business District (RBD), and the ramifications of urban sprawl for socioeconomic and environmental problems. The boom of hotel development and resort establishment in urban settings was a leitmotif of morphological studies in the 1970s. For example, Lamb (1983) suggests that the outer boundary of a city's day trip recreational hinterland could be used as an indicator to define the outer limits of the city's commuting sphere. Clark and Crichter (1985) provide an historical analysis of leisure and recreational forms in Britain during the nineteenth and twentieth centuries, with an emphasis on the urban forms and poetical factors, forms of social control. They adopt a cross-sectional approach to analyze key periods of tourism development, as well as how the evolution of urban places and recreational activities emerged.

The morphology of tourism exhibits a unique pattern where tourist destinations and local residences can be separate, mingle, or coexist. The overall result has been a tendency for a growing number of people to live and work in expanding towns and cities. Simultaneously, urbanization coupled with tourism results in some important changes in the characters and dynamics of the urban system, land use, social ecology, and built environment. The built form of cities is seen as embodying social, cultural, and economic relations by structuring "patterns of movement, encounter and avoidance" (Hillier and Hanson 1984: ix). From this perspective, the built fabric emerges as a highly intelligent artifact with an intricate, dynamic, and multifaceted system for the storage and retrieval of information related to a wide range of societal processes. Government policies, legal changes, city planning, and urban management may eventually address such problems, stimulating changes that, in turn, affect the dynamics that drive the overall urbanization process.

The 1980s–2000s: tourism business district

Urbanization continued to transform the environment in a profound way in 1980s and became a driving force for social changes. The spatial patterns of tourism facilities and the ways in which they cluster became a central concern for scholars of tourism. For instance, Smith (1987), drawing on country-level data, analyzes four basic tourism regions, including urban fringe tourism. Other studies include Wall and Sinnott's (1980) account of urban recreational facilities as attractions; Boyer (1980) on the evolution of second homes in suburbs for recreational purposes; and Vedenin (1982) on changes in recreational systems. Mullins (1991) further suggests that tourist cities represent an extraordinary form of urbanization, in which cities are built solely for consumption.

In addition, political economic factors, along with the built environment, are closely associated for tourism development as dynamic processes are emphasized. Due to the complexity and uncertainty of urban forms, morphological analysis tends to link environment-behavior studies to gauge tourism impacts on districts and specific destinations. Regarding the basic categories of public open spaces that are addressed to tourism, Boerwinkel (1995: 251–255) suggests two fundamental types of spatial order underlying the formal variety: (1) successive arrangement, in which the observer experiences a step-by-step uncovering of space through both sight and movement; and (2) simultaneous arrangement, in which buildings and open spaces are arranged in such a manner as to encourage relatively "free exploration" of space by the individual. Grainger (1995), through a survey of national land-use morphology, proposes a basic geographic concept and a key element in the emerging theory of human–environment relationship and the modeling of global environmental change. He incorporates tourist flows to three applications, for example, international static comparisons, modeling generic nonspatial and spatial trends over time; and modeling global environmental change.

Perhaps one of the most important contributions to tourism studies in the 1980s is the Tourism Area Life Cycle (TALC), proposed by Richard Butler (1980). The TALC hypothesizes what might happen to tourist destinations as they develop and reach their limits in terms of carrying capacity. It is focused more on the spatial implications of the growth and development of tourist destinations than on the specific pattern and process of development in specific destinations (Butler 2004). Hall (2004) points out that the geographical concepts at the heart of the TALC were clear in the 1980 version, but in reality, the original form was much more spatial in its orientation. Wolfe (1982) proposes an alternative curve of destination development (which he labeled the "Ellis Curve"), comprising axes of economic and environmental quality, with positive and negative components. A typical trajectory for a destination, he argues, begins positive for both elements, passes through a stage where only the economic aspect is positive, to a point at which both elements are negative, as tourism begins to negatively affect the environment and fails to generate sufficient return on investment.

Building on Stansfield and Rickert's earlier resort-based concept of RBD (1970), research began to shift in the 1990s towards a growing interest in exploring Tourism Business Districts (TBD). This shift is evident in Getz's (1993) work on how contrasting planning systems, one regulatory and the other proactive, have resulted in markedly different tourism developments in Niagara Falls in both Canada and the US. For example, in both border cities, older "downtown" areas have been eclipsed; on the US side, tourist-oriented facilities and services have been consciously mixed with normal central business land uses, forming a well-defined TBD. The establishment of the TBD clearly indicates the changing landscape due to impacts of tourism, where the meaning of landscape is created, recreated, and contested in social processes (Ringer 1998).

Ashworth and Tunbridge (1990, 2000) establish a model of the tourist-historic city as an attempt to understand the role of historic city tourism within the urban mosaic of forms and functions, and to consider the impacts of the spending and behavior of tourists upon historic cities. Through case studies of several tourist cities, they uncover distinct patterns, such as clustering and linear distributions in the inner city, which may be explained in terms of such factors as accessibility, land use, zoning restrictions, and proximity to other tourism-related phenomena. They employ distributional studies to delineate urban hotel location, where hotels may be clustered as a function of proximity to inner-city historical attractions and businesses, or with regard to transport termini and highway access. Larkham (1996) further proposes to use tourism as a tool for conservation as a tourist city has transformed at various stages of development. Land-use intensity and resort restructuring strategies were widely discussed to better understand the impact of tourism businesses. In Asia, Kuala Lumpur, Malaysia, was used as a case study to explore urban hotel location and changing patterns in various periods of times (Oppermann et al. 1996).

Morphological analysis in the 1990s mainly addresses complex, diverse, and dynamic issues about tourism relevant to urban forms and society at large. As Jansen-Verbeke and Ashworth (1990: 619) contend,

> tourism development depends upon concentration rather than on dispersal, functional combination rather than segregation, and multifunctional environments rather than monofunctional ones. Success depends upon the functional integration of facilities within multipurpose clusters, which necessitates more attention being paid to the nature of integration.

In the meantime, tourism researchers have responded to the phenomenon of destination morphology in various ways. For example, Pearce (1979) traces the development of geographical interest in tourism and raises possible research avenues and theoretical developments. Six major areas of interest are identified: spatial aspects of supply, spatial aspects of demand, the geography of resorts, patterns of movements and flows, the impact of tourism, and models of tourist space. Smith (1983) initiates the patterns of restaurants and dining out as a new way of geography of tourism business. Wall et al. (1985) draw attention to the significance of large cities as tourist destinations and to the importance of accommodation establishments as a component of urban fabric. Using accommodation directories as the major source of information, they describe the changing numbers and types of accommodation, and analyze the spatial distribution of accommodations using the methods of point pattern analysis. Lew (1987) stresses the importance of studying travel attractions/regions and identifies three perspectives that could be adopted in morphological studies: (1) a cognitive perspective that examines how tourists perceive attractions and travel regions, (2) an ideographic perspective that explores a site's "unique" attributes and its "universal" (in the sense used above) attributes, and (3) an organizational perspective that examines geographical aspects such as the relationship between the location of a region and its spatially dispersed markets.

The 2000s and beyond: impacts of tourism on morphology

Since the 2000s, attentions have switched to modeling of destination morphology (Nepal 2009), as well as concerns about the potentially detrimental effects of overtourism on existing urban forms. A tourist destination is seen as a complex dynamic in which changes to the design of one region will affect changes to the morphology and economy (Prideaux 2000, Andriotis 2003, Lohmann and Duval 2014). For example, Nahm (1999) traces the transformation of central Seoul in Korea and the development of manufacturing-tertiary-quaternary industrial complexes. Tourist attractions change the characteristics of downtown to a more flexible and volatile system. The teritiarization and quaternarization of tourism, in the name of urban renewal, become a nucleus for economic performance. Morphology of tourism turns into the concrete outcome of social and economic forces. Kneafsey (2001) analyzes the process of cultural commodification in the rural tourism economy of Brittany, France, and discovers that the cultural economy is clearly evident through the commodification of the landscape, which results in the production of an "idealized countryside" and "vernacular buildings."

The last two decades have witnessed a phenomenal growth of the urban-rural fringe and explanations about the spatial pattern of tourists' movement around destinations. Many researchers have used four factors—population, economy, sociocultural factors, and the geographical landscape—to measure urbanization and suburbanization (Fang and Yao 2006, Chen et al. 2010). For instance, Weaver and Lawton (2001) explore residents' perception of tourism in the urban-rural fringe; Lew and McKercher (2006) depict the spatial movement patterns of tourists within a destination based on urban transportation modeling and tourist behavior, in order to identify explanatory factors that could influence movement. Wu and Cai (2006) coined the term Recreational Belts Around Metropolis (ReBAM) in order to describe the spatial patterns of urban residents' leisure travel to suburban areas, and to measure recreation and tourism development in these areas. Using the case of Shanghai, China, and applying the concepts of a tourism matrix, Wu and Cai demonstrate that growth of domestic demand, policy-driven supply, and transportation networks constitute the three determinants underlying the formation of the ReBAM. A spatial interaction model reflecting the concept of distance decay and land lease rates is constructed for tourism planning. Zhang et al. (2013) measure the relationship between levels of urbanization and hotel growth from the perspectives of urbanization, tourism demand, and policy. The results show a positive relationship between urbanization and hotel growth. In a similar vein, Luo et al. (2016) examine the impacts of urbanization on tourism development in four regions of Guangdong Province by utilizing time series data in China, ranging from 1996 to 2011. Results show that urbanization has been operationalized by a wide variety of attributes, such as population, economic forces, geographical landscape, and sociocultural dimensions. In general, these attributes facilitate tourism development; however, they do not affect different regions in Guangdong Province uniformly. Tourism development tends to receive different impacts from urbanization.

In the meantime, there are a growing number of historic cities being used as case studies by scholars of tourism morphology (Xu 2000). For example, the city of Suzhou in China was built on an orthogonally designed water-based grid, connecting the Grand Canal and Tai Lake (Breitung and Lu 2016). This water grid once played an important role in commercial activities and social interactions in the city, but over time, more and more canals were filled in to pave roads and build houses. The transport system has now almost entirely switched to the street grid. Drawing on historical maps, chronicles, artwork, and existing studies, it employs urban morphology as a method to understand the significance of waterways for the identity of Suzhou. Tourism development is presented as a chance to reactivate the water grid for the purposes of heritage conservation, transportation, and the enhancement of tourist experiences. In a similar vein, Sheng et al. (2017) trace the island city of Macau, China, which has expanded and become increasingly connected to the Mainland over the centuries. The reclaimed land is used for casinos and tourism development, which causes further urban fragmentation. The study shows that urban morphology is necessary to better understand rapid urbanization and the growth of coastal cities.

Spatial analytical tools have been used in recent years to plan tourist spaces, as well as to quantitatively analyze the relationship between morphological features and tourist preferences (Li et al. 2016). The rapid development and increasing availability of Geographic Information Systems (GIS) and space syntax analysis have led to a growing volume of spatial research in general, and tourism studies in particular (Allen et al. 1999). The primary function of the GIS serves to collect, capture, store, retrieve, and analyze spatial patterns, with the objective of providing a systematic record of the way in which destinations evolve in space over different periods of time. It has advantages over conventional methods in integrating various data sources, performing spatial analysis, modeling spatial processes, and mapping the results in land-use change studies. However, the application of GIS in tourism research has been minimal, even though GIS technology has been widely discussed in the tourism literature for over a decade (Urry and Larsen 2011). Thus far, tourism planning, recreation and park management, and visual resource assessment are the three tourism-related fields that have most frequently made use of GIS (Tremblay 2005).

As noted in Chapter 1, space syntax analysis has contributed to a better understanding of how spatial configuration affects movement flows, the location of economic activities, and the numerical levels of street life (Karimi 2000, 2012). It differs from classic urban morphology because it focuses on open space systems to pursue a form of spatial representation in which three types of distance metrics are adapted: topological (fewest turns paths), geometrical (least angle change paths), and metric (shortest physical paths). Space syntax measures the morphology of tourism through the spatial configuration of street networks, buildings, and accessibility of attractions. In recent years, there is a trend to utilize space syntax analysis for tourist space and provide a visualized and quantitative approach coupled with the application of GIS. Li et al. (2016) apply this strategy and develop research on tourist space organization in Gulangyu Island, China. The relationship between street network integration and the urban fabric as well as tourist preferences collated from data mining are explored. Urban morphology is presented as a chance to reactive heritage conservation, transport, and the enhancement of tourist experience. In addition, technological advancements in morphographic shape, such as the invention of aerial photographs, have led to a new era in longitudinal studies of urban form (Hussain and Ismail 2015).

Elements of urban tissue for tourism

The delineation of urban morphology, as addressed in Chapter 1, has many different meanings. This polysemy can be found at least in three different approaches leading to the study of tourism morphology: (1) the use of formal models, such as fractals or cellular automata, to link tourism development to larger cycles of urbanization, suburbanization, deurbanization, and reurbanization (Malfroy 1995); (2) deriving a GIS and space syntax from the observation of human behavior in a given urban environment; and (3) the deployment of a historico-geographical approach, combined with architectural typo-morphology, to produce temporal and historical meanings of urban changes.

These approaches express dynamics of expansion and contraction characteristic of modern areas closely related to tourism development. In terms of urban growth, the saturation of tourists in an urban center in a phase of urbanization causes overcrowding and congestion. Residents who are displaced to neighboring areas as a result often face the lack of infrastructure in a phase of spontaneous suburbanization along with the excessive dispersion in deurbanization and the conflicting patterns of old and new development in the stage of reurbanization. Therefore, tourism, as an exogenous factor, deconstructs the definition of the urban morphological process and alters spatiotemporal changes as well as perceptions of urban tissue. Camacho-Hubner and Golay (2007: 97) differentiate between "spontaneous consciousness" and "critical consciousness" in urban development. The former refers to the vernacular changes that occur every time a building operator finds himself or herself working in continuity with the inherited cultural experiences, while the latter indicates a systematic experience that leads a building operator to choose among different existing alternatives. The characterization of "critical consciousness" engenders the evolution of urban forms, as "historical events" morph into "tourism events" and eventually into "morphological events."

Tourism measures three principal changes in the definitions and uses of urban tissue: (1) tracking variations in the forms of concepts that have remained central to urban development over time, in order to trace the empirical evidence of a morphological process. For example, the concept of plot, a parcel of land representing a land-use unit defined by boundaries on the ground, is a shared concept in every morphological analysis, but the forms taken by this concept shift according to different periods or places, and the evolution of this form is analyzed as the process of plot pattern metamorphosis; (2) change of concepts when the evolution of a concept is most difficult to interpret. For example, a road is a quasi-permanent concept with many sub-concepts to differentiate a path from a highway. In the meantime, "cultural turn" has undergone a radical change when a concept disappears or a new one emerges catering to tourists; and (3) change of meaning which relates to changes in the context of enunciation, in which the sign takes on another value and becomes the vector of some different information.

Given the complexity of urban processes, Oliveira (2016) proposes to simplify the elements of urban tissue and offers an effective framework for identifying and describing the physical characteristics that contribute to the general and historical character of towns. The purpose of this framework is to identify the most relevant temporal elements for under-standing morphological processes, and to analyze the evolution of the re-lationship between theoretical concepts and concrete instances in order to describe the plurality of urban forms throughout history. In general, urban tissue comprises both physical elements of coherent neighborhood morphology (open spaces, buildings) and functions (human activity). Neighborhoods exhibit a recognizable pattern in the ordering of build-ings, spaces, and functions (themes), within which variation reinforces an organizing set of principles. Four key elements are identified for further study: (1) natural context; (2) street system; (3) plot system; and (4) build-ing system. The emphasis of four elements centers on a series of signifying physical changes over time.

Specifically, the natural context is the first condition for the establish-ment and organization of the different elements of urban form. The ter-rain, the quality and suitability of soil, the climate, and the solar and wind exposure are key factors influencing how a settlement is established from its foundation. Morphological studies pay attention to the basic forms of land relief, as well as endogenous forces originating from the geomorpho-logic formation of the continents. The structuring lines of the territory, the ridge lines corresponding to imaginary lines, and thalweg lines are closely associated in branched hierarchical systems forming the orographic and hydrographic systems. All these lines are adapted for tourism development, thereby reshaping the urban form. One salient example of this process is the renovation of the Cheonggyecheon stream in Seoul, Korea, which was com-pleted in 2005 (Lee et al. 2014). A group of municipal officials and urban designers decided to remove roads, buildings, and other built structures in order to create an artificial waterway that joined up with Seoul's under-ground river. The purpose of this project was to create a pedestrian-only public space bringing water and vegetation into the center of a large met-ropolitan area, where a traffic-filled stretch of elevated freeway used to stand. The 3.6-mile-long water corridor now acts as a major flood-relief channel and draws more than 60,000 visitors each day, transforming an area of Seoul previously renowned for deterioration (Figure 2.1). Known as "daylighting," projects that expose the physical tissue of the city are part of a broader global movement towards rediscovering urban rivers and revitalizing inner cities worldwide. Daylighting boosts the attractiveness of the town center and ultimately helps surrounding businesses to grow with high influx of tourists. Examples also include Zurich in Switzerland, where urban river restoration has been used to complement local architecture and heritage.

The street system is another important focus of morphological studies. Hillier (2009) argues that the livability of the streets is probably the most relevant indicator of the presence of a strong civil society. Gu and Ryan (2012) undertake a comparative study of residents and businesses in Shi Cha Hai Hutong (a type of narrow street in Beijing, China) and illustrate

Figure 2.1 The Cheonggyecheon Stream in Seoul, Korea, for Changing the Natural Context. (Source: authors)

the impacts of tourism for residents. The findings show that from a temporal perspective, streets are the most stable element of urban form, yet tourism drastically alters the street system, and may even cause permanent transformation. It also represents the microscale of analysis of out-of-home leisure epitomized in major cities by colorful open markets and leisure shopping areas, where tourists, shoppers, and residents meet (Hall and Page 2014). Streets provide the spatial setting for these transitory and performing events that create a unique identity and sense of place, often transformed by these performances. Duffy (2009: 91) comments that "festival and spectacles [on the streets] formalize space, time and behavior in ways that distinguish these events from everyday events." The oft-cited example of the Zócalo, the main square in Spain and Mexico, illustrates the significance of street system and its impact on tourism. A well-developed street system creates better opportunities for people to dwell, interact, relax, and perform leisure activities through enhancements such as public art and performance, street shows, and related soundscapes (Hall 2000, 2004).

The plots system, on the other hand, is an essential element of the urbanization process, the definition of which has remained relatively stable over time. The plots system serves the purpose of separating the public and the private domains. Nonetheless, the role of this system is often neglected by the main agents and stakeholders in the process of city building, largely because of the reduced urban visibility of plots over different periods of times (Oliveira 2016). In general, the dimension of street blocks and of plots increases as one moves from the historical center to the peripheral parts of the city. Correspondingly, tourist flow tends to move from the center of the destination towards surrounding areas. The plots system coincides with the Burgage cycle, which is the progressive built occupation of the back of the plot culminating in a significant reduction of the open space, resulting in the need to release this space and a corresponding period of urban fallow, preceding a new development cycle. One of the salient examples is the Fatehpur Sikri (the City of Victory), located in the northeast of India. It was the first planned city of the Mughals, marked by tombs, residential and religious buildings, mosques, and living areas. The city was rectangular in plan with a grid pattern of roads and by-lanes, which cut at right angles. The plot system has evolved over centuries, largely due to the abandonment of the city and its ensuing revitalization. It has become a major destination for tourists interested in the Mughal Empire (Figure 2.2).

The last one is the building system, one of the most important elements of urban form and probably the most visible of these elements. In morphological terms, architectural changes across time and space have been studied in two distinct fields, for example, vernacular changes due to local adaptations of the way of life; and codified changes which transform the built landscape from exogenous forces. Teller et al. (2007: 101) suggest that vernacular changes stem from spontaneous consciousness, while

Figure 2.2 Fatehpur Sikri (the City of Victory) in the Northeast of India. (Source: authors)

codified changes belong to critical consciousness. In particular, ordinary buildings and exceptional buildings are two major categories, which can be distinguished by their form, as well as the manner in which they are used. Typically, ordinary buildings are common in residential areas, while exceptional buildings represent the vernacular architectural style of a given city. Although, in the past decades, there has been a powerful trend towards an increasing uniformity of buildings on a global scale, a great diversity of architectures across different countries becomes the symbol of the cities. The ethos and spirit of these buildings are the draws for tourism development. A range of exceptional buildings practically tell tourists about the whole development of architecture in the city's history and heritage. Selective demolition *in situ* and trying to maintain architectural features and layering of urban fabric *ex situ* turn into tourism planning along with exposed tourist infrastructure. An example is the Murray House located in Hong Kong, China (McKercher et al. 2005). Dismantled brick by brick in downtown and reassembled in Stanley, the countryside near the waterfront in 2001, this classic colonial building was first built in 1855 as officers' quarters for the British army. It is now a popular tourist destination, uprooted from the original location but filled with restaurants and shops.

Classifications of tourism facilities

The morphology of tourism can be classified in many ways. Examples of such classifications include, but not limited to, natural, human-modified, built and resource-oriented, etc. The majority of research today focuses on the supply side: largely on interpretation, conservation, and other elements of resource management, as well as the support services that accommodate tourists at various locations (Oliveira 2016). In the analysis of tourism patterns and trends, the complexity of existing destinations requires some form of classification to improve the understanding, thereby simplifying the prevailing complexity.

Wall (1997: 240–243) suggests that attractions be divided into three types based on their spatial characteristics: points, lines, and areas. Each set of spatial characteristics has different implications for tourist behavior, as well as different potential and management strategies if a balance is to be achieved between resource protection and commercial exploitation. Point attractions concentrate large numbers of tourists in a small area, for if the point is not visited then the attraction is not experienced. Examples of such sites include vernacular buildings, monuments, landmarks, historic and archeological sites, museums, galleries and theaters. Concentration results in opportunities for the commercial exploitation of tourists, for, when many people are in close proximity they can be catered to efficiently and the minimum thresholds of successful business operation are most likely to be exceeded. Hillier (1996: 4) argues that many buildings "constitute the social organization of everyday life as the spatial configurations of space in which we live and move." Point attractions and their organization are entangled in an intricate way, as they depend on context, culture, and character. Sailer and Penn (2009: 6) observe that individuals in point attractions may relate to each other by means of closeness (spatiality) or conceptual closeness (transpatiality). The disadvantages of point attractions are possible dangers of congestion, overdevelopment, reduction in the quality of tourist experiences, and degradation of traditional urban forms. These problems are evident in Macau, China, where tourist congestion overruns the area around the landmark site of the Ruin of St Paul (Lee and Rii 2016). In this way, a point attraction may enact a vicious circle schema, resulting in the commercial expansion of the tourist area, a high proportion of shorter visits, congestion, and a downgrading of the quality of tourism products.

Linear resources, such as the San Antonio Riverwalk in Texas, or the Las Vegas Strip with its high density of hotels and casinos, encompass coastlines, lakeshores, rivers, scenic byways and trails, and other various landforms. The corridors of tourist movement can also become linear attractions by physically linking multiple points of attraction (Ashworth and Tunbridge 2000). Some of these resources become attractions with linear properties; others are routes which channel tourists along particular paths. In both cases, large numbers of tourists are concentrated along a narrow strip of land or a transportation corridor. The concept of tourism corridor has emerged in recent years to illustrate the significance of strategic alliances along linear properties. The concentration of tourists tends to attract considerable commercial development, which eventually leads to "creative destruction," "destructive creation," or "creative enhancement" (Mitchell 2013: 375). Timothy and Boyd (2014) propose that linear resources derived from a series of individual nodes (point attractions) require the successful implementation of networks and social capital building. It is noted that linear resources can easily be overdeveloped because a large number of tourists are drawn to narrow strips of land and water. The enforcement of setbacks is often a useful strategy in coastal areas but, more generally, breaking up lines into a series of nodes and links, or nodes and less developed or underdeveloped areas, may be a more appropriate strategy to pursue.

Areas may attract large numbers of people, but their spatial distribution may permit and even encourage the wide dispersion of tourists. Such places include parks and protected areas, wilderness, and scenic landscapes. In some areas, tourism turns out to be the lifeblood for regional economic development. Caribbean countries, including Antigua and Barbuda, Dominica, the British Virgin Islands, Turks & Caicos Islands, and Anguilla, are typical "areas" of tourism development. Pearce (1998), in a careful morphological examination of Paris, France, posits that a marked clustering of tourist-related service is evident in a polycentricity and a certain level of synergy is apparent between the sectors. The synergistic relationships and agglomerative effects are especially evident with regard to the emergence of tourist-oriented shops and services in close proximity to major attractions, as well as the linear concentration of similar businesses. In tourist destinations such as Paris, they create tourist concentrations, for instance, at access points, scenic overlooks, or interpretation centers, to impart information to tourists, to monitor them, and to provide facilities which tourists may require.

One concern of area planning is the possibility of overtourism as a consequence of urban tourism where tourists flood fragile historical cities. It is possible to identify such conditions of crisis at an early stage and their potential impact on urban form, such as the saturation of an urban center due to overcrowding and congestion from tourists, lack of adequate infrastructure in a phase of mass tourism, the excessive dispersion in a phase of tourism planning, and conflicting patterns of old and new development in a phase of reurbanization. The representative example is the city of Venice in Italy, which has experienced a sharp population decline from over 170,000 inhabitants in 1951 to 56,000 in 2015 (Settis 2016). Yet the surge of visitors outnumbers Venetians by 140 to 1. It is estimated that as tourism development continues apace, the city center may soon have no residential lodging at all. The changing morphology is evident as souvenir shops have replaced grocery stores, while luxury hotels have occupied medical offices. A pattern of "tourist monoculture" has emerged, which "banishes its native citizens and shackles the survival of those who remain to their willingness to serve." To make matters worse, globalization and the mobility of capital make Venice an ideal second-home investment, where homeowners' average stay lasts only two and a half days per year. The second-home owners, who have hoovered up every building or apartment with a winged lion on its door, aggravate the community identity with mindless urban expansion. At the same time, Venice shows another side of the tourism industry, where cruise ships blight the scenery, ravage the canals, and disgorge their day trippers. The situation coincides with Calvino's (1978) description of "Invisible Cities," in which the spaces of Venice are devoid of vernacular features and local populations. The primary meaning making referents for a tourist city is transformed into time, place, history, and memory.

The three types of attractions—points, lines, and areas—occur on multiple scales as well as the essential elements for the morphology of tourism. At the scale of the country, destination areas, such as coastal resorts or national parks, may be viewed as a series of points. On the other hand, a single destination area may be viewed as a combination of points, lines, and areas, or as a series of nodes and links. Therefore, this model of spatial distribution provides some flexibility with respect to scale. In addition, points may be viewed as essentially unidimensional, lines as two-dimensional, albeit with some depth, and areas as multidimensional. The inclusion of points, lines, and areas is a useful way of viewing a wide range of heterogeneous tourism attractions because it encourages consideration, at the same time, of specific attributes of the resource, tourist behavior, and spatial distribution, as well as the potential for commercial development and the associated transformation of urban form.

It must be noted that the points-lines-areas model has been gradually adopted in the field of urban morphology, particularly in tourism studies. Sarri (2016) undertakes a comparative study of the Old Truman Brewery in London and Technopolis in Athens, and proposes to view tourist sites in three major scales: urban, neighborhood, and buildings. She investigates tourism activities on a citywide scale using the DepthmapX (Varoudis 2012) software based on different metric radii, those being 400, 1,200, and 2,000 meters from the center. The first radius is based on Hillier's (2016) proposal for analyzing pedestrian movement in areas similar to market-places, the second radius investigates normal urban pedestrian movement, and the 2000-meter radius is used to produce a patchwork pattern map, which depicts the metric density of each urban structure (Hillier et al. 2007), revealing the relationship of each site to its foreground and background city networks. On the neighborhood scale, Sarri conducts a morphological analysis of the urban blocks based on land uses and frontage/boundaries in order to understand the current growth and adaptation of tourism. A classification of frontage boundaries for each neighborhood is conducted. The research of morphological frontages includes active frontages (including retail/service facades and premises with window shops), doors and windows, doors only, windows only, non-permeable fence, permeable fence (see-through screen), low fence (not higher than 1.50 meters), and blank wall (Trigueiro 2005). Finally, the building scale focuses on a frontage/boundaries analysis studying the interface between buildings and public spaces. Using the snapshot method, it records the tourist patterns during events, weekdays, and weekends. In addition, a survey including qualitative questionnaires and mental maps in the form of short interviews was undertaken to ascertain visitors' perceptions and attitudes towards destinations.

Towards an integrated approach to the morphology of tourism

"City" looks like a "machine," a system modified by man, inside of which he lives, where for living it means the performance of all those activities characteristic of human being (Caglioni and Rabino 2007). Davis (2001: 127) argues that "histories, cultures, power relations, aesthetics and economics all combine at a place to create a context." Using this kind of definitions, tourism activities in an urban/rural setting can be studied at three observational levels: (1) the physical level, comprising all structures, networks, and artifacts in a given territory; (2) the socioeconomic level, which encompasses all activities performed by hosts and guests in a given destination, as well as relationships between stakeholders; and (3) the mental level, which concerns the perceptions and images of a site. Every one of these levels is important and constitutes key elements for developing a useful framework for the morphology of tourism.

Unfortunately, much of the existing literature seeks to understand the morphology based on singular approaches, such as typo-morphological, configurational, historico-geographical, and spatial analysis. What is missing is an overarching framework in which these useful approaches can be interconnected. Furthermore, the spatial analytical tools used in recent years do not involve the traditional morphological analyses of urban fabric and functions over different periods of time (Li et al. 2016). Urban morphology and tourism are interwoven, but their respective literatures have remained unengaged with each other, which constitutes a double lacuna. First, although tourism is recognized as a central feature and a driving force that reshapes urban form and impacts urban tissue, the link has been weakly theorized. Secondly, changing morphology is a direct result of tourism development, evident in terms of mobility, transnationalism, and urban regeneration. The range of resources that function as tourist attractions is extensive, and the types and dimensions are manifold. Very often, tourist landscape has local, endemic, insider meanings, and broader, pandemic, outsider meanings (Lowenthal and Prince 1972). There is a conscious attempt to provide a stronger theoretical base to the morphology of tourism, which would both be informed by and contribute to contemporary social theory. In other words, what happens when tourism represents (metaphorically) the city as something "woven" (*tissue* in French refers to a woven textile)? The study of the complex processes of tourism morphology needs a conceptual construction robust enough to be applicable to many different scales.

This chapter seeks to highlight the elements of morphology, characters of tourism, and its impacts documented in previous ones. It explores how the relationship between morphology, tourism, and their impacts can be conceptualized, thereby mapping out future tourism research agendas. Figure 2.3 offers one such framework using the key issues discussed in the book as the starting point from which to consider the interrelatedness of urban morphology, tourism, and their impacts on a destination. This framework is infused with multidisciplinary perspectives that draw on a variety of subjects, including urban form, planning, and geography, in order to develop a coherent strategy for describing the morphology of tourism. Using a gearbox as its model, this framework illuminates the interconnectedness of urban morphology, tourism, and its impacts. The traditional foci of morphology, including natural context, street system, plots system, and building system, set tourism development in motion, and the cogs of that gear, in turn, drive the sociocultural, economic, and environmental impacts of the tourism industry. The subjects of analysis for tourism should include at least three spatial characteristics, for example, points, lines, and areas. These are themselves influenced and mediated by urban tissues and the institutional arrangements that govern the process of tourism development. They can move, or be moved by, the transformation of the morphology. The impacts that stem from the intersection of tourism and morphology propel further

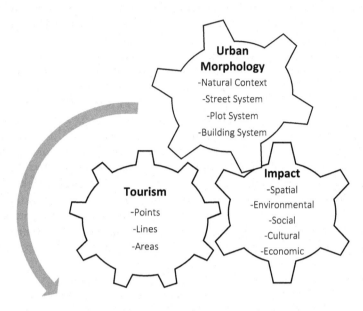

Figure 2.3 Conceptual Framework of the Morphology of Tourism.

changes in urban form and its distinctive elements. Eventually, a new morphology emerges, reshaped through the influence of tourism.

Urban morphology, tourism, and their concomitant impacts do not exist in isolation; instead, each element is directly related to the other. The interaction of urban morphology, tourism, and their impacts is the nexus of this investigation, and it is what the morphology of tourism confronts. Tourist cities are an outcome of highly structured sets of socially, economically, culturally, and environmentally related systems in space (Penn 2009). Traditional morphological studies, constructed in the modern world, hinge on the reification of a place in the landscape. The natural context, street system, plot system, and building system arise from the interaction between commercial development and placemaking. On a larger scale, the temporal-spatial relationship defines its morphological changes from a complete interaction with tourism activities. The changes are intimately related to the places impacted by these activities.

The proposed conceptual framework presents the conjunction of urban morphology, tourism, and their impacts. Tourism has long been developed as an alternative to the existing urban form, and grew out of an ideology that has a minimal impact on historicity or the characteristics of tourists and their repercussions on the configuration of physical settings. Whatever their intentions, tourism's tendency to decentralize urban growth is not proportionate to the pressure that drive the formation of tourist districts. The discontinuity between the modes of aggregation of spontaneous construction in morphology and those derived from the impingement of tourism become a challenge for urban planning. In the meantime, the movement to restore and recontextualize major monuments, vernacular architectures, and historical buildings for tourism purposes has become the heart of the concern for preservation. Therefore, the justification for this framework rests upon these three axioms: namely, that tourism in its various forms has played, and continues to exercise, a critical role in urban morphology; that elements of urban tissue form an equally critical part of a growing tourism industry; and that tourism's impacts have become a major force in the restructuring of the modern city.

Summary

While it is widely accepted by the contemporary society that cities must change, one of the key problems is how to cope with these changes while retaining originality and structures in which past generations have invested so heavily (Oliveira 2016). Spatial arrangements often reflect typical social structure, behavioral characteristics, and cultural connotations (Soja 1980). Rather than just refer to an external intervention or an exogenous force, tourism is being used to expand commercialization and mobility so that the core power exerts a strong influence over the destination morphology. The subjects of tourism and morphology are ones in which the disciplines of geography and planning intersect, with implications for destination development. It is a rich field of further enquiry, exploring issues about the use of morphology from both theoretical and practical perspectives.

Despite the growing importance of the morphology of tourism, which is associated with the physical characteristics of the urban landscape as well as the process of urban transformation, few studies have offered significant explanations about the spatial pattern for tourism purposes. An understanding of tourist flows, and the spatial patterns of tourism facilities, can help tourism planners and policy-makers provide better services and facilities to cater to the needs of tourists. The functional and spatial associations of tourism and other related phenomena are not illustrated by empirical examples, and the basic characteristics of the spatial structure in tourist destinations are not fully developed. Few empirical studies have been completed, and a conceptual framework seems nonexistent.

The proposed conceptual framework sets out to fill the void and explore aspects of the spatial and functional structure of tourism in selected cities, resorts, and destinations, as shown in the following chapters. As part of a broader study of the morphology of tourist destinations, it attempts to identify the characteristics, structure, and functioning of these locations and examine how these form part of the broader urban fabric. It is assumed that each component of the framework can adjust over time, while the selection of tourism-related phenomena links any morphological change. For example, analysis of the distribution of accommodation, shopping and dining, attractions, and supporting facilities in a tourist city mirrors the evolution of urban form over different periods of time. Similarly, examination of the emergence and functioning of tourist points, lines, and areas, particularly with regard to heritage and history, demonstrates the multifaceted character of tourism. The spatial and functional association of tourism's diverse components reveals that the sociocultural, economic, and environmental aspects of a given place may shape, or be shaped by, the development of a tourism destination.

Another challenge is to cast a penetrating light on the way in which understanding the conceptual framework can have a wider value: how it can, for instance, inform and give direction to the way in which the current challenges that face societies can be met. In particular, morphology can engender a greater appreciation of how understanding the composition, origins, processes, and effects of tourism can strengthen urban form. This entails not only enhancing the conservation and regeneration of existing tourism resources, but also improving the ways in which entirely new tourist destinations are brought into existence, and the quality of the new environments that result. In the present context, there is scope for building upon and promulgating historico-geographical approaches such as the morphological periods to tourism (Borsay 2006). These bring realism not only to concentric zonal interpretations of development around tourist destinations but also to other configurations. Though the growth of many tourist cities is indeed broadly concentric around an initial core, much less evident in research and practice hitherto has been wider appreciation of the fact that what is created on the ground reflects the spasmodic way in which tourism grows.

The following chapter traces the development of the morphology of tourism in Fiji, specifically, as the evolution of the seaside resort is a popular topic for case studies concerned with the rise and fall of tourism destinations (Hall and Page 2014). The historical geography of Fiji has provided a focal point for echoing the proposed conceptual framework, where a range of factors explain why the destinations developed, where they did, how they developed, and the pace and scale of change. The study of morphology is an evolving resource for tourist destinations.

3 Morphological changes and the evolution of coastal resorts

Introduction

The juxtaposition of land and water has long been identified as a very important factor in attracting tourists to coasts, lakes, and rivers (Andriotis 2006, Valls et al. 2017). Seaside resorts are acknowledged for their natural beauty and rich biodiversity; at the same time, they are highly vulnerable ecosystems (Kitolelei and Sato 2016). The exponential growth in coastal tourism is associated with higher disposable incomes from tourists, better modes of transportation, and more available time for leisure activities. Coastal resorts evolve from their natural state to an increasingly urbanized state through tourism-induced development. In addition to promising tourists access to the beach, these destinations have established an integrated resort model accommodating recreational, retail, and entertainment facilities.

Coastal tourism brings foreign exchange to the government, and incurs social, environmental, and political changes. The development, in turn, has triggered a rising coastal property market as resorts proliferate and expand along the coastlines. Tourism has the potential to cause immense ecological disturbances, from the construction stage through to its daily operations in coastal systems (Bidesi et al. 2011). Very often, rapid construction of hotels and secondary housing cooperatives as a result of income expectations leads to the degradation of fertile land, creating aesthetic pollution (Burak et al. 2004). The impacts of tourism have also been empirically linked to marine pollution, habitat degradation, and a loss of place identity (Movono et al. 2017). At its height, coastal tourism leads to socioeconomic polarization, until overdevelopment, high competition, and low occupancy rates cause overall economic decline. Smith (1992: 209) points out that inadequate resort growth planning eventually leads to a "proliferation of environmental and social problems, poor infrastructure provision and deteriorating resort ambience."

From a morphological perspective, the issues that accompany coastal resort development can largely be attributed to the cumulative effects of a piecemeal approach to land use and zoning (Honey and Krantz 2007).

Most tourist developments are constructed as close to the beach as possible, with minimal to no governmental guidance, resulting in a development pattern incompatible with beach dynamics and environmental functions (Nordstrom 2000). While small-scale land-use decisions may have minor effects in isolation, a number of them when combined produce major changes and predominantly negative consequences (Collins and Kearns 2010). Most resort developments are undertaken without assessment or consideration of potential impacts, except for anticipated economic benefits (Butler 1993, Huffadine 2000, Prideaux 2009). Coastal settlements have increasingly commercialized as a result of legislative and institutional incentives to encourage further tourism investment. They tend to face congested populations coupled with unbridled economic expansion from the surrounding areas.

This chapter aims to understand the process and consequences of land-use change resulting from coastal tourism in order to minimize its negative impacts and sustain coastal resources. It employs morphological analysis in order to enter the territory of coastal resort development, outline the phases and impacts of a coastal resort's urbanization process, and identify ways in which land-use planning can be employed for the better. A lack of geomorphological awareness can bring many socioeconomic disadvantages to coastal areas engaged in resort planning (Inskeep 1988, Nordstrom 2000), as morphological changes have profound impacts on recreational amenities and dispersal of the natural environment. The current research examines morphological changes on Denarau Island, the island in Fiji with the highest concentration of tourist accommodations. The stages of tourism development on Denarau Island were evaluated by utilizing Smith's Beach Resort Model (BRM) in the context of physical, environmental, and social characteristics to ascertain the changing process.

BRM and conceptual framework

Most morphological studies of coastal tourist sites focus on the physical characteristics of coastal areas, as land and sea are composed of a very high level of biodiversity and some of the richest and most fragile ecosystems. The theoretical morphology initially served the purpose of preserving the shoreline and satisfying the vital needs of residents for access to water. Put simply, roads should not be built parallel to the shoreline or within one mile of it; instead, all access roads should run at right angles to the shoreline and be far apart (Liu 2008). In recent decades, there has been much contention and debate over what makes coastal areas a tourist destination. Therefore, morphological studies have increasingly preoccupied themselves with the classification and categorization of coastal areas. For example, Anfuso et al. (2014, 2017) provide coastal scenic values of 100 sites along coastal Cuba by the use of a weighted, fuzzy logic-based checklist containing 26 physical/human factors. Sites are categorized into five classes from Class I, top grade scenery, to Class V, poor scenery. Beaches belonging to Class I tend to be minimally impacted by human activity and high scores of natural parameters. Most Class II beaches are located at international resort areas; have white coral sand beaches, turquoise water, and vigorous vegetation; and are located and designed in a manner that lessens the ecological impact of tourism development. Classes III, IV, and V denote a wide variety of beaches with lower scores, which were linked to a poor environmental setting. These classifications of beach resorts allow for improvements of beach management and formulate for current international tourist destinations.

Table 3.1 presents a chronology of studies in resort morphology. Both resort morphology, in general, and an evolutionary model of resort morphology, in particular, were first introduced by Gilbert (Butler 2011). These two concepts later separated and advanced in different directions until the 1990s, during which they once more intertwined together and became a single evolutionary model (Brent 1997). According to this evolutionary model, changes in coastal resort areas proceed according to a series of discrete developmental stages that, over time, form a life cycle. Several common features of resort morphology, such as the significance of the seafront to the building structure and location of the commercial core, were initially identified as the "distinct zonation" of visitor accommodation and residential areas, and an extension of settlements parallel to the coast (Pigram 1977: 525, Getz 1993: 584). The model follows a zone of frontal amenities comprising tourist facilities followed by a gradual decrease in tourist-related activities as the distance from the central beachfront increases, creating a "concentric pattern" of architectural and social stratification (Smith 1992b, Meyer-Arendt 1993). This pattern of development exemplifies the growing market value of the land. In general, coastal land use for tourism commences with minor modifications to the natural landscape and small-scale resort development, the success of which initiates further development and extensions until the coastal landscape has been completely transformed (Xie 2003). It is argued that coastal resorts and urban fringes experience the most rapid land-use changes of all populated areas (Allen et al. 1999), the impacts of which may be both positive and negative, depending on the level and nature of influence exerted upon land use, tenure, and values.

In order to trace the morphological change, Lavery (1971) presents a schematic diagram of a typical coastal resort, consisting of a mixture of tourism-based land use and buildings from studies of Western Europe (Getz 1993). Lavery's schema proposes that certain features, such as larger hotels occupying the prime frontal locations with gradual changes in land value and tourist-oriented functions away from the seafront, are typical of coastal resort development. By classifying resorts into eight types and associating them with certain landscape characteristics and features, Lavery stresses the spatial and functional separation of the Recreational Business District (RBD) and Central Business District (CBD) in resort redevelopment. However, these morphological claims are inadequate at the present time. Perhaps the greatest disadvantage is that the first line of development often consists of high-rise structures, forming barriers both visually and physically between the inner residential zones and the coast. The vehicle path creates a further barrier for the pedestrians by disrupting their flow to the coast. The linear development pattern itself is often displeasing and degrading, both aesthetically and environmentally.

Of equal importance is the role of decision-makers, such as the Territorial Local Authority (TLA), that control resource management and planning. As the coastal landscape shows a pattern of urbanization which leads to concerns about environmental, social, economic, and cultural degradation, the decline and failure of the resorts begins. At the same time, the impacts of drastic landscape modifications raise governmental and public concerns with regard to sustainable development and management. Ultimately, morphological changes lead to the expansion of physical buildings and infrastructure. In Europe and America, resorts grow from their exploration stage, to a stage of commercial involvement and infrastructure development, followed by settlement expansion and further intensification of developed sites (Wu and Cai 2006). Only at the end of this period of expansion and intensification, after all potential developable land has been urbanized and incoming tourist rates have stabilized, is "human induced environmental degradation" recognized and translated to government controls (Nordstrom 2000: 10). The government response includes the creation and implementation of land-use regulations to stabilize and control market demand due to uncontrolled development. Urban development policies are crucial as they exert influence over morphological changes and a community's capacity for sustainable development.

Evolutionary methods of plan analysis have gained attention on tourism development in coastal communities at various stages (Agarwal 2012). Clave and Wilson (2017) explore the notion of path plasticity in Spanish Mediterranean destinations and propose a reactive-creative-transitive stage of development. The evolutionary trajectory shows incremental tourism urbanization derived from an axis of selective and spontaneous governmental intervention. For example, in Thailand, the initial stage of development involves the construction of simple low-budget visitor dwellings, later upgraded as visitor numbers increase, and then procured by developers who construct hotels to meet increasing demand (Nordstrom 2000). Andriotis (2006), using Crete as a case study, suggests that changes in Cretan coastal resort morphology can be understood via the following characteristics: road network, lodgings and infrastructural facilities, beach width, residential areas, faming land, aesthetics, and architecture. Each characteristic of Cretan coastal resort morphological evolution is developed based on the stages of Butler's Tourism Area Life Cycle (TALC). Andriotis' case study of Crete illustrates how the morphology changes in different stages while morphological changes of its coastal areas as the resort undergo urbanization through tourism-induced development.

Table 3.1 The Development of Resort Morphology Research

Year	A Chronology of Resort Morphology	
1930s	Gilbert (1939)	Early work in the field delineates the basic
1940s	Gilbert (1949)	morphological characteristics using map
1950s	Wolfe (1952), Barrett (1958)	scheme as well as distance decays for the resort planning.
1960s	Stansfield (1969)	Stansfield adopted Barrett's (1958) theory and applied it to North America.
1970s	Stansfield and Rickert (1970), Lavery (1971), Pigram (1977), Pearce (1978)	Research in the theory and related concepts such as the theory of evolution resort, land use, the CBD, and the RBD. Identify CBD, RBD, public service, accommodation, residential, park space, and functional morphology zonation.
1980s	Mathieson and Wall (1982) TALC Model (Butler 1980)	The review of the tourist destinations; see how they change over time and respond to the changing demands of the tourism industry. The literature recognizes that changes in morphology are influenced by socioeconomic factors.
1990s	Jeans (1990), Meyer-Arendt (1990), Getz (1993), Brent (1997), Agarwal (1997), Wong (1998) BRM (Smith 1992)	The classifications of Tourism Business District, RBD, and CBD, including tourist behavior, the basic physical, transport opportunities, policy issues, and environmental impacts. The BRM is introduced, an assessment of the suitability of TALC model and related research functions in the formation of the Regions.
2000s	Gospodini (2001), Agarwal (2002), Liu and Wall (2009)	These studies further the relationship between the resort and the restructuring of the relationship between the host, guests, politicians, and morphology.
2010s	Agarwal (2012), Anfuso et al. (2014, 2017), Clave and Wilson (2017)	Studies on the evolution of coastal tourism destination using a path plasticity perspective; changes in the intensity of land use, contact spatiality in the restructuring of the beach resort, and the trajectory of tourism mobilities for path-dependence or path creation.

Despite the broad application of the evolutionary method in tourism planning, there is a similarity in terms of models' contexts and contents. Most new iterations of the evolutionary method are improvements to a previous model, incorporating changing philosophical views and new understandings of how resort morphology changes. There is no succinct model that incorporates specific features, such as physical, environmental, and social characteristics. In response to the lack of applicability of the historic research and resort evolution models, Smith (1992) put forward a revised model to bridge the gaps of the previous research in form of the BRM. The BRM traces the evolution of contemporary coastal resorts established after World War II (Smith 1992), and it incorporates aspects of previous research into new unpredictable patterns of development to produce a refined and strength-ened schema. In particular, this model provides generic plans for each stage of development and identifies the factors that mark evolution from one stage to another. The six elements of change are morphological, physical, envi-ronmental, social, economic, and political. The evolution of coastal resorts is categorized into eight stages: (1) pre-tourism data; (2) the construction of second homes, which typically marks the first stage of tourism develop-ment; (3) the construction of the first hotel improving visitor access; (4) the establishment of a resort, marked by an increase in hotel construction and the intensification of strip development; (5) the establishment of a business area, an increase in non-hotel business growth, and an increasing awareness of cultural disruption; (6) the construction of inland hotels, accompanied by rapid residential growth, the emergence of a tourism culture, and the pro-duction of a governmental master plan; (7) the transformation and decline of tourist culture, marked by an oversaturation of accommodations and a de-crease in visitor expenditures; and (8) the establishment of a fully urbanized city resort, confronted with serious pollution and other urban problems.

The advantage of the BRM is that it generally captures the different elements of coastal resorts, and the associated effects (positive and negative) of coastal development once the accommodation of tourism becomes the dominant driv-ing force. The use of the BRM to analyze the stages of coastal resort evolution reveals that most coastal resorts are fueled by waves of external investment, and planned minimally if at all by centralized governing authorities (Prideaux 2009). Additionally, the BRM enables scholars and policymakers to take into account all of the necessary parts of morphological change, as they apply to coastal resorts. As suggested by Faulkner (2002), the model presents a more holistic approach, taking into account economic, social, and environmental considerations. Andriotis (2006) echoes that three most important elements of morphological changes are guests (who are the main cause of induced develop-ment); hosts (who by supporting development and by being involved in tourism contribute to the success of a destination); and politics (which influence overall development). The BRM embodies these key elements by integrating planning policies at all levels of government. It also accounts for the unique historical context of contemporary coastal resorts, which evolved in the era when motor vehicles expanded tourists' access to new destinations (Weaver 1993).

The existing research on morphological changes in coastal areas places less emphasis on decision-making from the TLA's perspective. Conceptual mod-els such as spatial structure by Pearce (1998), spatial evolution by Lundgren (1974) and Oppermann (1993), and temporal change by Butler (2011), result-ing from coastal resort and tourism studies (Agarwal 1997, 2002), mention the influence of territorial local authorities only briefly, if at all. In particular, the importance of the local authority policies, such as the adaptation of a master plan, has been neglected in the context of morphological changes. The present research has developed an evaluative research framework using a partial ad-aptation of Smith's BRM and the existing literature (see Figure 3.1). As noted

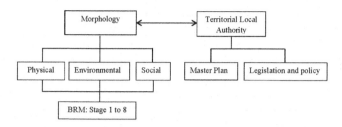

Figure 3.1 Conceptual Framework for Denarau Island, Fiji.

in the literature review, the reason for adopting the BRM as a framework is that this particular resort evolution model appears to be an accurate account of how and why a resort evolves, as well as the implications of the development process. The evaluative criteria of this particular study focus on physical features, enabling a morphological analysis of the developmental form and land uses from their initiation to the present time; environmental features, including the changing landscapes due to the development of tourism along the coast; and social features, which significantly impact local communities.

The morphological analysis will therefore be undertaken using a modulated form of Smith's BRM of Evolution. This analysis will be mapped to the eight evolutionary stages of the BRM, and then measured against the three identified key features, for example, physical, environmental, and social, which are derived from the existing tourism literature to explain the morphological transformation of a coastal resort. The mapping exercise involves recording major changes in the destination resort in these three key areas. The aim is to explore whether these features and phases outlined in the tourism literature and resort evolution models are present in the case study area, and to what extent. This will test whether the BRM and theories of resort evolution are global or area specific. In addition, the impact of the TLA and its legislative policies are linked to the framework in order to understand how guidelines are conceived. Particularly, the implementation of urban planning policies, such as a master plan, at various levels of governance is included. The pattern of development over the history of the resorts against the respective legislations, perceptions of the developers, and the market stance of the time are thoroughly investigated. The differences are then analyzed from a resource management and planning perspective.

Methodology

Coastal resorts are shaped and influenced by the era in which they are established, especially in terms of their architecture, form, function, land use, culture, and other characteristics. The first fieldwork in Denarau Island was undertaken during April and May 2008. Two additional follow-up field trips were undertaken in Fiji during May 2009 and 2010, where the

Denarau site was revisited for updates and intensive detailing of coastal developments and the natural environment. The elements of the built and natural landscape of this case study were mapped onto plans. These included buildings, roads, the sea and waterways, beaches, mountains, open spaces and parks, jetties and boat ramps, bridges, boardwalks, pedestrian pathways and crossings, trees, recreational activities, tourist accommodation units, commercial activities, second homes, and residential areas. Information sources for this mapping project included Google Earth, site inspections, advertisements, historical photographs, aerial photographs, journals, websites, locality maps, tourist brochures, and handbooks.

Interviews were conducted with local tourism advisors in order to gather information on resorts that are high in demand. Plans for upcoming projects and access to tourism planning information, such as journals, guides, and national programs, were included in the interviews. While undertaking fieldwork and cartographic analysis, informal meetings were held with the landowners in order to ground the research in concrete, verifiable information about sources of resource management and planning processes. These meetings led to a more formal meeting with the TLA to obtain information such as council reports, community guidelines, historic photographs, and aerial images, in order to ease the cartographic mapping task set for the respective time periods. The master plan was examined and reviewed, as it provides a detailed layout for a site. This layout includes roading patterns, as well as commercial, business (industry and office), residential (including high-intensity residential areas such as apartments, or low-intensity residencies such as detached dwellings), open spaces (parks and reserves) and special purpose land uses (community facilities, schools, etc.). These types of plans are normally used to depict the general structure and land-use typology of an area that is either undergoing rezoning or is about to have a rezoning proposal attached to it. Additionally, private resource management and planning firms familiar with tourism projects were consulted to ascertain the technicalities and planning experiences surrounding tourism developments, and in order to seek directions as to where detailed information could be found.

Morphological analysis

Physical characteristics

Denarau Island is situated on the western side of Viti Levu, the largest island of the 300-plus islands in Fiji's archipelago, within the township of Nadi. It is a private island, consisting of 684 acres of lush tropical garden, connected to Viti Levu via a causeway. The island is not only a departure point for cruises and transfers to the Mamanucas and the Yasawa Islands, but also serves as a major transit harbor and a gateway to Fiji tourism. Additionally, Denarau Island is the largest integrated resort within the South Pacific, fringed with coral reefs and housing a world-class golf course, a tennis complex, Port Denarau, and residential precincts fronting canals with boat berths. Recreational activities such as swimming, snorkeling, diving, surfing, river rafting, sailing, and exploring the surrounding natural beauty are the main sources of adventure and attractions on the island (Telecom New Zealand Company 2008, Visitdenarau 2009). Australians, followed by New Zealanders, comprise the majority of Fiji's annual tourist flows (Fiji Islands Bureau of Statistics 2011), since the destination is approximately three to four hours away by air, attracting both business travelers and holidaymakers.

Figure 3.2 presents a comparative analysis of morphological changes on Denarau Island from 1977 to 2007. These changes reflect the impact of legislative policies set by the TLA over three decades of coastal resort development. There are two key legislations in Fiji that govern physical planning: the Town Planning Act of 1946 and the Environmental Management Act (EMA) of 2005. The Town Planning Act of 1946 introduced town-planning controls in Fiji's urban centers, and later expanded to include rural areas across the country. There are 12 declared cities and towns, and 15 rural town planning areas in Fiji. As of 1971, the planning regulations are applicable to all land outside the town planning areas except for land within the Fijian villages (Department of Town and Country Planning 2007), making all land subject to the requirements of the Town Planning Act.

Forward planning and development control comprise the two main mechanisms of planning on Denarau Island. Forward planning encompasses a more visionary approach to goal setting, identifying uses of different parts of the country that are most appropriate. This informs the preparation of planning schemes and advisory plans alongside scheme amendments, such as rezoning. Development control planning involves the creation of subdivisions, development assessments, and master planning. The purpose is to manage the extent and nature of growth, and to balance competing needs at the same time (Department of Town and Country Planning 2007). Developmental controls are zone-specific; thus, they are implemented in a variety of manners, according to the requirements of a specific forward planning module. Limits imposed by developmental controls may include allotment size, infrastructure requirements, building setbacks, building height, car parking requirements, and so on.

Table 3.2 provides a summary of morphological changes on Denarau Island, and compares them to the physical, environmental, and social changes outlined in the eight stages of the BRM. The initial development of Denarau Island began more than 40 years ago when the island was established on reclaimed land on the western coast of Nadi (Gale Group 2006, Tabua Investments Limited 2010). Tabua Investments Limited, primary developers of Denarau Island, reorganized the land ownership into a mixed model. For example, hotel properties were designated as iTaukei lease lands, which is a collective lease arrangement; residential properties were designated as freehold, which is individual interest/ownership in perpetuity; and recreational and commercial lands were designated as state-owned, which

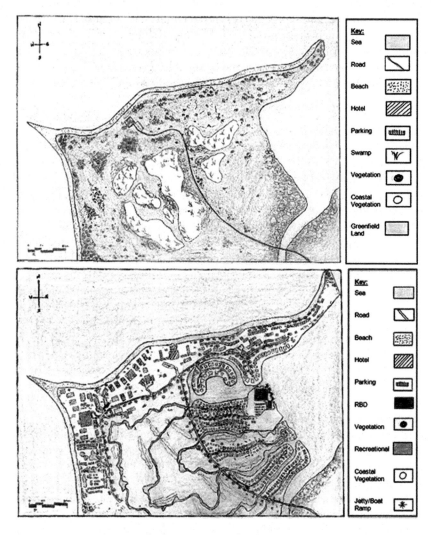

Figure 3.2 Cartographic Representation of the Morphological Elements of Denarau Island from 1977 to 2007.

is administered under the Crown Lands Act, but can also be leased out.
In 2006, the passage of the Qoliqoli Bill proposed to transfer proprietary
rights of qoliqoli areas, such as beaches, lagoons, and reefs, from the State
to ethnic Fijians. Under the Charter of Denarau Island, Tabua Investments
Limited became Denarau Corporation Limited, which continues working
on land development and coastal management. However, the mixed ownership model on Denarau Island is significant as it closely relates to tourism
development and impacts morphological shift.

Table 3.2 The Morphological Changes in Denarau Island, Fiji

Stages of Resort Evolution	Physical	Environmental	Social
Stage 1 Pre-tourism	An existing dirt road connects the island to the mainland (Viti Levu).	High concentration of original natural landscapes until 1969.	A few residents reside in the vicinity of the island.
Stage 2 Construction of second homes	Infrastructure works begin as a preliminary to resort development in 1969. These include roads, drains, and utility services. No second home constructions appear on maps of Denarau Island during this period.	Major alterations of landscape and vegetation result from infrastructure works.	Tourists are introduced to the area and became central to the lives of the locals.
Stage 3 Construction of first hotel	The Regent Hotel opens in 1975. A new road is constructed, running parallel to the northern and western coasts. It leads to the new hotel site.	Non-native plant species are introduced to the island for the purpose of beautification. Major sections of mangrove forest are cleared to allow access to the waterfront and to progress reclamation.	The locals are offered jobs with better income. Recreational opportunities are promoted for both locals and tourists, including the proposed golf course, marina, and rugby stadium.
Stage 4 Establishment of a resort	The Sheraton Denarau villas open in 1999. A small commercial complex opens in 2001, situated adjacent to the villas along the primary access road opposite the waterfront. The Golf Terrace apartments open in 2005, close to the Marina and backing onto the enclave water system.	A vast amount of landscaping is undertaken throughout the island as development and stages of the master plan are completed.	Local tourist and resident populations increase as new accommodation facilities are completed.

(continued)

Stages of Resort Evolution	Physical	Environmental	Social
Stage 5 Establishment of a business area	More hotels started to occupy the northern and western beachfronts. Residential development continues within the gated subdivisions on the eastern face of the island. The Port Denarau Retail & Commercial Center opens in 2007, consisting of offices, retail shops, restaurants, and other businesses catering to tourists.	The rise of intensity of the area causes an increase in vehicles. An integrated planting scheme is implemented to retain the natural vibrancies of the island atmosphere.	As beachfront sites are developed, the public is visually and physically excluded from using this resource. New services and goods are provided that reflect the needs of the tourists, implying that a cultural shift is on the horizon.
Stage 6 Construction of inland hotels	N/A	N/A	N/A
Stage 7 Transformation of tourist culture	N/A	N/A	N/A
Stage 8 Establishment of urbanized resort	N/A	N/A	N/A

The Westin Hotel originally opened as The Regent Hotel in 1975, and is the oldest resort within the group. The Sheraton Fiji Resort opened in 1987, followed by the Sheraton apartment villas in 1999 (Birchfield 2004, Tabua Investments Limited 2010). The first residential neighborhood was also constructed in 1999 with the opening of a small shopping complex adjacent to the Sheraton villas in 2001. The Sheraton Fiji Resort was refurbished in 2003, and more internationally acclaimed hotels, as well as the Port Denarau retail and commercial center, opened between 2006 and 2007. Further development is planned including a rugby stadium with associated training and accommodation facilities, a residential beach park, marina accommodation, hotels, and resorts.

Physical change induced by tourist development is readily apparent on Denarau Island. In the early stages of tourism development, it was marketed and promoted as a golf destination. Initial tourism development was undertaken far away from residential areas. Although the master plan for this development does not directly restrict public access to the coast, it nevertheless creates a barrier between the public realm and residential population via the internal roading network to the coast, as the layout is such that only visitors can gain access to the resort. This is mainly because there is no road parallel to the coast, as typically seen in other coastal resort areas. In addition, the master plan offers integrated resort development strategies that depict and anticipate the location and type of developments that can take place on Denarau Island. In accordance with the master plan, a range of tourism facilities are provided, including hotels, a marina, leisure and recreational retail, golf courses, residential areas, and various types of water-based recreation. These facilities share infrastructure, such as roads and drains, recreational features, beaches, marinas, open spaces, and transportation facilities. Although the tourist facilities share an integrated infrastructure, including an open bus service, each hotel development is a separate project from all the others. Geographically, the island is accessed via a road from the south, which divides the land use as follows: (1) the eastern side consists of residential dwellings, mainly vacation homes for foreigners within gated subdivisions, apartment buildings, a commercial and retail center with restaurants, nightclubs and specialty shops, and a marina; (2) the southern and central areas are designated for recreation, including the golf and the racquet clubs and the proposed rugby stadium; and (3) the western and northern sides comprise a vast variety of hotels and resorts with their own retail and recreation activities, overlooking the bay and abutting the beach.

A series of interconnected canals have been constructed across Denarau Island, providing tourists and residents with boats and easier access both to the sea and to the island's many dwellings. The layout is innovative and has garnered some comparisons to Venice's famous canals. The difference, however, is that Denarau Island's canal system primarily caters to recreational and leisure purposes, with quaysides and mooring berths bordering the island. These canals, constructed to flow next to dwellings built virtually on the water's edge, allow residents and tourists to literally step out of their dwellings and onto their boats. The residential development retains a set form, with the canal, berth, accommodations, and vehicle access, providing a holiday ambience throughout. The tourist villas and hotels also carry a similar layout in which the canals are replaced by the beach. The purpose of the design is to retain a holiday atmosphere and to enhance the amenities and quality of the resorts. The system of islands provides greater mooring spaces and waterfront lots. The height of tourist villas is limited to two storeys, which allows for clear sightlines to the ocean and to the surrounding islands, providing an aesthetically desirable environment.

Each of the tourist complexes receives visitors' cars at their entrances. Tourists then continue and experience the resort on foot, creating a calm atmosphere with predominant movement on foot and moderate use of canal travel. The dominance of pedestrian traffic in Denarau Island's resorts brings the tourist in close contact with the maritime environment and separates vehicles and pedestrians, providing the foot traffic with unimpeded access to the water. In particular, the hotels and resorts overlooking Nadi Bay do not follow a ribbon development, which is a typical morphological pattern in costal tourism planning. The new layout inevitably avoids traffic and pedestrian conflict, reduces congestion, and maintains a distance between car traffic and the sea. To encourage pedestrians, a vast series of landscaped footways have been built, and to reduce private vehicle movement, an open bus service is provided within the island that moves from resort to resort and to the marina and other recreational facilities. Because the beach constitutes the principal attraction, a local ordinance promoting low-rise development, and limiting the height of buildings to two storeys, effectively avoids overcrowding and obstruction of beach views.

The Port Denarau Marina marks the border of the CBD and the RBD. The Marina accommodates the retail and commercial center of the island, while hotels provide accommodations in its vicinity. The commercial and retail center resembles a mall structure, formed in a circle shape with an arena at its center, surrounded by retail activities such as shops, restaurants, and the occasional handicraft market. The second floor is mainly used for commercial purposes, namely offices, nightclubs, restaurants, and an emerging new retail center. The central dome holds a fountain that resembles an aquifer, shooting water skywards. The Port Denarau Marina attracts visitors through its setting that is steeped down from the ground level and its dominant use as a stage for cultural performances; thus, it acts as the focal point of the commercial and retail center. The arena layout also is more aesthetically pleasing than a typical horizontal shopping or commercial strip, as there is enclosure, which creates a communal space. The ground and upper floor activities are not restricted in orientation to only face the center, but also have faces on the outer side, with the backdrop of the waterfront and pedestrian access all around the commercial/retail complex and the marina. This ensures great use of the available resources, as well as safety and surveillance all around the center.

Environmental characteristics

Coastal resort development, particularly in the absence of planning regulations, tends to sprawl along the coastline. Terms such as "architectural pollution" describe a failure to integrate resort infrastructure with aesthetically pleasing characteristics of the natural environment (Wall and Mathieson 2006). Tourism adds to environmental stresses which are already imposed on fragile coastal resources. The environment of Denarau Island was intact until 1969, as the hotel industry moved onto the periphery of the island. The advent of tourism, and the concomitant development of infrastructural works, altered landscape features and vegetation alike. At present, the primary challenge to Denarau Island's environment is that local infrastructure is unable to cope with the intensity of tourist visitation at peak periods of the year.

As the first hotel was established on the island, many plants, and even white sands, were imported for the sake of beautification. In addition, major sections of mangrove forest were cleared to allow access to the waterfront. Resort development did not take place along the transport nodes, but cul-de-sacs extended from the main arterial link to service the new residential allotments. There was no commercial hub within this locality. As a result, the current development model, one favoring the needs of resorts, has been put in place. Although commercial land use existed prior to the development of resorts, the general consensus is that the current commercial area was initiated to accommodate the needs of the tourist population, and the integrated marina, office, and commercial hub are oriented towards entertainment and catering for high market customers. Therefore, beautification is necessary to attract tourists.

Access to the western coast of the island is restricted due to the arrangement of hotel developments along the coast, which do not provide access to the general public beyond the main entrance of the hotel or resort. The spatial separation of tourist areas from the rest of the resort carries a number of consequences for the ecology of Denarau Island. A vast number of landscaping projects undertaken throughout the island have put pressures on traffic congestion. Although the public can gain access to the coast via pockets of accessible public beaches, one is always under the impression that the beach and coast behind the resorts are under private ownership, solely based on the development layout, unless one knows about the legislative requirements of the locality to confirm that this is public land. As a result, the local authority may want to hold negotiations with the resort owners in order to guarantee a joint collaboration. The cost to local authority in return is that it will need to take responsibility for infrastructural supplies such as water supply to the island, drainage of water and wastewater, and roading, in exchange for the provision of a public in the form of beach access.

The Fijian government passed the EMA in 2005 to provide for the effective enforcement of environmental standards and create an administrative framework for the Department of the Environment. This Act creates a legal framework for environmental impact assessment, integrated natural resource management, waste management, and pollution control. Regarding coastal resort developments, Schedule J (Requirements & Dispensations for Integrated Resorts, Tourist Villas and Over Water Development) of Provision 9 in Chapter 139 (General Provisions) of the Town Planning Act 1946 is of relevance. This section facilitates resort development planning through the provision of integrated resort developments. It stipulates that the minimum site area for such a development to occur on is 40 hectares, that not less than 70% of the area must be utilized for tourism, not more than 25% for residential, and not more than 5% for commercial developments (Town Planning Act 1946, Schedule J(1)(i)). In addition, integrated resort development laws list specific structures that are either permitted (such as hotels, marinas, mooring areas, recreational structures, and residential sites), conditional (such as multi-units, service stations, airstrips, and civic structures), or non-permissible (all other buildings). It should be noted that before a proposal reaches this stage of specific land and redesign requirements, if the land on which a resort is to be developed is not zoned for such activity, which generally is the case, it needs to be rezoned.

From the perspective of the BRM, environmental changes on the Island end at Stage 5 with the intervention of the EMA. Despite the stipulated act, massive coastal tourism development has already displaced the adjacent farming and local populations further inland because extant policies and planning regimes are not specific enough to avoid this. The apparent economic benefits of tourism, therefore, potentially come at the cost of environmental degradation through loss of the natural landscape and the social costs of local people's displacement away from the coast. The planning authorities, however, are generally willing to accept such developments to gain funding in the form of property taxes. Furthermore, although there are development controls for this island destination under the master plan, these are limited. Consequently, the governance of and final decisions pertaining to beach development fall upon the owners of the island but not the local authority, which is a major power shift. This resort development is situated away from the urban areas of the town and contains a large touristic accommodation inventory. Thus, the majority of tourism activities and consumption take place away from the urban areas. As a result, the local authorities can face a number of problems, such as delivery of utility services (water, electricity, and gas), natural disaster (flooding and sandflies), overdevelopment of the coastal environment, pollution from effluent discharges, erosion and deforestation, loss of mangroves, damage of fragile ecosystems, and uncontrolled exploitation of adjacent reefs (Honey and Krantz 2007, Prideaux 2009).

Sociocultural characteristics

The social effects of Denarau Island's coastal development are unique due to the rural setting of the resort and the period for which it has been functioning. Resort development on the island is still not fully complete and work is still being carried out in Stage 5. Many vacant allotments for hotels along the west coast remain to be planned despite the fact that the resort has gained major recognitions for its creative ideas, layout, and planning. A social benefit for coastal tourism is job opportunities for the locals, especially for unskilled workers within the construction and hospitality industries. However, job creation has slowed due to rising labor costs and demands from hotels. Another issue is that the majority of the development within this integrated planning is owned by international investors. This can affect the local economy in the form of income leakage to foreigners, as opposed to growth within the local economy.

Denarau Island has distinctive characteristics due to the fact that a few residents reside and tourism has become central to the lives of the locals. Land ownership continues to be an ongoing issue regarding land leases and accrual and dissemination of benefits. In recent years, security has become an issue as thefts from hotels and private housing have increased. Interviews conducted with the locals suggest that residents embrace tourism-induced job opportunities and were prepared to accept the inconveniences of tourism. There is a common consensus that local residents are cognizant of tourism benefits to the community. Because the vast majority of new developments are constructed far from the residential areas in early stages, their impacts on the locals tend to be negligible. In particular, the development of beachfront sites excluded public involvement from using the resources.

Mitchell (1998, 2013) uses the term "creative destruction" to describe the sequence of circumstances by which small destinations are transformed by tourism. The commodification of tradition is initiated with accelerated external investment. In return, local residents who remain must learn to adjust to this new situation where a previously uncommodified rural landscape is replaced with one that is congested and crowded by tourists. The concept of "creative destruction" applies well in the context of Denarau Island. The levels of resident response and threshold levels to the degree of tourist impact remain small in comparison with other coastal developments. The reason for this is that beachfront and strip development are controlled by external resources with little input from local residents. The spatial separation between the development zone and residences provides little interaction between tourists and the locals. Services and goods provided to hotels reflect the needs of tourists, such as indigenous souvenirs and local fruits, but the supply is tightly controlled by the hotel owners and foreign companies. Therefore, tourism as a result has a minimal social impact on coastal resort development mainly because its linkages with the domestic economy are weak.

Macleod (2004) suggests that an island's remoteness, insularity, cultural traditions, "Otherness," unique environment, and character present an ideal context for tourism development. On the other hand, tourism development leads to changes in the sociocultural and political structures of local communities. However, islands often face structural handicaps due to their peripheral locations and a high degree of dependency on such external forces as tourism as a major source of income. Denarau Island is a new type of enclave in which the foreign domination and ownership of tourism facilities has led to the repatriation of tourism revenue, domination of management positions by expatriates, and lower salaries for locals (Mbaiwa 2005). Furthermore, temporal-spatial division prevents social interaction between locals and tourists. Behaviors adopted from exchanges with tourists, as well as the tourism work setting, are difficult to be carried forward into local communities. There are recreational opportunities being promoted for both locals and tourists, including the golf courses and the proposed rugby stadium; however, the primary benefit of tourism for the community of Denarau Island appears to be providing job opportunities for the locals.

Research implications

The changes on Denarau Island bear a resemblance to morphological patterns in other small island settings. Construction began on the RBD, particularly the port Denarau retail center and the commercial hub adjacent to the Sheraton villas, in the early stages of the island's development into a tourist destination. The first hotel triggered a tourism boom in the form of a planned resort development concept, creating a catalytic effect for the major job opportunities that emerged in response to tourism development. In spite of similarities, it appears that Denarau Island does not fully concur with the BRM. Stage 2 of Denarau Island's development as a tourist destination did not include the construction of second homes. The current development ends on Stage 5, with the development of the business center. Another noticeable fact is that the components of change outlined in the model do not occur at the same stage in reality. There have been mismatches of some elements for this case study.

It is suggested that the BRM cannot predict the changes that will occur to Denarau Island at a given point in time. The evolutionary model does not have universal applicability as stated in the existing literature; thus, it cannot explain the processes that an individual coastal resort experiences. One of the major reasons for the mismatch of the BRM is the influence of the master plan undertaken following the construction and commercial success of the first hotel on the island. The master plan has been, and continues to be, implemented in stages with most of the anticipated developments now complete. The development has been conceived under the plan and is therefore at its maximum capacity. Furthermore, Denarau is unique where a "land swap" was implemented and mixed land ownership is the defining feature of tourism development on the island. The pattern of development at this destination is therefore quite distinct from what the tourism literature or the evolution model anticipates, for the following reasons:

1   There was no resident settlement prior to the establishment of a resort; therefore, no pre-resort commercial area exists. From its inception, the commercial area grew in response to tourism, with the opening of a small commercial center very early in the development scheme, followed by the construction of larger commercial and office spaces.

2   There was no change in the use of coastal village buildings such as dwellings or huts. All development started up fresh, and no relocation or redevelopment scene was created in residential areas. Residents

were not displaced from the vicinity of the resorts; rather, they were attracted to the hotels for jobs.

3   The exploration stage did not exist, given the implementation of the master plan. The coastal resort was the initiator of development that brought residents from foreign countries, rather than existing residents' settlements attracting tourism development.

4   Due to the mixed ownership of the island, tourism development focuses on "distinct zonation," in which the expansion of international hotels occurs only in selected areas. The zoning plan tends to minimize the disruption of local populations. In terms of access, there is a primary road with feeder roads leading off it to the gated residential communities and the marina; there is no variation to this network.

5   The master plan outlines the prospects and limitations of future development; thus, urbanization has yet to be a concern here. This is in part because the island is privately run in terms of governance, and therefore changes can occur in response to high demands.

Despite the uniqueness of Denarau Island, its development has faced several challenges. For instance, environmental pressures and conflicts are not assessed on an ongoing basis, which likely means that environmental policy and management are not adaptive; and limited planning activity reduces the likelihood of identifying and reconciling inter-sectoral issues and pressures (Lane 2006: 11). Therefore, there is clearly a need for improvement of Denarau Island's land-use planning, especially in the coastal environment where there are increasing developments and a potential for urbanization. This would only succeed if rationalization of the institutional responsibility takes place at the level of central government, and if municipal authorities are granted a substantial mandate for area planning, inter-sectoral planning by intergovernmental taskforces increases, and a change in government structure takes place (Uniquest Party Limited 2010).

The master plan governing the coastal tourism development areas would need to allow flexibility for the district plans where particular standards such as design criteria can be met and checked. Eventually it would allow for variations at the development stage within the scope of the anticipated environmental outcome under the master plan. In response, the legislation should identify the necessary elements of a master plan, particularly in precinct areas. These areas would then have specific controls added to them for activities, development and design requirements, protective measures such as covenants and encumbrances on heritage areas and outstanding natural features, demarcating public and private domains, and so on. Identifying precinct areas will inevitably protect and enhance the urban characteristics of the coastal resort, while maintaining and growing tourist values. This will provide planners with the opportunity to proactively plan for tourism developments.

Setting a maximum limit for specific activities such as commercial use as a portion of the total landmass of the resort will control sprawl and urbanization, as the limits and the carrying capacity of the development site are proactively determined. This will also contribute towards planning for adequate infrastructure and the future viability of the resort itself by maintaining an attractive environment, both natural and built. The process will also need to go through the public notification process, where the community can have a direct influence on matters of concern to them and their locality. Any modification to the original controls set as part of the master planning process will need to be negotiated and go through the same series of steps as the original.

Summary

Coastal resource management and developments are very complex in nature. However, exploring a particular situation via a case study provides an opportunity to generate a holistic framework for coastal tourism. The applications of morphology in urban geography provide a means to understand the form and spatial configuration of coastal resorts by relating each development to the visual and psychological context in which it took place. Thus, morphology can be utilized as a tool to assess coastal resorts. The success of coastal tourism in destination rejuvenation process is ideally based on the existence of a shared strategic vision and in-depth involvement of key stakeholders in building an atmosphere of political, entrepreneurial, and social consensus. The case study of Denarau Island presents a conceptual framework to understand the developmental stages and examines coastal resort development patterns by investigating past activities and evolutionary changes. Prideaux (2009: 252) notes that "small island communities experience difficulties in translating planning objectives into practice because of conflicting governance issues, lack of finance, and resistance to change." Tourism planning in an island setting includes studying the impact of tourism on communities, heritage and culture, sustainability, transportation, employment, and external threats.

Denarau Island represents a unique coastal development model in which tourism development begins with international hotel construction. As demand for tourism development in the area rises, rapid development and subdivisions immediately follow. Development begins in a steady and sustainable manner, but soon after, the natural components of these areas are lost and resort quality declines. More than the economic component, there are adverse effects on the environment, such as erosion, coastal inundation, loss of flora and fauna, degradation of the marine environment, and increased vulnerability to natural disasters. On Denarau Island, mixed ownership, largely controlled by the local government, is one of the reasons that morphological changes do not follow the traditional BRM. In turn, both these components have a social effect on the local residents. However, this study observes a need for legislative reform to require a spatial plan that maps areas suitable for tourism developments, conservation, and protection. This, coupled with a mandatory master planning approach for all tourism developments, will proactively guide the construction of destination products and place a lock on the maximum development capacity. The final thread to sustaining coastal resources and allowing for tourism activities on the coast is setting up a coastal commission who, in consultation with the TLA, assess and make decisions on tourism development proposals, and ensure continuous monitoring of policies and objectives.

Coastal planning is crucial, given the ability of beach resort development to alter land usage, the natural and built environments, local lifestyles, and the economy. Most importantly, it is essential for achieving sustainable development in a fragile island setting. For example, Coastal Zone Management (CZM) is a subject area first introduced and implemented in 1972 with the US Coastal Management Act (Cicin-Sain and Knecht 1998, Kay and Alder 2005), who seeks coastal zone sustainability by ensuring that the environment and landscapes are in harmony with economic, cultural, and social development. Tourism is encouraged in much of Fiji as a tool for attaining long-term prosperity and sustainability (Movono et al. 2017). The ideal planning process should recognize the need to adopt integrated regional plans for maintaining coastal resources. In addition, individual coastal developments need to confirm compliance with the coastal management plan in which natural scenic and cultural resources need to be protected. Community involvement in the planning process, manageable objectives for CZM, monitoring and evaluation of impacts, and educating employees, resort operators, and developers are also necessary for resource management and planning.

4 Destination morphology in an ancient Chinese city

Introduction

The management of historical urban landscapes has regained prominence in recent decades. Much ink has been spilled on various aspects of urban conservation, notably relating to the allied topic of "heritage" (Veldpaus et al. 2013). The substance of what has become known as tangible heritage consists of the historic parts of the urban landscapes, which are objects of investigation by urban morphologists. It could be readily argued that urban morphology offers a substantial part of the fundamental research base that should logically be drawn upon in the recognition, delimitation, and management of World Heritage Sites (Whitehand 2007). Yet, despite the burgeoning expenditure of energy on these activities, little research is undertaken into the morphology of heritage sites, or the role tourism plays in that morphology.

The response to this challenge relies on the two primary schools of thought within the field of urban morphology, which have become associated with two different disciplines: the Conzenian school, within which the principal movers have been geographers (Conzen 2004), and to a lesser extent, the Muratorian or Caniggian school, which has received its main impetus from architecture (Caniggia and Maffei 2001). Both approaches were developed in Europe examining a wide range of geographical scales, with a particular emphasis on streets, blocks, plots, and buildings, and in the case of the Conzenian approach, building types, materials, architectural style, and land use. While the broader concern of both schools of thought is the long-term morphogenesis of cities that explicates the physical form of change, their focus is an investigation of the spatial structure of the urban ground plan, which is recognized in urban methodological literature as "plan analysis." Specifically, consideration is given to the implementation of key decisions leading to the skeletal structure of ground plans, the modular design of street systems, and characteristic building arrangements within this larger matrix.

From a cultural geographical perspective, M.R.G. Conzen was the first scholar to relate a particular significance to the historicity of the urban landscape, namely, its historical expressiveness (Whitehand 1977). In this context, the city is viewed as a long-term asset whose importance extends far beyond its contemporary functional value. The urban landscape is an invaluable source of tourist experience, particularly because it constitutes the predominant environment of a large proportion of cultural and heritage sites. The fact that the urban landscape is a highly visual and, for many tourists, practically omnipresent experience gives it an advantage over many other sources of knowledge. However, realizing its potential requires appreciating societal activities and processes in what can be observed on the ground, and an important part of this appreciation is the uncovering of historical and geographical order.

Urban form is deeply imbued with a sense of the intrinsic importance of regionalization within geography. Together they have epitomized "critical regionalism" (Tzonis and Lefaivre 1990, Herr 1996, Powell 2007, Botz-Bornstein 2015), including the multiple contemporary and historic origins of the cities. Conzen (1988: 261) has coined the term "morphogenetic priority" to denote the existence of a hierarchy of urban landscape units, according to their resistance to change and consequent persistence across time. He suggests that elements present in the ground plan tend to display the highest resistance to change. Many old street systems are still recognizable in the landscape today and constitute a framework that powerfully influences the long-term historical development of the city's conformation. Land and building use, in contrast, tends to be much more ephemeral, while the buildings are, on average, intermediate in their resistance to change.

Nonetheless, the extant research on urban form has largely been confined to western, postindustrial cities (Vance 1990, Burgers 2000). Morphology posits an evolutionary cycle of the town and tracks a dynamic complex of changes across multiple time periods. In recent decades, economic clusters have been recognized as important elements of urban spatial planning (Yang et al. 2015). These studies offer an important decision-making process for planning and improve the existence of elements that create urban form, such as old districts, commercial streets, and development zones. However, urban morphology is emerging in China, where most cities still lack an accurate detailed plan. Consequently, the morphological study of Chinese cities has neglected what has come to be seen in the West as the fundamental unit of analysis: the individual plot of land (Whitehand and Gu 2003).

Given the importance of historical elements in urban morphology, there is an increasing interest in incorporating morphology into tourism studies (Gospodini 2001, 2004); however, the significance of applying morphology to urban tourism remains neglected by tourism researchers (Liu and Wall 2009). Furthermore, architectural heritage has been discussed in tourism literature, but little work has been carried out explaining its relationship to urban development (Lasansky and McLaren 2004). Gospodini (2001) advocates that architectural heritage reflects differences among cities and provides cities with a sense of historical and cultural authenticity. It not only provides a frame of reference that articulates the physical composition of an urban area, but also represents a place identity embedded with images and memories for tourist consumption. Architectural heritage is not limited to old houses, but also encompasses landmarks, such as city walls, characterized by their tourist-historic functions (Bégin 2000). These landmarks have integrated into the contemporary socioeconomic life of a city in which the past and present are inexorably intertwined.

This chapter explores the destination morphology associated with the city of Pingyao, an ancient walled city in Shanxi Province, China. It uses the city wall as a reference point to characterize three periods of urban change in Pingyao's history and eventual emergence as a major tourist destination in China. The purpose of this chapter is twofold: the first is the introduction of urban morphology in the context of China, as well as the sources that can be used in its investigation in urban tourism; and the second is to assess the historical development of the city wall in Pingyao, and to detail the impacts of tourism development associated with the wall.

Urban morphology in China

There is a growing and substantial literature about urban form in China (Yan 1995, Xu 2000, Gu 2001, Liu et al. 2005, Wu 2015). The late twentieth and early twenty-first century has witnessed the plight of demolition or irreparable damage for thousands of historic streets across China as a result of urbanization and redevelopment. A core of committed practitioners, academics, and enlightened local governments have begun to recognize the important historical legacy of these streets and are undertaking conservation and revitalization projects (Cheng et al. 2017, Xie and Heath 2017). The majority of research focuses on spatial changes and urban land expansion during the economic reform era (Lu 2006). Tourism planning is viewed as an essential component of economic development, which improves tertiary services.

Bégin (2000) conducts research in Xiamen, China, and identifies three stages of urban morphology in Chinese cities: renovation, expansion, and redevelopment. The old central core of the city tends to be too condensed to develop a modern Central Business District (CBD). Consequently, an initial form of "recreational business district" or a "tourist cultural district" was engendered due to the mixture of traditional residential areas and emerging business districts. Ashworth (1989) argues that there exists a transition zone between the newly developed business district and the old town. The transitional morphology can be seen in the glittering office buildings juxtaposed with dilapidated urban cores. In China, transition zones can be found on Maoist-era residential and industrial campuses versus the newly developed districts (*xingqu*). The dividing line between these stages of urban morphology tends to be marked by administrative boundaries or historical landmarks, such as the city wall.

Chinese cities are experiencing rapid urban changes as a result of economic development. Struggles between preservation and development continue as tourism becomes an effective means of economic growth. Influenced by urban designs for sweeping changes in the old core of the city, local governments face simultaneous pressures to modernize the city and preserve its historical architecture. Commercialization, such as tourism, has profoundly impacted spatiotemporal changes in urban cores and caused tensions between heritage preservation and urban conservation. Gospodini (2001) proposes that urban morphology faces three properties in relation to tourism development: the preservation of aspects of the city's past, authenticity in terms of spatial morphology, and richness in meaning. The architectural heritage of the city should not be viewed as static, but as a dynamic relationship between buildings and their beholders that evolves alongside the social and economic concerns of a given period. Historical architecture represents *genius loci* defining a city's identity.

The concept of "critical regionalism," proposed by Tzonis and Lefaivre (1990), upholds the individual and local architectonic features against the mainstream of the society. Many characteristics of local architecture may reflect critical-regionalist design, including material, plan form, wall surface, or construction mode. The emphasis is on the authenticity of the architectural elements. Frampton (1983) argues that critical regionalism represents the particularities of place with nostalgic reconstructions of vernacular architecture or urban elements. Herr (1996) and Powell (2007) suggest that by studying heritage architecture in Ireland and the US, these elements are idiosyncratic and emblematic for regional traditions, which require an extensive study. The medieval walled cities in Europe and North America, such as Quebec City (Evans 2002), have become an instant symbol of critical regionalism. The walls are used to promote "national identity" and to market its cultural heritage. They constitute a major contribution to the historical grain of a city and have significant implications for planning, especially conservation. It must be noted that differences exist between approaches to heritage building in the East and the West. For example, cultural heritage in Asian cities is largely shaped by philosophies and religious systems that emphasize the intangible rather than the tangible. Those differences are manifested in the 1994 Nara Documents and 2003 Hoi An Protocols.

Tourism can be used as a means to legitimize or to authenticate public culture (Xie 2003). Public culture can be refashioned by the needs of tourism to symbolize reconstruction of the existing entity. Hollinshead (1999: 267) calls this kind of modification "the legerdemain of tourism," where material symbolism has been continually reconstrued across multiple time periods. Heritage architecture is widely seen as representative of local culture and identity; however, history shows that the architecture is built or renovated to suit the political, economic, and sociocultural needs of a given locale. In many cases, this selective reinterpretation of architecture serves to legitimize a governmental viewpoint on those aspects of the past that are deemed important to remember or to market. For instance, Chan (2005) examines the multiple meanings of building the temple, Huang Da Xian, for Mainland Chinese, Chinese in Hong Kong, and Taiwanese. As a heritage temple, the Mainland Chinese regard Huang Da Xian as an ideal place to practice religious activities and to develop pilgrimage tourism. Conversely, for overseas Chinese, the construction of the temple is viewed as a nostalgic search for roots and authenticity. Finally, the Chinese government cites the temple as a symbol of nationalism to reinforce a Chinese identity. AlSayyad (2001: 4) calls this kind of regeneration "engazement"—a process through which the tourist gaze transforms the built environment into a cultural imaginary. In other words, the gaze is not the same everywhere, but its spatiotemporal dimensions change from place to place. Heritage identities have been reinterpreted by different stakeholders for the purpose of tourism development.

Various aspects of city walls have been the subject of research including their values in urban tourism planning (Knapp 2000, Le 2005). City walls are arguably the most prominent heritage landscape feature in a traditional Chinese city (Whitehand et al. 2011). During the twentieth century, many city walls in China, such as Beijing, were demolished, and their sites became important thoroughfares, encircling the core of the city (Ruan 2003). The restoration of existing walls serves a multitude of purposes. In particular, tourism remains a catalyst of change in the process of restoration and urban regeneration. The revival of ancient walls and their conversion into tourist attractions are often seen as "theatres of memory" (Samuel 1994: viii) in which a region's historic and cultural past is salvaged and reshaped. The restoration encompasses a sense of regional identity, and most significantly, rejuvenates a sense of place attachment in heritage architecture (Gu and Ryan 2008). Tourism represents a powerful option for preserving these walls and an effective means of making a visible cultural identity.

Urban planners and government officials in China have spearheaded efforts to conserve city walls since the 1980s. For example, in Xi'an, restoration of the city wall and development of a park outside the wall began in 1983 (Wang et al. 1999). In Beijing, the central government greenlighted two projects to restore the city walls and create city-wall parks in 2003. One result was the Ming City Wall Park—a 1.5-kilometer strip with an area of 12.2 hectares (Zhang 2008). The second project was the Imperial City Wall Park, which is 2.8 kilometers in length and has an area of 7.5 hectares (Dong 2006). Similarly, in Shanghai, where the sixteenth-century wall had been demolished almost entirely between 1912 and 1914, an Ancient Wall Park was created in 2002 (Whitehand et al. 2011). These are just a few examples of the widespread reinstatement in China of historical fortification zones that had been colonized for other uses during earlier periods.

Research setting

An ancient walled city

Pingyao was the original birthplace of the banking and financial system in China (Xiong 2003). A representative culture, *Jin Shang* (Jin Merchant or Shanxi business people), was embedded in commercial activities in Pingyao when the city was the financial center in the nineteenth century. Geographically, Pingyao is situated on the gently sloping plain between the River Huiji and the River Liugen in central Shanxi. It is one of the few Chinese cities that still retains large parts of its traditional layout and fabrics. In particular, it is one of the few cities that still retains its city wall: a structure that is 6.4 kilometers in perimeter, and is one of the oldest and largest intact city walls in China. The number of gates has remained the same despite the large increase in the size of the walled area in the fourteenth century: two each in the eastern and western stretches of the wall, and one each in the northern and southern stretches (Du 2002). The walls on the north, east, and west sides are straight except in the northeast corner, whereas the wall on the south side follows the former winding course of the River Zhongdu, later realigned and renamed the River Liugen. The base of the wall ranges between 8 and 12 meters in width, and 3–6 meters at its top. The entire wall is just over 10 meters high, and is protected by a moat. Textures made from the wall and streets inside the city look like a geometric pattern on a tortoise shell; as a result, Pingyao is nicknamed the "tortoise city" (Xiong 2003), as shown in Figure 4.1. The old core of Pingyao, comprising almost

Figure 4.1 An Aerial View of Pingyao. (Source: authors)

the entire city as it existed at the end of World War II, is still contained within a city wall constructed towards the end of the fourteenth century. Extending to a little over 2 square kilometers in area, this old core is some six times the size of the walled area of the old core of Como. This great difference in size is indicative of the major difference between China and Europe in the sizes of their cities in the medieval period.

Embedded within Pingyao's present walled area are earlier, formerly walled areas. Documentary and archaeological evidence of these former walls is minimal, but their positions can be hypothesized based on street alignments and other aspects of the city's layout (Whitehand and Gu 2007). The ancient core contains the city's administrative offices, located at the junction of the north–south and east–west axial streets (Zhaobinanjie and Xihujing Street–Zhengfu Street) (Figure 4.2). This is a type of layout noted by Chang (1987: 78) as one of the four most common street patterns in Chinese cities. The limits of this early settlement, almost certainly originally city walls, are followed now by streets, that is, Xiguojiaxiang– Domgguojiaxiang, Nandajie, Shuyuan Street–Xinanmentou Street, and Shaxiang Street. Having been developed along a fixation line, these are *consequent* streets (Conzen 1966: 124–125). These streets, and those following the lines of two subsequent city walls inside the present city wall, are shown in Figure 4.2. The present city walls, and many of the lines of former walls, constitute significant morphological frames that give a historical grain to the city. Some of those farther from the present commercial core are associated with scattered remnants of fringe belts or, in the case of the zone immediately outside the present wall, a continuously surviving fringe belt. Institutions, many of them religious or quasi-religious, are frequently located within fringe belts, having started as prominent elements of a zone of spacious plots at the rural–urban fringe, but later embedded in the growing urban area. In the south and east of the present walled city, a number of large institutional sites associated with the presumed previous edge of the city are not clearly distinguished from the pronounced fringe belt associated with the present wall, which is in large part extramural.

That the original western city wall continued to mark the edge of the city as late as the mid-thirteenth century is supported by a documentary reference in 1349 to the fact that the area west of Shaxiang Street was still outside the wall (Du 2002: 40–41). The suggested alignment of the northern wall at this time is the only continuous line of streets between the previous city limits and the present wall, but the layout of streets and plots at the eastern end of the alignment of streets provides no indication of how it might have joined up with the eastern wall. Much of the glacis fringing the present wall survives as various types of open space. The intramural component of this fringe belt, consisting of a mixture of quasi-agricultural plots, institutions, and factories, is much less continuous. It should be noted that substantial areas of intramural agriculture existed well within living memory. They were most extensive in the northwest, but also significant

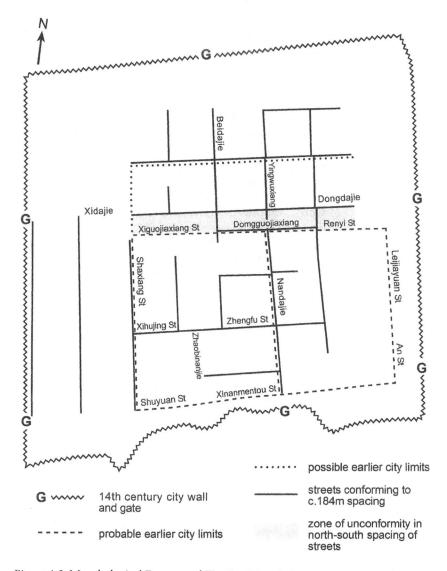

N

G

Beidajie

Yingwuxiang

Dongdajie

G

Xidajie

G

Xiguojiaxiang St

Domgguojiaxiang

Renyi St

Lejiayuan St

Shaxiang St

Nandajie

An St

G

Xihujing St

Zhengfu St

Zhaobinanjie

Shuyuan St

Xinanmentou St

G

G

········· possible earlier city limits

G ⌇⌇⌇ 14th century city wall
and gate

───── streets conforming to
c.184m spacing

- - - - - - probable earlier city limits

zone of unconformity in
north-south spacing of
streets

Figure 4.2 Morphological Frames and Fixation Lines in Pingyao. (Source: Whitehand
et al. 2016)

in the northeast. By 2007, the occupation road (cf. Conzen 1969: 127) just
inside the wall had become an almost continuous paved ring road.

Generations of streets, pseudo-streets, and agricultural legacy

Much of the layout of Pingyao within its present walls is a predominantly
square grid of narrow streets. The only extensive areas where this is not the

case are the later developed northern and western extremities of the city. Most of the grid is characterized by main streets spaced approximately 184 meters apart. The approximately square street blocks may well have been *fangs* until the seventeenth century, the *fang* having been the basic administrative unit in Pingyao until that time (Compiling Committee for Pingyao Gazetteer 1999: 69). In many Chinese cities, the *fangs* were walled until early in the Song dynasty (907–979). Such square street blocks are absented within an elongated area immediately north of Xiguojiaxiang–Dongguojiaxiang–Renyi Street, reflecting the existence of the northern fortification zone of the city here until the late fourteenth century. There are few deviations from orthogonal street lines (Figure 4.3).

In the course of city extensions, some consequent streets have become major axial streets lined by shop fronts, notably Xiguojiaxiang–Dongguojiaxiang and Nandajie, which have become the major commercial thoroughfares within the walled city. Conversely, several axial streets have decreased in significance as extensions to the city have brought new major thoroughfares into existence. A notable example of this is Yingwuxiang, which has long ceased to lead to a gate in the northern city wall and no longer has much significance, even within local patterns of vehicular movement. The present northern and southern gates are not connected by a single straight axial street. This asymmetry in the street plan is another common feature in Chinese cities (Chang 1987: 78).

Over practically the entire walled city, culs-de-sac are numerous. Within the oldest areas, they appear irregularly, and many of the culs-de-sac seem to have developed piecemeal as the interiors of street blocks became subdivided: alleys, initially private but eventually becoming public rights of way, were created to provide access. Thus, in the interiors of street blocks, there has developed what Conzen (1966: 129) termed a pseudo-street system, much of which is made up of culs-de-sac. At the end of a cul-de-sac, there is frequently either a stele bearing the inscription *Taishanshi gandang* or a stone lion, as a remedy for the inauspicious street end (Du 2002: 57). Otherwise, a dead end to a street is incompatible with *feng shui*, "the art of adapting the residence of the living and the dead so as to co-operate and harmonize with the local currents of the cosmic breath" (Chatley 1917: 175).

The essentially north–south-oriented rectilinear street plan in the northeastern corner of the walled city contrasts with the square grid that predominates elsewhere. It is most likely that this area was undeveloped until well after it was encompassed by the fourteenth-century wall. Here, in contrast to the older, square-gridded areas, the culs-de-sac are mostly integral to the original layout. The rectilinear street pattern has similarities to that in a smaller area just inside the wall towards the southwest corner, although there the alignment of streets is predominantly east–west. The three parallel north–south streets in the northeastern corner originally had

N
↑

0   500
metres

▬▬ Major axial streets and public spaces
▬▬ Direct through streets
▬▬ Alleys and culs-de-sac

Figure 4.3 Morphological Hierarchy of Streets in Pingyao. (Source: Based largely
     on an unpublished plan prepared in c. 2000 by the Shanxi Research
     Institute of Urban and Regional Planning and Design)

gates at their ends (Song 2000: 25). This arrangement was characteristic of
agricultural villages in the vicinity (Zhang and Song 1996).

Degrees of modification and the influence of feng shui

In Pingyao, plots are mainly metamorphic in the central and southern parts
of the walled city (Figure 4.4a). This is consistent with the very long time
span over which these areas have been exposed to forces for change. The
principal exception to this is in the zone of former northern and western

city fortifications, that is, north of Xiguojiaxiang–Renyi Street and west of Shaxiang Street (see Figure 4.2 for street names), where hypometamorphism is a characteristic. Here, it is evident that a more planned series of plots have been more recently laid out along the consequent streets, following the demolition of the city fortifications. In the vicinity of parts of the northern and western stretches of the present wall, plots are predominantly orthomorphic and hypometamorphic (Figure 4.4b and c). The greater regularity of the plots here, especially in areas remote from gates in the wall, corresponds broadly to greater regularity in the street system. Orthomorphism is particularly evident within a broad zone inside the eastern half of the northern stretch of the wall.

According to *feng shui*, a south-facing orientation of plots and buildings is especially auspicious, being most in harmony with the "cosmic breath." The large majority of plots and the courtyards that occupy them are therefore oriented north–south (Figure 4.4). Most entrances are at the southern end of their plots. On north–south-oriented streets, it is not uncommon for plots to display a long side to the street. In such cases, there is often a minor east–west orthogonal street, usually a cul-de-sac, giving access to a south-facing courtyard entrance. Such culs-de-sac are predominantly on the east side of north–south streets. Hence, west-facing entrances are fewer than east-facing ones: this is particularly evident in the areas of rectilinear street systems just inside the northern stretch of the present city wall.

Among the relatively few stretches of street in which there are significant series of east–west-oriented plots are those in the three principal north–south consequent streets: Shaxiang Street, Nandajie, and Leijiayuan Street–An Street. In many of these cases, including practically every plot in Nandajie, commercial premises front the street. For the walled city as a whole, south-facing entrances are the most numerous, followed by east-facing, west-facing, and north-facing entrances, in decreasing frequency. This accords with the view that *feng shui* exerts a heavy influence on the city's layout. However, in a sizeable settlement, especially one in which many plots contain shop fronts, there are practical obstacles to achieving a layout that complies in its entirety with the principles of *feng shui*.

Straight boundaries between series of plots that back on to one another are rare within the part of the city that was developed before the fourteenth-century wall was constructed. Practically, only such boundaries exist where plots were laid out along consequent streets. In contrast, many straight boundaries between plot series exist within those parts of the city that were developed between the mid-fourteenth century and late nineteenth century (Compiling Committee for Pingyao Gazetteer 1999: 74–77). The highly irregular plot boundaries in the oldest areas of the city are probably a reflection of the susceptibility of the large square street blocks in this area to various types of plot subdivision and the lengthy period during which processes of change have been at work here.

a. Metamorphic plots

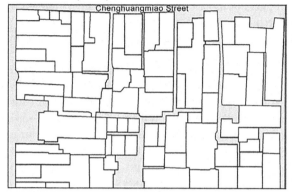

b. Hypometamorphic plots

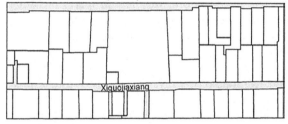

c. Orthomorphic plots

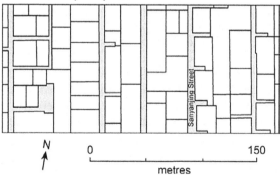

Figure 4.4 Plot Types in Pingyao.

Courtyard design, south-facing entrances, and tourism development

With the major exception of parts of the northwest corner of the walled city, much of which remained in some form of cultivation until after the Communist Party came to power in 1949, the walled city of Pingyao is, like the traditional parts of most Chinese cities, largely occupied by courtyards. These are constructed so as to afford a high degree of privacy and separation from the street. While in Europe the contrast in building block plans between the fringe belts and the large majority of housing areas is marked, inside the city wall in Pingyao courtyards are characteristic of both types of area. Both tend to have little vegetation. Although the physical form of Pingyao's institutions towards the end of the nineteenth century has been captured in a number of drawings (Wu and Wang 1883: 3–33), information about the physical character of Pingyao's housing areas is largely dependent on fieldwork in conjunction with recent plans. Unlike in the West, where observations from the street are a major source of information about the characteristics of buildings, in Pingyao, as, in Chinese cities generally, the plain relatively undifferentiated exteriors of courtyard buildings, which lack windows on to the street, reveal very little about what exists behind the street frontage. Furthermore, very few property records have survived from the nineteenth century to the present. Oral histories and fragmentary information in the possession of the present occupiers of sites are thus of especial value.

In this light, an area of six courtyard dwellings at the junction of Shaxiang Street and Xiguojiaxiang, investigated by Whitehand and Gu (2007: 104–106), is particularly valuable, allowing changes of building block plans and ownership boundaries to be reconstructed between the end of the nineteenth century and the early twenty-first century (Figure 4.5). Courtyard houses were apparently built in the area between 1736 and 1795 (Compiling Committee for Pingyao Gazetteer 1999: 756–757), but in view of the favorable location of this part of the city at the time, it is unlikely that these were the first such houses to have existed here. In the second half of the nineteenth century, the owner of one of the banks purchased all six courtyards, and undertook major renovations (Du 2002: 123–124), although the existing building block plans apparently remained largely unchanged (Figure 4.5a and b). The courtyard houses mostly retained their existing form until the 1960s, when they were taken over by the government. By the early 1990s, four of the houses had gradually become occupied by a total of 22 families, mostly those of factory workers. The new occupants sought to increase the woefully inadequate space within existing buildings by improvising structures within the courtyards (Figure 4.5c). This was a process reminiscent of that in the cores of many traditional British cities in the nineteenth century (Conzen 1960, 1962), although the results were markedly different, reflecting in particular differences of building type. In

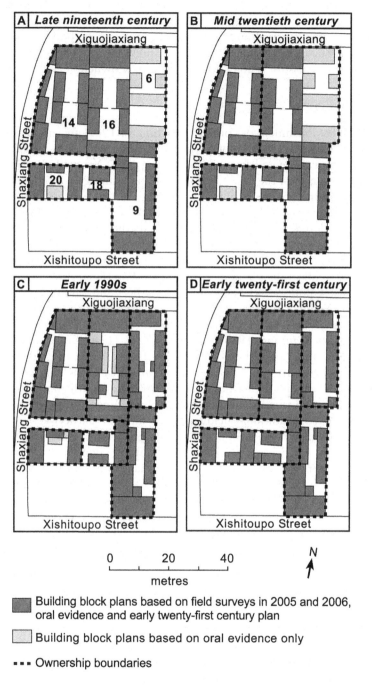

Figure 4.5 Changes of Ownership Boundaries and Building Block Plans in Ping-yao's Courtyards. (Source: Whitehand and Gu 2007)

Pingyao, the tourist potential of these traditional courtyard buildings was recognized during the economic recovery that began in the late 1990s. Renovation of the principal buildings and clearance of the buildings that had been constructed in the courtyards by the previous occupants (Figure 4.5d) provided the basis for a hotel business by a new owner.

Methodology

After the establishment of communist China in 1949, ancient city archaeology flourished as never before, and ancient city plans and excavation evidence became more widely available (Chang 1987, Yang 2003). Associated with the creation of the first School of Urban Planning at Tongji University in Shanghai in 1952, research on the history of Chinese city planning became an important subject (Whitehand and Gu 2006). Based on new archaeological and historical findings, the first edition of History of Chinese city construction was finished in 1961 (Dong and Li 1999). Disrupted by the Cultural Revolution, it was eventually published and adopted as a textbook for the students in the planning program in 1982 (Dong 1982). Along with Dong's work, four books in particular have been influential. Two were authored by Yeju He in Chinese: *A Study of the System of City Construction in Kaogongji* (1985) and *Collective Discourses on the History of Ancient Chinese City Planning* (1986). Based on these, *History of Chinese Urban Planning* was first published in 1996. The fourth book, in English, was *A Brief History of Ancient Chinese City Planning* by Liangyong Wu (1986).

Research for this chapter began circa 2000, during which a detailed survey of Pingyao's ancient core, including plot boundaries and block plans, was conducted. Additional fieldwork was undertaken between 2005 and 2015, including a longitudinal study of Pingyao as a heritage tourism destination, and extensive reviews of urban planning documents. Earlier cartographic representations of the city are diagrammatic: a map drawn in 1883 shows little more than the approximate lines of streets and the positions of special structures, such as the city walls. Changes wrought by urban tourism planning on streets and districts were carefully recorded and plotted. Governmental documents were compared to the historico-morphological shifts in three periods. Pingyao Urban and Rural Construction Bureau and Shanxi Research Institute of Urban and Rural Planning and Design were visited in order to obtain updated data on city planning. Selected local officials in urban and tourism development were interviewed, and their attitudes towards heritage preservation were observed. Finally, maps of changing morphology across three periods of time were drawn and compared.

As of 2001, the historical core of Pingyao had a population of approximately 35,000 (Xiong 2003). The city walls have drawn tourists internationally. Urban tourism plays a vital role in the improvement of both the local economy and the physical environment. A number of previous courtyard houses or institutions were redeveloped and converted for commercial uses. Concomitantly, there has been a widespread reinstatement of historical transition zones that had been colonized for other uses prior to the 1980s. The restoration of city walls began to be actively pursued by the planning authorities in Pingyao (Tongji University and Shanxi Research Institute of Urban and Rural Planning and Design 1989). Large-scale landscaping and housing clearance projects have been implemented in the zones immediately adjacent to the city wall, as well. Over the past two decades, development in Pingyao has mainly concentrated in the areas surrounding the fourteenth-century city wall. The rapid transformation of the urban landscape, mainly driven by tourism development, poses great challenges for the preservation of the cultural continuity and authenticity of this historic city.

The modern development of the city wall can be divided into three time periods: (1) From 1949 to the early 1980s, the wall demarcated the boundary between residential areas and the industrial zone. The impact of tourism was negligible since travel was widely viewed as a political activity. (2) In the period between 1980 and 1999, Pingyao evolved from a sleepy industrial city into a vibrant destination for cultural and heritage tourism. Tourism began to exert great influence on urban planning, as the wall was considered a heritage asset for marketing and promotion. (3) Since 2000, tourism has become a major source of income for the city of Pingyao, with the wall as its primary cultural marker. As such, projects to conserve the walled city have gained attention and support from local government and tourism planners alike, and commercial real estate development has been restricted in order to preserve architectural structures.

Stages of tourism development

The creation of Danwei (1949 to the early 1980s)

Until World War II, Pingyao was essentially preindustrial, following a vernacular architecture in an ancient city. The recognition of historical dwelling types in China is made difficult by the tendency for Chinese dwellings to have shorter lifespans than their counterparts in Europe. A number of factors, however, suggest that a few standard types of dwelling have been constructed and reconstructed over a lengthy period up to the middle of the twentieth century. The rigidity of the social hierarchy in traditional Chinese society until the establishment of the Republic of China in 1911 had a major impact on buildings. Ordinary dwellings were at the bottom of a building grading system in which many types of construction were permitted for upper grade buildings only. Hence, for the vast bulk of houses, changes in design were very limited. Other factors that tended to create a degree of uniformity in the physical form of dwellings and settlements included *feng shui*, which provided guidelines for the orientation of dwellings, standardized dimensions for bricks (the major walling material) and tiles (the main roof covering), and provided near-standard dimensions for wooden pillars and roofing structures, based on available timber. Established custom resulted in the widespread construction not only of houses of similar scale, but also approximately the same floor plan—living room, bedrooms, kitchen, and toilet tending to have specific positions. Standardization was perhaps further engendered by the fact that architects as members of organized professions scarcely existed, even in major cities such as Shanghai and Guangzhou, until the twentieth century. Much of the labor supply for building was provided by agricultural workers (Liu 2000: 120), many of whom were hired for brick laying and other construction work during quieter periods in the farming year. These workers revered their ancestors and maintained traditions passed down through countless generations. Speculative house building was not common until the 1920s and 1930s, when it was introduced largely by Chinese who had traveled overseas.

In 1949, Pingyao began to experience profound changes to its social and economic organization. Traditionally a service and administrative center, the city began to be transformed into an industrial city in accordance with the ideology of the new Communist China (Xie and Costa 1991). Socialist industrialization between the 1950s and 1970s significantly changed the physical environment of Pingyao. A key feature of this transformation was the creation, mainly between the mid-1950s and early 1980s, of *danwei*, or residential and industrial campuses. *Danwei* were an integral component of a centrally planned economy in which financial resources were planned by entire sectors (Ding and Gerritt 2003). Communities were created by local governments to revamp the old core of the city and to implement "social projects." Public housing was established to provide accommodations for the working class. Entire communities were constructed all at once, enabling workers to live close to their work. A railway line linking Taiyuan and Jiexiu and a railway station on the northwest side of Pingyao were built in early 1950s. The construction of this station limited city expansion in the northwest sector of the city, instead attracting the growth of *danwei* to the west of the walled city for citizens requiring direct access to transportation.

Bray (2005) suggests that *danwei* function not only as major purveyors of employment, wages, and other material benefits for the majority of urban residents, but also as an institution through which the population is housed, regulated, policed, and protected as a community. As such, the *danwei* has been the fundamental socio-spatial unit of urban China under Socialist policies, and has had an influential impact on morphology. Each *danwei* is typically a walled enclosure containing a workplace such as a hospital, school, or factory, residential accommodation for those employed in the workplace and services for residents, and it often includes a communal dining hall. The wall served as a divider between self-sufficient *danwei*. Outside the city wall, *danwei* largely occupied previously rural land, forming a major extension of the extramural residential belt. Before 1949, this part of the belt comprised little more than the glacis, the moat, eight religious or quasi-religious sites, and a military ground (Whitehand et al. 2011). *Danwei* were added to the extramural area in large numbers, mainly to the west of the wall. At the same time, large areas of high-density housing were created, and public buildings erected in places separating the open area outside the wall from the surrounding rural area, especially to the south of the walled city but also to a lesser degree on its eastern side.

While the organized industrialization that underlay the construction of *danwei* was strongly influenced by the example of the Soviet Union (Xie and Costa 1991: 281), their enclosed, gated form had antecedents in traditional Chinese courtyard layouts and in the gated communities of which physical relics still exist in the northeastern parts of the walled city (Song 2000: 25). The influence of the traditional courtyard layout is perhaps most immediately evident in the presence in a large majority of cases of a *zhaobi*, usually across and just inside the *danwei* entrance. This is a substantial screen, often decorated, constructed so as to obstruct a direct view and straight-line access into the courtyard. According to the precepts of *feng shui*, the *zhaobi* affords protection against evil spirits.

During the creation of *danwei*, tourism planning was nonexistent since it functioned as political propaganda. Few governmental organizations paid attention to the wealth of heritage buildings. Zhang et al. (1999) propose that, prior to 1978, the Chinese government used tourism solely to serve the needs of "Socialism rebuilding." *Danwei* were designed largely to accommodate members of the working class who clustered near factories, and offered easy access to stores. It also presented politics of identity in a region where industrialization was highly prioritized. *Danwei* were widely viewed as "modern" socialist products that were realized in both formal and functional terms, while simultaneously conveying an ideological charge that relied on the reinterpretation of deeply rooted traditions and the continuity of identity. In contrast, intramural buildings in the old core of the city were denigrated as instances of the insufficient architecture, devoid of social consciousness, that had been produced by and for the dominant "bureaucratic feudalism." Intramural buildings began to deteriorate as a consequence of negligence, poor maintenance, and an emphasis on *danwei* development. Vernacular architectural forms and decorative elements were likewise abandoned. Most temples in Pingyao were readapted and converted into elementary and high schools after 1949. For example, the *Wen Miao* (the Temple of Civil Culture) was transformed to Pingyao Middle School, which is the biggest school in the city; and the Taoist temple became the Bureau of Food Administration (Wang 2008). The original social and religious functions of the temples have disappeared and been forgotten.

However, the creation of the *danwei* unintentionally helped to preserve the vernacular architecture in the old core of the city. It was virtually impossible to build factories in, or to convince workers to commute to, the inner city. Most owners of the houses in the old core of the city fled after the Communist Party took power. Local policies sought to reoccupy and reconfigure extant buildings rather than build new ones. Land distribution and political agitation to solve the housing deficit resulted in a chaotic system. New residents living on government subsidies quickly filled these houses in inner city, deemed inadequate by Western standards. It was not uncommon to have four to six families inhabited in one old house without proper sewage or tap water. The lack of maintenance aggravated living standards in the old core of the city as more residents moved to the neighborhoods of *danwei*.

Modernization and tourism (1980–1999)

Tourism, which had previously been considered a political activity, emerged as a new pivot of economic development from 1986 to 1991. Local government sought to construct a new political identity in which tourism played a significant part. Tourism planning has been an integral part of master urban plans and conservation for Pingyao since the early 1980s. It has been particularly highlighted in the urban master plans in 1982 (Tongji University and Pingyao Urban and Rural Construction Bureau 1982), the conservation plan in 1989 (Tongji University and Shanxi Research Institute of Urban and Rural Planning and Design 1989), the provincial plan in 1999 (Shanxi Research Institute of Urban and Rural Planning and Design, the National Research Centre for Precious Heritage Towns and Cities at Tongji University, and Pingyao Urban and Rural Construction Bureau 2000), and provincial urban design in 2005 (Shanxi Research Institute of Urban and Rural Planning and Design 2005). The marriage of urban planning and tourism has been viewed as a driving force to revive this historical city. In 1986, Pingyao was added to the List of Precious Chinese Historico-Cultural Cities (*lishi wenhua mingcheng*) and was inducted into United Nations Educational, Scientific and Cultural Organization's (UNESCO) list of World Heritage Sites in 1997. This status is perceived to bring enormous prestige at both the global and national levels, as well as impacting future planning decisions at the local level (Smith 2002). The city has swiftly become a popular tourist destination to experience cultural heritage, urban landscapes, and traditional *Jin Shang* culture.

From 1992 to 1999, the provincial government regulated tourism as part of a "market economy" model and offered a wide range of freedom and flexibilities. Pingyao benefitted from a commercial ethos as tourism planning was implemented. The previously blank walls of the *danwei* were eventually replaced by continuous shop fronts bustling with petty-commerce vendors and private businesses. Local government officials and developers in Taiyuan, the capital of Shanxi Province, began to recognize that Pingyao, especially its city wall, had major potential for tourism. After Pingyao was designated on UNESCO's list of World Heritage Sites in 1997, the wall instantly became a valuable landmark to preserve the ancient inner city.

The wall's role as a mere line of demarcation defining *danwei* became a thing of the past; instead, it came to represent an authentic heritage asset and imaginable physical setting in urban planning. Tourism was widely viewed as a way of "de-constructing" identities for the city of Pingyao. The intramural and extramural were marked by front stage (where *danwei* was clustered) and back stage (where the old core of the city remained intact) for a growing number of tourists. The collective memory of industrialization reflected in *danwei* has been replaced by sense of place stimulated through the conservation of heritage architecture inside the city. Karimi (2000) uses the term "traditional anchor elements" to describe urban structures that possess a high degree of commercial and social meaning and accommodate major activities in a given destination. These anchor elements, such as temple of the City God, Taoist temples, the *Wen Miao*, and main streets, initially seem to be unrelated to tourism, but are affirmed by the images and representations of ancient Pingyao reproduced for domestic and international tourists (Wang 2008). Heritage architecture inside the city has been subjected to insistent and prolonged pressures from government planning to rejuvenate "old" buildings for new purposes. This political change signaled the beginning of a dramatic upheaval in how architecture was understood and practiced.

Profound changes have taken place in Pingyao since China's open-door policy, such that the city's wealth of heritage architecture and its wall have been recognized as important assets for local culture and heritage. Architecture was not always regarded as a formative part of city's cultural heritage until a stream of tourists was surprised by the vernacular buildings, a reflection of Pingyao's economical and architectural apogee. The original functions of these buildings have been restored with the support of local government. For example, the *Wen Miao* was revived as an example of symbolic architecture in the old core of the city, and the high school that once occupied the building was relocated. The replacement of *danwei* with a commercial housing market gives local residents greater freedom of location, but it also led to the deconstruction of communities in which work, leisure, and commerce are closely integrated (Ding and Gerritt 2003). *Danwei* was regarded as stylistically backward in terms of the conditions and functions of housing. The areas adjacent to the wall have been transformed into mixed-used complexes, housing a growing number of shops catering to tourists.

The promotion of traditional *Jin Shang* culture, once forgotten by local residents, has become a focus for tourism planners. The film *Raise the Red Lantern* was shot in a location approximately 30 kilometers from Pingyao in 1992. Despite the filming site's distance from Pingyao, the brick-walled compounds and housing styles featured in the film have induced many domestic tourists to visit the city. The influence of the film was so strong that

Pingyao decided to solidify the city's new image as the birthplace of red lanterns. Old buildings dealing with banks and merchants were quickly restored to ensure tourists understand the history of *Jin Shang*. Although the city itself provides little physical evidence about the nature of *Jin Shang*, it has nevertheless become a marketing tool to attract more tourists.

Urban tourism and commercialization (2000 to present)

Pingyao's successful tourism industry resides as much in the physical form of the architecture as in the methods of dissemination and promotion of that form. The success of the film *Raise the Red Lantern* and revived regionalism have refashioned planning adjacent to the city wall. Local government has invested heavily in the restoration of these buildings as the number of tourists has risen significantly. Heritage architecture, once occupied by local residents, has transformed into hotels or bed and breakfasts that are marketed as "living museums" for tourists. For example, the well-known Yide guesthouse was converted from a courtyard house built in 1736. It provides air-conditioning, heating, and private bathrooms to accommodate tourist needs. Other courtyards have been turned into museums, such as Baichuan Tong and Rishengchang, where old banks were located.

In the 2000s, the forces of urban tourism development have precipitated two major developments. First, the local government has passed several new, strict regulations, dictating building height, façades, materials, signs, and architectural designs. These regulations have been negotiated with real estate developers specifically to ensure that buildings do not reduce the visibility of the walled city, and have resulted in the demolition or reconstruction of several buildings in the city. For instance, by 2006, large amounts of single-story, high-density housing that had recently begun to mushroom on the south side began to be demolished in order to reopen views of the wall. In the spring of 2009, a new multistory building, some 900 meters west of the wall and highly visible from afar, was in the process of having four stories removed (Whitehand et al. 2011). These demolitions and transformations have changed the extramural areas into "green belt" to beautify the old core of the city.

The second development involves the traditional CBD. In contrast to western cities, where the expansion of CBD is a major influence on urban development, virtually all of the traditional CBD in Pingyao is situated along the fourteenth-century wall, next to a large residential zone. The CBD in Pingyao has, over the past two decades, especially since the mid-1990s, become increasingly tourist-oriented, to the extent that the tourist trade is now its prime function. As a result, the original *danwei* districts have further shrunk, and tourism businesses have extended significantly into the interiors of street blocks.

The wall has transformed into a boundary dividing the "tourism zone" and the "non-tourism zone." It has morphed into a marker and a gateway to define tourist flows. Residents living inside the wall, who previously were employed in other ways, are now working for tertiary sectors, and traditional *danwei* units have been commercialized. There is a growing debate questioning whether the architectural renovations are "truthful" in the sense. Cultural continuity and authenticity have become issues as an increasing number of structures inside the wall turn into tourist attractions. Wang (2010) argues that the problem in Pingyao is whether the city retains its "spatial spirit" as its past has been re-scripted to serve contemporary tourism needs. Numerous courtyard houses have been transformed to cater to the curiosity of tourists, while historical accuracy is of relative interest to urban planners. The temples are open to tourists for a fee, and the rituals performed therein have become "disneyfied." Emphasizing *Jin Shang* culture allows Pingyao to construct interesting heritage sites and architectures. However, this culture has never been materialized in reality as various stores compete for the government's sanction as the birthplace of *Jin Shang*.

The growth of tourism has had a profound impact on the urban setting. Figure 4.6 shows the evolution of urban morphology in Pingyao since the establishment of the wall in the fourteenth century. The encircled wall delineates the boundary between *danwei* and intramural heritage architecture. The main intramural zone is a mixture of temple sites, many of them redeveloped from *danwei*, along the northwest edge of the walled city. There are roads bordering the wall, particularly inside the wall and outside the moat, that are now almost complete ring roads. With the advent of tourism, this entire zone is being beautified, notably by tree planting in areas just inside and outside the wall. Large portions of this zone were previously occupied

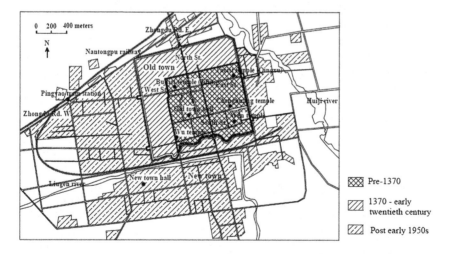

Figure 4.6 Evolutionary Morphology in Pingyao. (Source: authors)

by agriculture on the northern side, military barracks on the western side, and housing on the southern side. *Danwei* occupied the west and east sides, just outside the wall. These distinctive components have given the city a distinctive character which should be an important consideration in determining planning priorities, especially at a time of major urban growth and accompanying pressures for urban conservation (Whitehand et al. 2011).

Summary

Half a century ago, M. R. G. Conzen set out fundamental morphological bases for the management and conservation of urban landscapes. These principles relied on a combination of detailed mapping and the conceptualization of historico-geographical processes. In this chapter, we have sought to build on those foundations, in an academic and practical environment that shows signs of becoming more congenial to such an approach than the one in which Conzen was working. By applying a systematic approach to uncovering fundamental aspects of the historico-geographical structure of Pingyao, notably by identifying and mapping unitary areas of plan elements, a contribution has been made to the necessary morphological basis for decision-making concerning the conservation of major types of inherited assets. Through a systematic analysis of the morphological composition of Pingyao's historical cores, this chapter sheds additional light on the role that the built environment plays in answering such larger questions. More immediately, it has identified those features of urban form that contribute most to the heritage of the historical destination. Herein lies the basis for more informed decisions about its future conservation, particularly in light of the pressures that historical cities like Pingyao are experiencing from the rise of intensive tourism. This is not only a question of urban economics but of the survival of cultural authenticity.

Morphology in Pingyao epitomizes to a great extent the process of urbanization. Urban transformation in Pingyao bears similarities to other Chinese cities: as in other cities, Pingyao's urbanization is marked by the emergence of CBDs and the rise of tourism and shopping opportunities. Simultaneously, the socio-spatial templates inherited from previous eras, such as the influence of *danwei*, continue to shape post-reform urban development (Lu 2006). This chapter maps urban transformation by highlighting tourism development, which has significantly impacted city morphology. Tourism development centered on Pingyao's ancient walls has precipitated the development of "urban tourism precincts" (Hayllar et al. 2008: 9), where a number of attractions aggregate alongside tourism-related services, providing Pingyao with a particular spatial, sociocultural, economic identity. Six decades of Chinese socialist policies have altered the way Pingyao uses public spaces and accommodates the growing number of tourists.

As far as the city wall is concerned, the proliferation of the *danwei* between the mid-1950s and early 1980s was exceedingly significant. Extramural development indirectly helped preserve the intramural buildings and architecture. The extensive fringe-belt zones of various *danwei* are Pingyao-specific features and deserve further research exploration. *Danwei* are the primary urban structural units in many Chinese cities. However, spatial changes occurred as tourism became a more viable source of economic growth in the late 1980s. The ancient wall has evolved and been developed in a variety of ways, ranging from the demarcation of *danwei* to the preservation of the old core of the city with a strong tourist element. The importance of the wall in urban tourism reflects its commercial value and serves as the delimitation and symbol of the World Heritage Site. The local government's effort to reduce the number of stories in tall buildings and to increase the visibility of the walled city highlights the importance of preserving the landscape for tourism. The morphology of tourism becomes a process of placemaking when heritage is framed not only by professional priorities but by wider societal values. In contentious political contexts, this is manifested in the way in which the walled city is represented in the collective memories that underpin identity and historical conflicts. Although a cultural ambivalence to architectural legacy of the wall remains, attitudes have become predominantly inclusive. This shift is substantially underpinned by local collected memories connected with place identity, and has implications for placemaking processes (Parkinson et al. 2017).

Although the city wall has existed for centuries, changes both inside and outside the wall provide an interesting case study for the impact of tourism on urban morphology. The wall is an expression of cultural identity and a representation of critical regionalism in Pingyao, which has increasingly become a neutral and interchangeable unit that facilitates tourism development. The wall should be viewed as a line of demarcation, imaginable physical setting, and a marker to define tourist flows in three different time periods. The balance between the preservation of architectural heritage and economic development has become a crucial problem. Architectural heritage sites, such as temples, have been reconverted to their original use; however, the *genius loci* have disappeared due to the encroachment of tourism. The traditional rituals and ceremonies that occurred in these temples have been replaced by performances exchanged for admission fees, which have changed the meanings of these rituals. The courtyard and traditional civil dwelling houses were transformed into hotels and bed and breakfasts to cater to tourists. Wang (2008) suggests that historical preservations based on the European model need to be modified in the context of China. The revisions and displacements of architectural heritage have challenged the process of preservation. Due to tourism's significance to urban planning, future studies of tourism should integrate concerns about urban morphology, and vice versa. The concepts of authenticity and sense of place should be considered in tourism marketing.

The historic city of Pingyao is in a state of flux. From a morphological perspective, the urban landscape is a historical phenomenon: past, present, and future are indissolubly linked. In particular, intramural and extramural zones have experienced greater pressures to change for the sake of tourism development. Major urban renewal and tourism projects have taken place in both zones as a result of the dynamic relationship between shifting economic priorities and concerns about the authenticity of architectural heritage. Pingyao's city wall embraces the elements of critical regionalism despite its mixed use of public spaces and responses to different governmental policies. The wall reflects a distinctive blend of urban tourism, economy, and social changes in the context of modern China.

5 Morphological processes and impacts of tourism

Introduction

Port cities all around the world face challenges as they seek to redevelop their urban waterfronts in the interest of economic competitiveness, place promotion, and tourism. Once primarily occupied by ports, warehouses, factories, and transportation authorities, urban waterfronts have undergone a reorientation in recent decades from brownfields to commercial, residential, and recreational areas. Obsolete and derelict industrial structures on the waterfront, owing to the relative decline of shipping employment as a result of deindustrialization, are emerging as ideal host environments for spatial rebranding (Hutton 2009). There is a tendency to combine waterfront transformation with urban festivities, in order to underwrite the "growing aestheticization of urban space" (Kipfer and Keil 2002: 243) and, in so doing, offset the decline in manufacturing jobs (Jayne 2006). Such processes prompt the creation of newly commodified waterfronts, which act as "themed backgrounds" (Law 1996: 20) for entertainment, conferences, and shopping. This transformation also serves to reimage the postindustrial city in order to harness competitive advantage and attract tourists and businesses. The practice of waterfront revitalization has reached new heights of commodification in the creation of themed landscapes, with some of the major examples including Docklands in London (Wood and Handley 1999); the Baltimore Waterfront in the US (Vallega 2001); the Tokyo Waterfront City, Odaiba, in Japan (Murayama and Parker 2007); and riverfront development in Singapore (Chang and Huang 2011).

Research on urban waterfront transformation has been concerned with changing political-economic frameworks, urban planning and design, spatial and land-use changes in waterfront districts, the role of history and heritage, and ecological issues concerning waterfronts (Hoyle et al. 1988). Roberts et al. (2000) argue that waterfront regeneration is evolutionary and can be traced through various decades, such as reconstruction in the 1950s, revitalization in the 1960s, renewal in the 1970s, redevelopment in the 1980s, and regeneration in the 1990s. This evolutionary process has shifted from physically oriented renewal schemes towards a more comprehensive form of policy and practice which prioritizes environmental and social sustainability. Sairinen and Kumpulainen (2006: 121) attribute urban waterfront redevelopment to a number of factors: (1) technological changes after World War II, which led to the abandonment and deterioration of thousands of acres of industrial land across waterfronts; (2) the historic preservation movement to promote heritage; (3) heightened environmental awareness and water cleanup; (4) consistent pressure from the public to redevelop central city areas; and (5) urban renewal including state, federal, and municipal assistance.

It is fruitful to use the methodologies of urban morphology to understand waterfront development practices. Traditionally, these practices have consisted of an array of plan-led and market-driven approaches in which the derelict waterfronts of postindustrial cities have been transformed (Galland and Hansen 2012). These changes have closely associated with urban morphology to take place in port cities and are concerned essentially with the spatial impact on the physical environment for new development, as well as the spatial coordination of the various functions and activities that they would require in relation to the urban fabric at the all-important junction of land and water. The morphology is intimately connected to the changes of the built urban environment in general. Spurred by increased capital mobility and interurban competition (Malone 1996), a growing number of regeneration projects have influenced waterfront policies all over the world. Waterfront redevelopment affords cities the opportunity to remediate brownfields, restore natural shorelines, spur economic growth, and enhance transit, pedestrian, and bike connectivity (Spector 2010).

Given the importance of historical elements in urban morphology, recent years have witnessed a growing interest in incorporating morphology into tourism studies (Hall 2000, Gospodini 2001, 2004). Although architectural heritage has been discussed in tourism literature, little work has been carried out explaining how tourism relates to the morphological process (Lasansky and McLaren 2004). There is a lack of research on the spatiotemporal effects of tourism in the context of waterfront redevelopment. In particular, examples of clearly formulated methodology and effective planning implementation are quite rare (Xie and Gu 2011). Morphologically, waterfront redevelopment has tended to force existing sectors like boat building, fishing, and some port activities to relocate, in order to accommodate new types of activities (Craig-Smith 1995). Consequently, it creates new leisure and tourism quarters as a basis for further regeneration initiatives (Jones 2007). A reconstituted waterfront with amenities and considerable investments in leisure-oriented infrastructures proves to have profound impacts on contemporary society.

This chapter serves to address the morphology of the waterfronts in Auckland and Wellington, New Zealand. It compares morphological processes and challenges facing current planning management on both waterfronts. It describes the changing waterfront landscapes and seeks to explain the physical changes in terms of the key morphological agencies at work and their evolving roles in the development and implementation of waterfront planning and design. Based on extensive reviews of urban planning documents in both cities, it draws on qualitative and quantitative data that were collected as part of a longitudinal and ongoing study of the waterfront's redevelopment. The purpose of this research is to enter the territory of waterfront revitalization and, through a morphological analysis, outline the phases and impacts of urbanization process in order to identify ways waterfronts can be employed for the better. By using an evolutionary analysis of the spatial structure of the waterfront landscape as the basis for development coordination and control, it demonstrates that government agencies, public participation, and tourism are key agents of change in influencing waterfront development.

Waterfront redevelopment and impacts of tourism

Policies for urban regeneration are generally inspired by exploiting the cultural potentials of historic and industrial districts (Jansen-Verbeke and Lievois 1999) with little emphasis on the scale of tourist spatial structure. Although the resulting morphological and socioeconomic implications vary in different cities, they have gradually become instrumental to understanding tourism impacts at spatial levels. Particularly, the relationship between morphological periodicities and the stratification of waterfront development is important to the understanding and planning of urban areas. In this connection, a morphologically based inquiry into the modes of decision-making that underlie the spatial character and dynamics of the waterfront landscape offers a sound footing for tourism planning. The consequences of tourism and the evolutionary process of waterfront regeneration can be fully recognized and analyzed through urban morphology.

Under the current economy, tourism is the primary objective behind most urban waterfront development (Griffin and Hayllar 2006). It is an integral part of "the production of space," a procedural character of socio-spatial relations in which life is in a state of perpetual change, transformation, and reconfiguration (Lefebvre 1992). Waterfront redevelopment articulates different processes of exclusion and polarization, and creates new social orders through prompting new temporal and spatial power relations, such as job creation and destruction, the dynamics of housing markets, financial mechanisms, and public participation or the absence thereof (Moulaert et al. 2005). Harris and Williams (2011) show that regeneration demonstrates the transformative power of capital increasingly focusing on attracting potential tourists. It tends to foreground the consumption of pleasure as a city's most important scheme for growing local economies. Massey (1993) refers to tourism as a "power geometry," through which the multiple relations of domination/subordination and participation/exclusion that constitute social space are reorganized. It proves to be a powerful leitmotif for planners and politicians to shape landscapes in their desired image. Tourism-induced urban design pays attention to facadism and pastiche streetscape recreation, or an over-sanitization of both the history and the life of an industrial town. As a result, Orbasli (2000) explicates that tourism is no longer an outcome of conservation, but conservation becomes a product of tourism.

Event tourism is of great spatial attribute and serves to restructure urban spaces (Dwyer et al. 2005, Andersson and Getz 2008). Hosting events both produce and reflect the existence not only of a growing mobile and affluent population who seek new and fashionable encounters with cultural experiences, but also a strong and effective series of marketing channels (Lane et al. 2013). Hallmark events, such as World's Fairs and Olympics, integrate local economic development with urban gentrification (Goldblatt 2005, Getz 2012). Daly and Malone (1996), through the study of Darling Harbour in Sydney, Australia, find that waterfront projects are primarily driven by economic ambitions, spurred by a widespread assumption that urban renewal can be sustained by tourism rather than the financial or other sectors of the economy. Gotham (2005) conducts a study of New Orleans' waterfront in the US, and discovers that special events, such as Mardi Gras, constitute one of the primary "cultural strategies" to promote travel and to reestablish a city's image. Robinson et al. (2013) propose that events are especially important in the context of building a legacy, or longer-term impacts after the event. Cities can use event hosting as an opportunity to raise awareness, build community, improve local image, and enhance economic activity. Waterfront redevelopment has long been used to refurbish former industrial areas and set space aside for commercial use. Special events have transformed these landscapes within a space-time framework, and eventually lead to the creation of a gentrified waterfront.

Waterfront development is also an accumulation process that is intertwined with the nation-state, the local government, and the port authority, as well as other urban interests (Desfor and Jorgensen 2004). Smith (2009) comments that a mixture of residential, recreational, and cultural developments results in a gentrified space that is largely occupied by urban professionals, suburban communities, and tourists. Material symbolism has been constantly construed in various time periods to refashion the city's image. The initiation of waterfront development through the hosting of special or hallmark events is a typical public project supported by governments and businesses alike (Adamietz 2012). Successful examples include Barcelona, Spain's waterfront redevelopment prior to hosting the Olympic Games in 1992 (Jones 2007), the Brisbane Southbank renewal in conjunction with the World's Fair in 1988 (Fagence 1995), the waterfront renewal of Fremantle, Western Australia, in honor of the 1987 America's Cup defense (Hall and Selwood 1995), and the celebration of Australia's bicentenary and the Olympic Games in 2000 for Sydney's Darling Harbour (Daly and Malone 1996). These hallmark events were closely associated with the improvement of a derelict waterfront, the establishment of recreation and tourism facilities including conference and exhibition centers, and the generation of income and employment (Craig-Smith 1995).

Gospodini (2001) proposes that morphology is particularly conducive to clarifying three aspects of tourism development: the preservation of aspects of the city's past, authenticity in terms of spatial morphology, and richness in meaning. Sairinen and Kumpulainen (2006), through their study assessing the social impact of the waterfront in Helsinki, Finland, reveal that communities make use of waterfront areas as part of local identity and that localized gentrification stemming from tourism development elevates the social status of the entire city, changing its reputation and generating pride and investment on the part of the communities. Furthermore, by providing access and commercial activities along the waterfront, regeneration improves the social sustainability of land-use plans. The significance of shifting urban waterfronts from industrial sites to tourism sites is "as profound as the initial eighteenth and nineteenth century of development of harbors and shores for industry, and their use in earlier times for shipping, storage and shipbuilding" (121). Krolikowski and Brown (2008) suggest that the waterfront provides a linkage between a sense of place and pedestrian tourists and eventually a "tourism precinct" is formed. These precincts perform a number of functions for tourists, most notably providing an environment where they have more freedom to wander and explore (Hayllar et al. 2008). The redevelopment of waterfronts that predominately function as tourism precincts eventually impacts spatiotemporal changes in urban cores. All these transformations can be described and characterized with morphology, aided by the use of surveying, mapping, and analytical techniques (Conzen 1960).

The morphological process of the waterfronts in Auckland and Wellington

Auckland, with a population of 1.57 million in 2015, is the largest city in New Zealand. The geographical boundary of its Central Business District (CBD) is traditionally defined by the southern edge of Waitemata Harbour on the north and the region's motorway system on the other three sides. Wellington, New Zealand's national capital, has a population of 203,800, approximately 13% of Auckland's population, where the CBD is generally defined by a motorway to the west and south, a railway yard to the north and Lambton Harbour to the east (Page 1996a). Auckland and Wellington's economic prosperity has always been intimately linked with the trade through their ports. The commercial waterfront areas are rich in Maori and European colonial heritage (Auckland Regional Council and Auckland City Council 2005). The dynamic relationship between city and sea resembles that in other cities, such as Sydney, Cape Town, Vancouver, and San Francisco. However, the commercial waterfront areas in Auckland and

Wellington are similar to each other in their size, history, and political-economic contexts. On the other hand, the contrasting dynamics of waterfront redevelopment in the two cities, especially in the past two or three decades, has resulted in quite different patterns in their built environment and different socioeconomic consequences.

Figure 5.1a shows Auckland where the Fergusson Container Terminal is in the foreground to the right, while Figure 5.1b shows Wellington, the Overseas Passenger Terminal and Waitangi Park are in the mid-ground to the right and left, respectively. Both waterfronts were created by a series of land reclamation schemes starting in the mid-nineteenth century. Their development before the 1980s can be divided generally into three phases. The first extended from the mid- to the late-nineteenth century, dominated by an augmentative process of land reclamation to satisfy increasing demands for marine transport, industries, and services. Beginning already in the 1880s, the reclaimed land began to be used to accommodate the early railway development of both cities. The second phase extended from the early twentieth century to the 1950s, when rapid economic growth, especially during the interwar period, stimulated further waterfront expansion. The third phase lasted from the 1960s to the late 1970s, when containerization led to the expansion of existing loading areas and the creation of larger wharves (Auckland Harbour Board 1973: 4–6, Anderson 1984, McClean 1997, Wellington City Council 2005). By the early twenty-first century,

Figure 5.1a The Waterfront Areas Adjacent to the CBDs in Auckland. (Source: authors)

Figure 5.1b The Waterfront Areas Adjacent to the CBDs in Wellington. (Source: authors)

total land reclaimed amounted to approximately 328 hectares and 360 hectares, respectively, in Auckland and Wellington. While Wellington has 13% of Auckland's population, its land reclamation area is slightly larger than that of Auckland's harbor region. The scarcity of flat land in Wellington's central area largely explains its pressing need to reclaim land.

As shown in Figure 5.2, both waterfronts were created by a series of land reclamation schemes starting in 1866 when the basic morphological structure was set. Their transformation can be divided into four stages. The first stage, beginning around 1895, was dominated by an augmentative process of land reclamation to satisfy increasing demands for marine transport, industries, and services. As early as the 1920s, the reclaimed land began to be used to accommodate the initial railway development of Auckland and Wellington, as a station and transportation hub was established near the waterfronts. The second stage extended from the 1920s to the 1950s, when rapid economic growth, especially during the interwar period, stimulated further waterfront expansion. Several wharves were identified, and both cities were expanded to cope with shipping and transportation. The third stage lasted from the 1950s to the late 1970s, when containerization led to the expansion of existing loading areas and the creation of larger industrial wharves (McClean 1997). Finally, the fourth stage started in the late 1970s

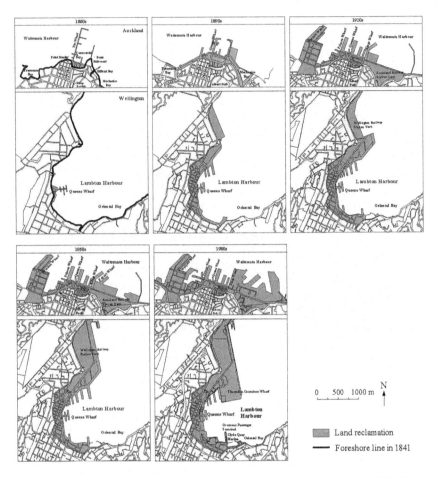

Figure 5.2 The Formative Processes of the Waterfront Areas in Auckland and
         Wellington. (Source: authors)

when the major land reclamations were completed in both waterfronts and
leisure spaces were emerged.

Figure 5.3 presents principal plan units in Auckland and Wellington. The
growth of both cities was fundamentally influenced by maritime history
and the shipping industry. The plan units are subject to cycles of adaptation and redevelopment, which usually involve a change of land use. While
significant waterfront territory, especially the docks and railway yards, remains in original use, many traditional land uses along the waterfront have
begun to be replaced by commercial buildings since the 1990s.

Auckland has been branded the "City of Sails" and its harbor is one
of its key geographic features. The Port of Auckland is an international
trade port on the Waitemata Harbour, spanning the central and eastern
Auckland waterfront. The entirety of Auckland's waterfront is divisible

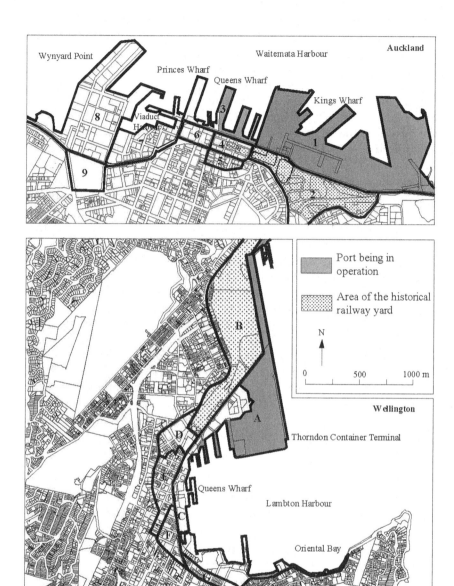

Figure 5.3 Principal Plan Units in in Auckland and Wellington Waterfronts. The Auckland waterfront: (1) Port unit, (2) Quay Park unit, (3) Central Wharfs unit, (4) Britomart unit, (5) Fort Street unit, (6) Central Area unit, (7) Viaduct Harbour unit, 8) Wynyard Point unit, 9) Victoria Park unit; The Wellington waterfront: (A) Port unit, (B) Railway yard unit, (C) Harbour Edge unit, (D) Whitmore Street unit, (E) Central Area unit, (F) Civic Center unit, (G) Wakefield Street unit. Based on author's field survey, 2008–15. (Source: authors)

into four distinguishing precincts: (1) the Port; (2) the Central Wharfs, including Princes Wharf and Queens Wharf; (3) Wynyard Point and Viaduct Harbour; and (4) Westhaven Marina. These areas, comprising a total of 55 hectares of wharfs and storage areas for containers, automobiles, and other large cargos, are essential to the economic and sociocultural development of the country. On the southern side of the port is Quay Park, the site of Auckland's former Central Rail Station. Once primarily owned by the New Zealand Railway Corporation, Quay Park is now reclaimed and administered by the Department of Survey and Land Information. Since the 1980s, contemporary apartments, an office park, Vector Arena, and intensive housing communities have been built, mainly along the edge of Quay Park. Land-use changes to Viaduct Basin, Princes Wharf, and Quay Park are characteristic of the alienations that have occurred independently. Since the 2000s, the waterfront has become a multipurpose harbor, boasting a number of tourist attractions and leisure sites.

Wellington's port is a major focus of economic activity along the capital city's waterfront. Tourism development is not the priority when revitalizing its waterfront. Following the demise and relocation of Wellington's port facilities in the 1970s, approximately 20 hectares of land and buildings became redundant. Not until in the 1980s did Wellington Harbour Board realize the waterfront's commercial potentials. The revitalization started with the railway yard area and spread to the neighboring units. Figure 5.3 demonstrates that Wellington's waterfront redevelopment is divided into seven units: (A) Port unit, (B) Railway yard unit, (C) Harbour Edge unit, (D) Whitmore Street unit, (E) Central Area unit, (F) Civic Center unit, and (G) Wakefield Street unit. In contrast to Auckland, the historical railway yard in Wellington is preserved and used as a buffer zone between the commercial waterfront and the CBD areas.

Methodology

This research is carried out in three stages. First, governmental documents outlining the waterfront development plan were compared to the actual historico-morphological shifts experienced by the waterfront in recent decades. These documents include the publication on behalf of the Auckland and Wellington Councils, Waterfront Auckland, and Wellington to oversee the revitalization of the waterfront adjacent to the city center, and the development projects drafted by the Councils to direct long-term development strategies. Various governmental development agencies were visited in order to obtain updated data on waterfront planning. Historical documents were examined in order to understand the morphological patterns of both waterfronts and the districts immediately abutting it. In addition, a recent proposal from Auckland City Council including a physical development plan and implementation guidelines for the Wynyard Quarter was collected to reflect the shifting policies towards tourism development.

In the second stage, changes in urban tourism planning on streets and districts were carefully recorded and plotted with the goal of assessing the variation of urban forms. Maps of changing morphology in these periods were drawn and compared. One striking outcome of the dynamics of waterfront expansion is the formation of contrasting "plan units" (Conzen 1969), as shown in Figure 5.3, used as a tool to analyze the morphology of built forms. The waterfront of Auckland consists of nine plan units, each of which contains a distinctive set of landscape characteristics, while Wellington has seven plan units centering the historical railway yard. Each plan unit represents an individualized combination of streets, plots, and buildings distinct from its neighbors, unique in its site circumstances, and endowed with a measure of morphological unity or homogeneity (Gu 2010). These units were built to act as extensions of former industrial sites and continue to exert significant influence on the morphological pattern of the waterfront.

Lastly, the Tourism Business District (TBD) through special events offering a geographical concentration of facilities and attractions along the waterfront was identified. In particular, the changing morphology, due to hosting of the hallmark events, such as America's Cup and Rugby World Cup in Auckland, was recorded. Ashworth and Page (2011) suggest that it is difficult to identify the TBD, largely because the users of urban services and facilities are not just tourists, but workers and residents may utilize or share the same ones. Therefore, the distribution of recreational facilities, such as Viaduct Events Centre and Voyager Maritime Museum in Auckland, as well as the Museum of New Zealand Te Papa Tongarewa in Wellington, was mapped since the majority of these tourist attractions are adjacent to the waterfront.

The impact of governance structures on morphological changes

Tables 5.1 and 5.2 show the key urban planning and design documents prepared for both Auckland's and Wellington's waterfront redevelopment. These documents illustrate the liberation of market forces under neoliberalism, in conjunction with new urban governance structures, to create the so-called "third wave new-build gentrification" (Murphy 2008: 2522) in New Zealand. Waterfront redevelopment in both cities is a process of urban intensification that has been directly influenced by statutory planning, including by the Regional Council and the City Council. Early redevelopment projects were propelled by individual development proposals and managed by separate project corporations (Auckland City Council 2006). The consequences of this neoliberal policy shift are evident in the Princes Wharf redevelopment project, the Viaduct Basin project (Eisenhut 2008), and the Lambton Harbour Development project, in which developer-driven market processes have been dominant (Oram 2007).

Table 5.1 Key Urban Planning and Design Documents Prepared for Auckland's Waterfront Redevelopment

Year	Title	Prepared By	Summary
1989	Auckland Harbour Edge Investigation Committee Report	Auckland Harbour Edge Investigation Committee	Detailed survey of Auckland's waterfront area and recommendations for future development opportunities
1991	Joint Harbour Edge Study Interim Report	Auckland Regional Council and Auckland City Council	Planning and design framework for waterfront redevelopment
2005	Auckland Waterfront 2040	Auckland Regional Council and Auckland City Council	Principles and implementation strategy to guide future development of the waterfront
2009	Auckland City Centre Waterfront Masterplan	Auckland City Council	A strategic framework to guide future proposals for buildings, spaces, movements, and water- and land-based activities

Due to changes in port operations, transport modes, and the progressive expiration of industrial leases in the reclamation lands over the course of the 1980s, many deteriorating waterfront areas in both cities began to seek alternative uses. Because waterfronts comprise transferable values, whether architectural, aesthetic, or social, the local government has advocated the preservation of the waterfront area, or at least partial restoration. In the case of Auckland, its development attracted wider public attention in 1989 when the City Council's Harbour Edge Project was announced. Substantial changes did not begin until 1993, when the "Whitbread around the World Race" led to the redevelopment of the inner wharf area by the Port of Auckland Limited (Gu 2014). The redevelopment projects along the waterfront that followed sought to meet the increasing demand for business growth and urban living. Urban intensification and mixed-use redevelopment were viewed as a priority by the local government and communities alike.

Before 2010, the main public agencies involved in waterfront issues were the Auckland Regional Council and the Auckland City Council. The former had a regulatory role in the coastal marine area below the mean high-water mark through its Regional Coastal Plan, while the latter agency was responsible for managing natural and physical resources above this mark through its District Plan. Those areas connecting water and land were the joint responsibility of both jurisdictions. The Auckland Regional Council included representation from the Auckland Regional Transport Authority

Table 5.2 Key Urban Planning and Design Documents Prepared for Wellington's Waterfront Redevelopment

Year	Title	Prepared By	Summary
1986	Lambton Harbour Development Concept	Lambton Harbour Group and Gabites Porter and Partners	Urban planning and design concepts and proposals for Wellington's waterfront and its character areas
1989	Lambton Harbour Combined Scheme	Lambton Harbour Group and Gabites Porter and Partners	Urban planning and design principles and management strategy for waterfront transformation
1998	Wellington Waterfront Public Spaces Concept Plan	Wellington City Council	Provision and design of public open spaces and retention and enhancement of existing buildings
2001	The Wellington Waterfront Framework	Waterfront Leadership Group	Visions, principles, and values that should govern future development and urban design of the waterfront and its character areas
2003–2010	Annual Waterfront Development Plan	Wellington Waterfront Limited	A work program to implement the objectives of the Framework, including how developments will be implemented, a phasing schedule and a financial model for the proposed work

and Auckland Regional Holdings (ARH), which were established in 2004. The ARH successfully completed its bid for 100% ownership of the Ports of Auckland Ltd in 2005, and most land and properties in the port area were owned and managed by the ARH. However, one of ARH's main functions was to produce returns from its investments to fund regional transport and stormwater programs. As a result, the financial targets and objectives of the ARH contributed very little to the realization of the City Council's socio-cultural objectives of waterfront redevelopment.

As shown in Table 5.1, Auckland did not have a comprehensive planning and design guide for the entire waterfront until 2005, by which time the major redevelopment projects in Princes Wharf and Viaduct Basin had already been completed. In the absence of an agreed-upon long-term plan and a clear investment direction (Cormack 2009), it is not surprising that new waterfront redevelopment projects tend to be inconsistent in the decision-making process. Although an integrated approach has been specified in the Waterfront Vision 2040 (Auckland Regional Council and Auckland City Council 2005), an effective management and sustainable policy framework is still lacking. The City Council attempted to remedy this by preparing the Auckland City Centre Waterfront Masterplan in 2009, but very limited research and implementation details have been included in the document. An effective system of waterfront planning and design, including a conceptual framework, development plans, and detailed design, is unfortunately absent.

Comparatively, in 1982, the Wellington Harbour Board and the Wellington City Council sponsored the Wellington Civic Trust to organize a competition and conference to plan the future of redundant port land, resulting from the technological change in the shipping industry (Doorne 1998: 137). Redevelopment of Wellington's commercial waterfront commenced in 1987 when the Lambton Harbour Development Project was established as a partnership between the Wellington City Council and the Wellington Harbour Board. As a result, major redevelopment projects took place during the 1990s. Adaptive reuse of historical buildings and creation of a landscape of services and leisure were the key goals. For example, Wellington cable car from Lambton Quay is used for tourism purpose and takes through flashing LED light-filled tunnels to Kelburn lookout.

The Wellington City Council deliberately chose a path towards redevelopment that emphasized the attraction of the waterfront (Page 1996b). The waterfront is designed to enhance the city's role in tourism and complement the promotion of itself as national capital of New Zealand (Page 1993). Many old warehouses, sheds, and maritime industrial facilities have been redeveloped as art galleries, arenas, museums, theaters, and sports clubs. Some vacant land and former public institutions have been transformed to individual commercial and residential buildings on a much smaller scale compared with Auckland's urban intensification projects. Waterfront redevelopment in Wellington establishes that a successful waterfront does not need to be expensive and luxurious, but rather a vital focal point for community identity and an important catalyst for inner-city improvement.

At the operational level, governance structures appear to be fundamental to formulating planning and design recommendations for the sensitive management of the waterfront landscape. However, the lack of a sound theoretical basis for interpreting and representing the landscape contributes to the disjunction between plan and reality. Doorne's (1998) study of the redevelopment of Wellington's waterfront in New Zealand identifies the City Council and property owners as key players in the process, but finds that consultations with other stakeholders have been inadequate. Larner and Craig (2005) observe that governmental policies have given primacy to market forces since 2000, putting too much stress on strategic interventions in order to promote the local economy. The governance structure demonstrates that New Zealand adopts policies that focus on the free flow of capital and labor. The shifting policies trickle down to the City Territorial

Authority, resulting in a laissez-faire attitude towards inner-city residential development as well as towards commercial uses (Murphy 2008).

In addition, redevelopment projects have not sufficiently protected heritage landscapes and public amenities. According to the Royal Commission on Auckland Governance (2009: 196), a government agency responsible for making suggestions regarding future urban development, the waterfront landscape in Auckland is fragmented and lacks historical integration, largely due to the poor quality of much of the built environment, which has significantly reduced the amenity value of the waterfront. These projects are frequently enclosed and segregated from the neighboring urban fabric as the new plans give little consideration to maintaining original industrial structure. In other words, new buildings on the waterfront have become ahistorical and succumbed to high-density commercial and residential developments, engendering a disconnection from Auckland's industrial heritage.

Morphological processes in Auckland and Wellington waterfronts

According to the conceptual framework proposed in Chapter 2, Tables 5.3 and 5.4 summarize the characteristics of streets, plots, and buildings of the plan units in Auckland's and Wellington's waterfront areas. Each of the plan units provides a particular type of mixed-use space, running the gamut from historical warehouses to contemporary industrial buildings. Large-scale waterfront redevelopment is designed and built with the intention of generating tourism and leisure activity, and eventually forms the TBD along the stretch of the waterfront. Murayama and Parker (2007) suggest that mixed land use creates an idealized "amenity environment" in which local residents can play, work, and live. It brings vitality back to the city, and the emergence of the TBD shows that recreational facilities in the waterfront are dominant elements. The relationship between redevelopment and the creation of the TBD should be characterized as market driven, where multifunctional land use directly responds to the needs of capital and seeks out tourists interested in maritime, historical, and industrial heritage. The resultant environment presents a broad distribution of the range of tourist-oriented functions.

The entire waterfront in Auckland is bounded by a railway yard, and plan units dedicated to transport, including Britomart and Central Wharf, account for approximately 50% of the total waterfront area. The plan units directly bordering Auckland's CBDs have smaller plots and higher building density. The built environment of these units, especially the Fort Street unit and the Central Area unit, appears to be natural extensions of the CBD. By comparison, Wellington's waterfront redevelopment appears to be more resistant to urban intensification and consequently its landscape

Table 5.3 Characteristics of Streets, Plots, and Buildings of the Plan Units in Auckland's Waterfront Area

		Streets	Plots	Buildings
1	Port unit	Occupation streets	Large singular plot	Mainly low-rise buildings serving cargo transport
2	Quay Park unit	Irregular curving streets	Medium-sized irregular plots	Mixture of commercial and residential buildings, mainly in contemporary style
3	Central Wharf unit	Occupation streets	Large plots	Mixture of contemporary and industrial buildings
4	Britomart unit	Through streets in grid pattern	Mixture of small- and medium-sized plots	Mixture of historical warehouses, public buildings, and modern and contemporary commercial buildings
5	Fort Street unit	Mainly through streets	Mixture of small through plots and irregularly shaped plots	Mixture of historical and contemporary commercial buildings
6	Central Area unit	Through street	Mainly medium-sized plots	Mainly modern and contemporary high-rise commercial buildings
7	Viaduct Harbour unit	Irregular through streets	Mixture of medium-sized through plots and irregularly shaped plots	Mainly mid-rise contemporary industrial and residential buildings
8	Wynyard Point unit	Mainly through street in grid pattern	Mainly medium-sized through plots	Mainly low-rise marine service and industrial buildings
9	Victoria Park unit	N/A	Large singular plot	N/A

appears to be continuous and coherent. It has been reinvented by the custodians, who have thereby attracted new flows of global capital, achieved a balance of economic growth and public benefits, and visibly strengthened the relationship between Wellington and its waterfront. The differences in political economy and planning culture between Auckland and Wellington go some way to explaining the contrasts between their new waterfront landscapes. In common with many port cities around the world, the morphological agents of change in transforming the waterfronts of Auckland and Wellington include a mixture of government agencies, port authorities, the development industry, professional groups, and the general public. It is

Table 5.4 Characteristics of Streets, Plots, and Buildings of the Plan Units in Wellington's Waterfront Area

	Streets	*Plots*	*Buildings*
A Port unit	Occupation streets	Large plots	Mainly low-rise buildings serving cargo transport
B Railway yard unit	Occupation streets	Medium- and small-sized plots along the edge of a large irregular plot	Mainly large public buildings
C Harbour Edge unit	Irregular through and occupation streets	Irregular medium- and small-sized plots	Mixture of public and commercial buildings
D Whitmore Street unit	Irregular through streets	Medium-sized irregular plots, but small-sized plots at south and west ends	Mainly historical, modern, and contemporary public buildings
E Central Area unit	Through streets in grid pattern	Mixture of medium-sized and small-sized plots	Mixture of contemporary high-rise and historical commercial buildings
F Civic Center unit	Irregular through streets	Mixture of medium- and small-sized plots	Mixture of contemporary and historical public buildings
G Wakefield Street unit	Through streets	Mainly back-to-back plots	Mixture of contemporary and historical commercial buildings

appropriate now to take a closer look at the interplay of these "actors" in the drama of waterfront redevelopment.

In addition, unlike the predominant process of morphological alienation in Auckland's waterfront transformation, Wellington's waterfront has largely maintained its original character. In particular, Frank Kitts Park was remodeled in 1990, along with the development of a lagoon. The Dockside and Shed 5 restaurants and bars opened in the early 1990s. The Overseas Passenger Terminal was transformed into an event facility in 1992. Chaffers Marina was completed in 1993. The creation of Queens Wharf Events Centre, with underground parking and the development of Queens Wharf Square, were finished in 1995. The Museum of New Zealand Te Papa Tongarewa was opened in 1998 (Waterfront Leadership Group 2001). The major waterfront projects implemented in Wellington are characteristic of local adaptation—the acquisition of waterfront by land uses of similar type and character. These developments have improved public access to open spaces, which cater for local residents rather than tourists.

The impact of tourism on morphological changes

The significance of capital city tourism in Wellington has been neglected as other urban destinations, such as Auckland, Queenstown, and Rotorua, have formed the focus of research in terms of tourist activities. Wellington is arguably a secondary destination in terms of international and domestic tourism. It is compact where the central area is just 2 kilometers across. Wellington has not attracted the same amount of interest among tourism researchers as the city never intends to be commercial. It is promoted as a region of immense diversity but lacks a distinctive, identifiable tourism product beyond its main role as a short-stay destination for business travels (Page 1993, 1996a). Comparatively, the impacts of tourism on morphological changes are evident in the case of Auckland, which has made a particular effort to foster itself as a cultural and economic center. The following focuses on the impacts of event tourism in Auckland and traces the transformation at different stages.

From a marketing perspective, strategies to rebrand and promote Auckland typically include recasting the waterfront as an "arts, culture, and entertainment" district, as part of a larger plan to grow the city's tourism, fashion, and creative industries. The objective of the redevelopment, as stated by Auckland Waterfront Development Agency (2010: 5), is to create "a destination that is recognized for outstanding design and architecture, public spaces, facilities and events; a place where we can express our cultural heritage and history, and celebrate our great achievements as a city and nation." The underlying assumption of these efforts is that through the reconstruction of the waterfront spaces, Auckland will be able to attract more capital and people.

Event tourism thus plays a key role in generating interest in this developmental process: most notably, Auckland's selection as the 2000 and 2003 host of the America's Cup Regatta, an international yacht race that awards its champion the world's oldest sporting trophy. The hosting of the Rugby World Cup in 2011 has also influenced the tourism economy, and more recently, the Skycity Badminton Open in 2014 and FIFA under-20s in 2015 have brought additional public and media attention. One of the most tangible outcomes of these events is that their success has fostered the country's confidence in its ability to host large-scale international events and to speed waterfront regeneration.

The regeneration efforts that accompanied event tourism in Auckland attempt to enhance the natural character of the waterfront area in order to boost tourism and the local economy. The America's Cup match was a major tourist draw and substantial contributor to the image of the city. The first area to benefit from the Auckland waterfront redevelopment was

Viaduct Basin, which prior to the late 1990s was primarily used for timber milling, boat building, cargo handling at the port, and fish processing. Major redevelopment took place after the first running of the America's Cup yacht races in 1998. The previously underutilized Viaduct Harbour was refurbished solely for the Cup, in order to build yachts and equipment, but also for visiting vessels and spectators. A large proportion of land was then transformed into apartments and commercial areas. In the same area, Princes Wharf was built in 1923 to accommodate wool bale stores. The resulting concrete structure was adapted in 1960 as a passenger ship terminal and parking garage. From 1999 to 2001, the redevelopment project created a high-density, multiuse complex that included restaurants, retail shops, apartments, a car park, and a hotel.

Privatization of the waterfront areas has obviously dominated in Auckland. However, public demands for heritage preservation and the creation of a desirable leisure environment occurred in the preparation of the hosting of the America's Cup and the subsequent arrival of tourists. The southern side of the port unit is viewed as an ideal "portscape" and the Cup acted as an added catalyst for public and private investment. The establishment of the maritime museum, renamed the New Zealand National Maritime Museum, was originally advocated by the public to commemorate Auckland's seafaring history, and it attracted approximately 160,000 visitors in 2017 (New Zealand Herald 2018). The new Viaduct Events Centre was established and heritage trams were reintroduced for the Rugby World Cup hosted in 2011. Auckland's successful bid to host the America's Cup led to the promotion of the waterfront as a tourist destination at which visitors could experience the competition, which, in turn, led to economic prosperity and regeneration.

Event tourism requires substantial investment from local government and businesses. The report by PricewaterhouseCoopers suggests that the redevelopment of Auckland's waterfront will generate NZ$4.29 billion in jobs and investment by 2040. The waterfront will house more than 40,000 jobs within the next 30 years, 17,000 of which would not exist without redevelopment work. This data delineates the waterfront as vital to Auckland's economic future, and as potentially the most important urban redevelopment project in New Zealand. The local government forecasts that the regeneration will revitalize the tourism and events industries, attract highly skilled workers and new businesses to the waterfront, strengthen the fishing and maritime industries, and draw visitors from all over the world. Additionally, an increase in international tourists and cruise ships using Auckland as a port of call or turnaround destination is directly attributable to an increased perception of the waterfront as an attractive location to visit. The city is developing a social, cultural, heritage, and environmental showcase on the success of the waterfront.

The hosting of the America's Cup in 2000 and 2003 provided ample opportunities for the government to upgrade the neglected Viaduct Harbour.

The Auckland City and Regional Councils supported the 2000 and 2003 America's Cup defenses as a means of inserting the city into a global circuit of tourism (Murphy 2008). The large-scale waterfront redevelopment cost NZ$60 million over the three years preceding the 2000 America's Cup, but the 2000 America's Cup Regatta generated NZ$473 million net additional expenditures for the Auckland economy and over NZ$600 million for the New Zealand economy (Page 2002). In a 2003 survey of New Zealand's main spending sectors, Market Economics Ltd reported that the hosting of America's Cup in 2003 produced NZ$523 million in net additional spending for the economy which the country would not have gained otherwise. The expenditure generated NZ$529 million in value added for the national economy, NZ$450 million of which Auckland received. Cup-related expenditures also had a substantial positive effect on employment, sustaining the equivalent of 9,360 full-time years of employment at the national level, and 8,180 full-time years in the Auckland economy. Another international event in 2003, New Zealand Fashion Week, staged at Viaduct Harbour, garnered NZ$23 million for the country and NZ$19 million for Auckland (Lewis et al. 2008). As visitor attractions, these events held on the waterfront were an undoubted success, drawing a large number of tourists.

Following the success of these hallmark events, waterfront redevelopment has expanded to the adjacent Wynyard Quarter, also known as the Tank Farm, located on the western end of Auckland's commercial waterfront area. The Wynyard Quarter was previously zoned predominantly for port and marine-related industrial activities. It covers an area of 35 hectares that was formerly reclaimed between 1905 and 1930 (Auckland Harbour Board 1973). It is a monument to Auckland's industrial past and remains a prominent harbor landmark. The aim of the redevelopment project is to optimize revenues while delivering a "world class waterfront development." It has gone through a variety of stages and is expected to continue for 20 more years (Auckland Regional Council and Auckland City Council 2005). The primary goal of redeveloping the Wynyard Quarter is to reflect Auckland's gritty maritime heritage in a new, revitalized public environment. The vision for the area is a mixture of residential, retail, commercial, and tourism facilities that will enable the growth of a diverse, vibrant, and sustainable residential and business community.

The vision for the waterfront set out by the City Council is of a destination that "excites the senses and celebrates our sea-loving Pacific culture and our maritime history, commercially successful and innovative, a place for all people, rich in character and activity that truly links people, city and the sea" (Auckland City Council 2006: 12). Hallmark events precipitated waterfront redevelopment by necessitating the creation of a so-called "Cup Village" filled with restaurants, cafes, bars, hotels, and recreational facilities. Tourism has been promoted by the New Zealand Sail, which specializes in tour operations and departs from jetties in the Viaduct (Oram 2007). Public spaces become a venue for city festivals, which draw tourists to visit the waterfront. The 1990s and 2000s were a period of intense morphological change in Auckland, initiated by event tourism: hallmark events drove the creation of more tourism-friendly public spaces and expanded the waterfront to the industrial end. These spaces created through tourism enabled the proliferation of festivals and encouraged developers to prioritize accessibility to the public in their construction efforts. For example, one major redevelopment project involved the creation of a promenade reaching from the western end of the waterfront at Harbour Bridge Park to TEAL Park at the eastern end. This promenade provides a convenient connection to the whole of the waterfront, linking areas that were once unreachable and disconnected from each other. Furthermore, a new bridge connecting the Wynyard Quarter with Viaduct Harbour was completed in 2011. A new bus route has been introduced linking the adjacent suburbs with the city center and the waterfront (Adamietz 2012).

The Wynyard Quarter connects Viaduct Harbour with the existing large Westhaven Marina and the Auckland Fish Market. Tourists and residents alike can enjoy a coherent waterfront redevelopment with commercial functions such as a working harbor, a ferry port, tour operators, hospitality businesses, and recreational facilities, including parks, seating, bars, and restaurants. The central part of the Wynyard Quarter has combined commercial office space and residential living in the form of mixed-use apartments and townhouses. Urban design proposals and planning documents for the future development of the Wynyard Quarter reveal that some relatively unconstrained open spaces are to be provided. This is much needed in Auckland's waterfront, though its size could be more generous. Future development will, to a large extent, continue previous patterns of urban intensification (Auckland City Council 2006). Accessibility and connectivity have become the principal themes in the current stage of waterfront renewal.

Summary

Waterfront redevelopment projects are derived from the replacement of traditionally industrial areas with recreated, revitalized, and reinvented landscapes of consumption for tourism and leisure (Harvey 1989). This chapter directs morphological analysis towards understanding the physical and tourism impacts on the revitalization of the waterfront in Auckland and Wellington, suggesting that tourism and governmental influences are behind the morphological changes of the waterfront at differing phases of development. Waterfront transformation has been directly influenced by statutory planning, including the Regional Coastal Plan and the District Plan. The statutory planning provisions are largely defined by the Resource Management Act (RMA), which was invented as part of a radical liberalization agenda of New Zealand in the early 1990s (Kelsey 1995). In contrast to the conventional "conforming land use" regulation, the current statutory planning adopts a "performance based" approach, expressed as the management of the environmental effects of land uses. The RMA establishes a planning regime that has in practice been more reactive than strategic, and this has limited the ability of local authorities to pursue socioeconomic or cultural goals (Oram 2007).

Waterfront regeneration is both politically and economically motivated. It illustrates the changing role of government in the context of economic restructuring and the embrace of tourism as a significant element in the local economy. The use of event tourism as an impetus for waterfront regeneration fills a gap between business and society, as it tends to establish a strong relationship between industries and the communities in which they are located. Both Auckland and Wellington have different approaches where Auckland is more proactive to use event tourism as a means to revitalize waterfront. Despite the success achieved in other port cities, waterfront redevelopment in Auckland has not lived up to its developmental, aesthetic, or promotional goals. As demonstrated by the city's shifting morphological patterns, this is due to the fact that Auckland's waterfront renewal tends to exclude existing users, and create environments which give limited consideration to the city's cultural or industrial heritage (Chang and Huang 2011). Recent construction in the Wynyard Quarter is likely to switch the site from a space of industrial production to a high-end consumption enclave. While the vision of the Wynyard Quarter articulated by development agencies is oriented around the themes of community inclusion and adaptive reuse in an attempt to produce distinction, each of these aspects is complicated by commercial intent. Aiesha and Evans (2007) comment that an imbalance in or neglect of an area's livability risks the commodification all too familiar in tourism and other monocultural usage of urban sites. To some extent, waterfront development forms an impediment to the dissemination of local and regional industrial histories and the potential for creative exchange. New projects have largely created isolated "landscapes of consumption" awash with gentrified cultural and recreational activities (Cooper 1993).

The top-down governance of space in waterfront redevelopment leads to a passive as opposed to an active mode of public participation. The policymaking process in both Auckland and Wellington is heavily influenced by government agencies specializing in urban planning. The advent of redevelopment envisaged a meaningful engagement with a space that carries a rich set of industrial histories, a strong visual aesthetic, the presence of a Convention and Visitors Bureau, museums, and a full range of cultural and leisure production and consumption. Wellington has been successful to transform waterfront to a user-friendly environment. While redevelopment has achieved significant improvement from Princes Wharf to the Viaduct in Auckland, the refurbishment of Wynyard Quarter results in an aestheticization of space as the destination is sanitized and purified under the power of real estate developers and government agencies. Although event tourism has inspired the creation of a more accessible and connected waterfront for tourists, changes made to the Wynyard Quarter for event tourism could be further improved. Jauhiainen (1995) observes that a market and property-led approach to waterfront development tends to be problematic when the public is expected to subsidize infrastructure improvements but is not given adequate opportunities to participate in the redevelopment process. Consequently, the waterfront has increasingly been stripped of its sense of place and its roots in industrial heritage and in danger of entering a state of "placelessness."

Waterfront investment is typically organized as a public-private partnership aided by heavy public subsidies, such as tax breaks. The lack of a theoretical basis for waterfront design and an effective implementation strategy between public and private sectors has directly contributed to the discrepancy between image and reality. This is particularly evident in recent years, in which a process of privatization has dominated Auckland's changing landscape, while Wellington is widely seen as public spaces for leisure. To counteract such a discrepancy, two tools are essential: (1) an appreciation for the importance of maintaining the integrity of industrial and maritime heritage; and (2) a holistic approach to development that encompasses the entire waterfront as opposed to isolated parcels of land. Jones (2007) advocates a blend of the more commercially oriented American approach and the more community-oriented approaches of Europe in order to better integrate waterfront revitalization into existing development. Galland and Hansen (2012), through tracing the waterfront redevelopment process in Denmark, propose a hybrid planning approach that goes beyond traditional plan-led and market-driven planning styles. The hybrid approach stresses a more comprehensive waterfront redevelopment and management framework based on a systematic investigation of waterfront landscape characteristics and on objective impact assessment.

At a more operational level, however, if waterfront development is to succeed, it is essential that an urban landscape management plan be based on an understanding of the spatial coherence and context of the built environment. The lack of a sound theoretical basis for interpreting and representing the urban landscape and its morphological processes contributes to the disjunction between plan and reality, which is a main source of frustration for urban planners and designers. Malone (1996) suggests that the waterfront is a "frontier" and that regeneration constitutes frontier development's contemporary counterpart. Both cities share a common basis in economic deregulation practices, ambitions for flagship projects, and the desire to compete successfully in the global economy. Waterfront development has been a key strategy in political agendas, given its ability to generate economic value, to revitalize localities, and the social value placed on being able to access coastal environments in urban centers.

In sum, this chapter demonstrates that establishing a systematic understanding of morphological change creates a sound base for landscape management and tourism planning. As the waterfronts in Auckland and Wellington were still largely public assets before the beginning of the large-scale redevelopment, the government agencies and port authorities have been the key morphological agents of change in influencing the waterfront redevelopment. While Auckland and Wellington are similar to each other in their planning and institutional contexts, two cities have created contrasting new waterfront landscapes, especially Auckland has utilized special events as a catalyst for landscape changes. The subsequent waterfront privatization and the developer-driven development took place more widely than these in Wellington. It is apparent that in the decision-making process, the influences of the "hidden" agendas and the individual leadership within organizational structures are considerable. To achieve an objective and accountable policy process, transparency, dialogue, and debate are fundamental and the medium and public involvement should play a more critical role.

6 Urban fringe belts and the tourist-historic city

Introduction

European cities have a distinct spatial form and function, shaped by a unique historical evolutionary process with its concomitant endogenous and exogenous forces. Due to the unique pressures placed on these cities over time, many of them not only display examples of ordinary dwelling types that have survived from distant periods, but have also managed to preserve considerably more historical artifacts. Several European cities have built strong reputations as tourism hubs with distinct morphologies, through the continued interaction of the sociocultural environment, the political-economic structure, and the ecological environment (Conzen 2004). This is evident in the form and extent of newly developed landscapes, which attract a more discerning community and global travelers who seek to immerse themselves in different cultures and establish deeper connections with each visit.

The redevelopment of historical cities has long been a focus of study for urban morphologists (Slater 1990, Whitehand 2007). However, the lack of a theoretical basis to urban landscape conservation is a major concern with which urban morphologists in the West have been wrestling for many years. A workable solution in a European context has been outlined by M. R. G. Conzen (1966): similar to *genius loci*, a city's landscape engenders the "objectivation of the spirit" of the succession of societies that has inhabited it. This objectivation spans from the smallest detail of a single building, such as a molding over a window, to the configuration of an entire town or city as viewed from the air. Observable features are "expressions" of societies' aspirations, efforts, and experiences, and embody a form of accumulated experience to be viewed as an asset. Conzen (2004) distinguishes three aspects of the objectivation of the spirit from which individuals and society could benefit: the practical, the aesthetic, and the intellectual. The last aspect, the intellectual, goes beyond the practical aspect of providing a framework of visible objects whereby people orientate themselves in space, but forms a framework of historical meaning through which people orient themselves in time. Therefore, the historical expressiveness, or historicity, of the urban landscape is fundamental and germane to establishing conservation priorities.

In recent decades, tourism has become a driving force of regeneration for historic cities (Edwards and Gryffin 2013). Three types of tourist-historic cities worldwide have emerged as a result of these regeneration efforts (Judd and Fainstein 1999): (1) Those created from the ground up with tourists in mind. A primary example of this variety of tourist-historic city is Cancun, Mexico: originally a historic site for Mayan culture but fast becoming a purpose-built destination for American tourists who actively seek beaches. (2) Traditional historic cities that possess a cultural identity and a historical past, such as Paris, Amsterdam, and Prague in Europe. These cities, under the influence of tourism, adaptations, and redevelopments, have become distinctive urban zones, definable by a mix of morphological, functional, and perceptual characteristics. They encompass a delimitable physical area with a traceable extent that could be as large as the whole city or, at least theoretically, as small as a single building (Ashworth and Tunbridge 2000). (3) Cities in which selected areas have been developed as tourist attractions, presenting a contrast with other non-tourist parts. For instance, in cities such as Barcelona and Venice, tourist zones and non-tourist areas are clearly defined. All these cities have undergone a huge change in their spatial structures as new investments in transport, shopping, cultural, and amusement infrastructure have further altered their original urban tissue. It must be noted that these changes are not always programmed, monitored, and controlled by city authorities; many alterations are spontaneous in response to the growing number of tourists.

The combination of tourist-historic city is conceived largely to understand the role of tourism within the urban mosaic of forms and functions, as well as to consider the impacts of tourist spending and behavior on a given city (Ashworth and Tunbridge 1990). There is a growing and substantial literature on tourist-historic cities, ranging from the development of a theoretical understanding of the tourist-historic city's form and function using the tools on urban morphology; to focusing on both a particular type of city and a specialized morphological-functional region within a city; to studying both a particular use of history as a tourism resource and the use of tourism as a means of supporting the artifacts of the past, as well as justifying attention to the historicity of cities (Ashworth and Tunbridge 2000). Based on the above research subjects, a series of intra-urban structural models have been proposed to address changes incurred by tourism and ascertain the evolutionary phases of such cities. The key argument is that tourist-historic cities are not separate functional zones in the same sense as shopping districts, nor can they be delimited in purely morphological terms corresponding to their buildings and spaces. Rather, they are an integral part of the formal and functional complex that comprises a city's central areas. Therefore, the study of tourist-historic cities should be an extra dimension of that complex, instead of viewing them as a physical function alongside an existing central area, or a spatially demarcated district.

The variations from the intra-urban structural models were later confirmed by Kotus et al. (2015) who propose a model of a tourist-city's spatial structure-resident triad, implying that the city contains limited possibilities for physical expansion within the central area. An increase in tourism demand leads to an intensification of tourist usage within the existing infrastructure. As a result, there is a surge of demand to expand lodgings to accommodate tourist needs, but much of this expansion is peripheral to the central area. More recently, the emergence of Airbnb has allowed residents to host tourists in a spare room and a traveler to live as locals do in the central area. The creation of Airbnb, however, is not just competing with traditional lodgings for tourists but often challenging locals for space. The complex and problematic relationship between tourist attractions and supporting services is visible in virtually every tourist-historic city.

This chapter adopts the intra-urban structure model (Ashworth and Tunbridge 2000) to analyze the historic city of Como, Italy. It advocates using the concept of fringe belts as a means of understanding the physical form of urban areas, comprising both the process of outward growth and internal changes (Whitehand 1988). As noted in Chapter 1, the idea of fringe belts, a typical meso-level morphological concept, is instrumental in complementing urban form analyses at the macro-level concerning the size and shape of entire urban areas. They represent degrees of fragmentation, mono-centrism, and polycentrism on individual land-use categories and their isolated patterns. In his investigation of the growth and physical form of Berlin, Germany, Herbert Louis (1936) first recognized that, though the outward spread of housing is dominant, the urban landscape is punctuated by standstills where types of land use, alongside other physical characteristics, are created at the fringe of the built-up area. After renewed residential growth, these land uses become embedded in the urban area and tend to remain distinctive continuous or discontinuous zones, namely, a fringe belt, marking the selective survival of character areas with important heritage features, ecological areas, and places for tourism development.

This chapter attempts to address the morphology of tourism by examining the forms, changes, and pressures that have shaped the fringe belts in Como, Italy: a city that faces similar challenges to other destinations in Europe due to a lack of planning and unregulated urbanization. Drawing on research into the ancient plans of Como's streets, buildings, and plots, it explores the long-term effects when tourism plays a role in managing urban development. The physical features of Como, including fortifications and grid streets, have long defined urban forms and later rapid economic improvement. Three patterns of fringe belts are identified based on Como's historical and spatial arrangement.

Research questions are raised, such as, how do Como's fortifications exert influence on the formation of fringe belts? Do contrasting urban processes, including morphological periodicities, political-economic ideologies, and tourism planning influence the fringe belts in Como? What is the pattern of the tourism-related development of spatial structures? Finally, to what extent does tourism contribute to urban landscape management? Through extensive field work, this chapter demonstrates that Como's fringe belts have retained much of their historical character and position within the urban center, while historic streets, plots, and buildings gradually morphed into tourism resources. It starts with an overview of the city of Como, and then provides a breakdown of streets, plots, and buildings from a historical perspective. The impacts of tourism are addressed and the relationship between morphology and tourism is detailed.

The historic city of Como

The city of Como sits in the heart of Italy, at the base of Mount Brunate, and approximately 45 kilometers north of Milan, Italy's second largest city and largest metropolitan area. For centuries, Como has been strategically located on commercial routeways, and since medieval times it has been a key Alpine pass to northern Europe, accessible by boat, funicular, or car. Its proximity to Lake Como and the Alps has made it a prominent tourist destination, containing numerous works of art, churches, gardens, museums, theaters, parks, and palaces. Historically, it is the first holiday site recorded in Europe and a vacation spot year-round. Since the sixteenth century, the lake area has been a popular destination for the Milanese nobility, and by the end of the eighteenth century, Lake Como was an exclusive destination for the international elite with a cluster of second homes (Scheidel 2009). The whole region is designated as a World Heritage Site from UNESCO out of recognition for its historic landscape including the old town of Como.

Urban life in Como dates back to the beginning of the second century BC, when a Roman frontier fort was established to guard the route from the Italian heart of the Roman Empire to northern Europe across the Spluga and Settimo passes through the Alpine mountains. The settlement was enlarged to a municipality by 51 BC, and its growing urban function, which combined defense and trade, was maintained well into medieval times. Como develops a regional market center in Lombardy and serves as an entrepôt between the Milan hinterland and the mountain communities bordering Lake Como to the north. Its own locality benefitted from an early iron trade, followed by wool weaving, and later silkworm cultivation and the craft production of silk textiles. The industry became heavily mechanized during the second half of the nineteenth century, and prospered until the later part of the twentieth century, when global competition closed down the factories. There is still a significant business presence in textile design, however, largely supported by training programs in local vocational institutions. Como's beautiful natural setting has always drawn tourists, elite at first but increasingly democratic, and the city has become a growing center for cultural tourism in recent decades (Delaney 2009).

Initially, a near-square fortified Roman town, Como, was enlarged several times, so that by the fifth century, a large rectangular city (measuring approximately 440 × 560 meters) faced the southern end of Lake Como with its short side facing north-northwest. When medieval Como was fortified with a new town wall in 1127, it was placed a few meters beyond the perimeter of the Roman wall fortifications (Caniggia 1963), with some slightly irregular extensions to a new shoreline, measuring roughly 490 × 650 meters and enclosing a town of approximately 35 hectares (Figure 6.1). Urban accretions began to cluster outside the city gates along the three main arterial roads. During the fourteenth and fifteenth centuries, monasteries began accumulating, not only within the inner edges of the walled town, but also as fortified isolates on the urban fringe, some on routeways, others not (Caniggia 1963: 27–28). The closeness of mountains and hills on three sides and the lake on the fourth side forced urban expansion out along the lakeshore to the north and through a narrow gap to the south, beyond which modern development has concentrated.

The Roman town developed on the basis of an evolving street grid, with small *isolati* or urban blocks that clustered in superblocks of approximately 70 × 70 meters. This larger grid survived to determine the dimensions and orientation of most of the medieval blocks, although in phases of rebuilding the street lines lost some of their rigid straightness (Caniggia 1963). As a result, the majority of Como's streets within the *Città Murata* (walled town) are essentially "consequent streets," most of them over 2,000 years old. Because the medieval wall had only three town gates aside from the harbor entrances, urban development beyond the medieval wall was irregular, albeit composed of small street grid elements where the terrain allowed. Once the town wall lost its defensive function, numerous "breakthrough streets" were created to connect intra- with extramural districts. Within the old town, the areas surrounding the cathedral, castle, and old harbor were redeveloped during the nineteenth century to accommodate a modern business district and a formal landscaped waterfront.

The architecture in Como has undergone so many phases of alteration and refurbishment that tracking its age is difficult and largely irrelevant. However, the plot structure and fundamental building type within the walled town is based on subdivisions of the square urban blocks into generally square-sided *cortile* or courtyard cells, containing long-developed elaborations of the Roman *domus*, or house with enclosed portico. Building in the courtyards of the walled town was intense during late medieval and early modern period, resulting in extensive multistory buildings (Gianoncelli and Della Torre 1984). The Christian church has long been instrumental in Como as an organized, hierarchical institution, with specialized structures such as a cathedral, a bishop's palace, parish churches, monasteries, and convents constructed throughout the old town and beyond. Outside the walls, several linear suburbs developed, displaying a mixture of courtyard house types and newer forms, as well as large detached villas situated along

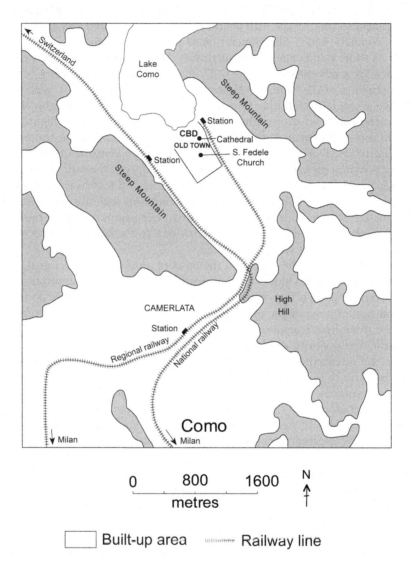

Figure 6.1 The Main Built-Up Areas and Topography of Como. (Source: Conzen et al. 2012)

the lakefront. Old field patterns defined some of the land parcels colonized by residential and later industrial development.

Like many European cities, Como has experienced a series of expansions of its city walls over history. The early core of the city was walled, compact, and dominated by ecclesiastical land users. Probably due to the geographical constraints, the walled area of Como in the twelfth century as a result of final city wall expansion was just 1.3 times larger than its original core.

Finally, the growth of commercial activity and prosperity led to an extension outside the walls in the early modern period, mainly for the factories and industrial movement. Beyond this, the city has primarily expanded in order for residential areas to accommodate both the rural immigrants and the suburbanizing inhabitants of the old town. The urban expansion processes and the patterns of morphological periodicities had a profound influence on the forms of the fringe belts in Como. The physical fabric of a city reflects its underlying sociocultural values and can be considered as the tangible expression of a society's political and economic structure. An authoritarian control with power may explain the regular plan derived from a rectangular grid of streets and the axial system in the historical cores of Como (Castagnoli 1971: 120, Scheidel 2009). Como also reflects the importance of the role of military (Kostof 1991: 108) and the application of the standardized fort plan in the original plan.

Methodology

Sauer (1925: 30) suggests that the morphological method rests on "the form of synthesis," which conveys an essential approach in the study of morphology and tourism. The purpose of the form is to distinguish key elements that exist within tourist cities and investigate their internal spatial relationships. The classification schemes for streets, plots, and buildings, as well as the levels between land-use parcels and plots (McGlynn and Samuels 2000), are employed to understand the morphological process holistically and to reflect the complexity of the historic city. Specifically, three identified fringe belts are used to examine the impact of tourism over different periods of time and urban functions for tourists.

Conzen et al. (2012) and Whitehand et al. (2016) have undertaken extensive research in Como and revealed the traces of fringe belts in this ancient city. They are of a great variety of shapes and sizes, whose boundaries often follow a field boundary, perhaps a rural property boundary. Compared with residential areas, fringe belts have considerably larger average plot sizes, less hard surfaces, and fewer road crossings, which are less permeable to traffic. Changes over time in the amount of housebuilding and associated fluctuations in land values are major influences on the formation of these fringe belts. Whereas high-density housing is characteristic of housebuilding booms, when land values are high, fringe belts tend to form during housebuilding slumps, when land values are low. When fluctuations in housebuilding are being considered, periods of little or no growth also leave indelible marks in the landscape. The fringe-belt model emphasizes the historical grain of the city, especially the very different zones that tend to be created during periods when the outward growth of the residential area has been arrested due to a slump in housebuilding, or some other obstacle to residential development such as a physical barrier.

Additionally, the approach of historical expressiveness is adopted for this study, largely because the continuous transformation, addition, or lapse of functions happen to individual buildings, plots, or larger regions from time to time. Historical narratives (Kropf 2011), in terms of observation, comparison, and classification of tourist districts, are taken into account to consider the local community as a whole socio-geographical group and to examine the socioeconomic functions of Como as expressed in its spatial patterns. They are essential for linking the form or pattern of the tourist city with its functional characteristics. However, several challenges emerge when applying historical narratives to the morphology of tourism. The first one concerns data, when inadequate data sources, low accuracy, and a confused writing format are the norms for tracing history and heritage. Insufficient historical data can be complemented by spatial alternatives, with an assumption that nearby historic cities will demonstrate similar relations between evolutionary stages and morphological characteristics. In the case of Como, it often confuses the city with Lake Como, where a lakefront resort is solely devoted for tourists. The second challenge is concerned with how to describe the geographical changes distinctly while maintaining the perspective of continuous change. Integrating fringe belts with discussions of the mechanisms of change is warranted in this case, but not necessarily accurate. Finally, causality between urban morphology and the context in which it operates is often not fully understood (Conzen et al. 2012). Morphology is commonly regarded as a response to social, cultural, economic, and political factors in the literature; however, reasonable explanations for tourism can be derived by means of qualitative as well as quantitative analyses.

Streets, plots, and buildings in Como

Variants of morphological approach have been applied in a number of towns and cities in Europe, mostly within England (Barrett 1958). They are reliant on source materials to which urban morphologists are accustomed to having access. These include ground plans, which show streets, plots, and the block plans (or "footprints") of buildings for a number of cross sections in time. Ground plans may span the past 200 or 300 years of a city's history, and occasionally, though less accurately, longer.

The greater part of Como's circulation system within the walled city has provided public rights-of-way for 2,000 years. While the morphological framework established by the Roman street system is simple, the full pattern of the ultimate street network is not quite regular. In the Roman module, main streets were spaced approximately 84 meters apart, with slight variations in the southern portion near the walled area. Subsequently, convenient shortcuts, particularly quasi-diagonal paths that crossed terrain not yet rebuilt following the post-Roman urban collapse, were added, and eventually became permanent streets. At the same time, some links in the former grid fell into complete disuse, leading to a few discontinuities.

Como's streets are grouped according to the traditional, albeit somewhat artificial, three-part analytical hierarchy of streets, alleys, and culs-de-sac. Most of the parallel main streets on the long axis qualify as axial because they each offer direct transfer from the city's commercial center near the lake to the major regional exit route beginning at the southern end of the walled city. They act, in effect, as super-through-streets. The axial streets in the commercial center near the lake connect highly frequented locations, several of which are large open spaces, such as *piazzas* (city squares) and marketplaces. The irregular geometry of this pattern is partly a reflection of modern traffic control and the direction of tourist flow, in which some short links are part of an awkward one-way vehicular circulation system. The most peculiar axial street is the narrow combination of street segments, including some zigzags, leading from *Piazza Cavour* at the lakeside to the main southern gate, *Porta Torre*. Lined with shops and service establishments of all kinds, it is the major pedestrian and commercial thoroughfare of the city's historical core, as well as the major tourist attractions.

In terms of plots, many European cities were traditionally arranged into rectangular plots with their short sides facing the street, with no particular concern for their orientation to the cardinal points of the compass. Como's plot history illustrates this tradition, while simultaneously demonstrating the processes by which lateral property accumulation could transform linear plots into approximately square ones, large enough to permit the formation of courtyard assemblages and serial aggregations. Plots vary in the extent to which they diverge from a regular rectilinear form, probably reflecting in almost all cases the degree to which the boundaries of plots have been modified since they were originally laid out. For example, the plot pattern along *Via Vittorio Emanuele II* includes remnants of ownership boundaries first defined in the medieval period, and thus suggestive of orthomorphic survival. But these are intermixed with numerous plots that have undergone a mixed change. The plot series in *Via Alessandro Volta* contains many amalgamations, which created opportunities for full courtyard development, producing a hypometamorphic pattern. By contrast, the plots fronting *Via Grassi* display a metamorphic pattern full of reconfigurations, which coincides with the creation in the late nineteenth century of the *Via Giulio Rubini*, a new breakthrough street. All three examples contain buildings associated with large institutions, such as convents and palazzi, that provide an accessible route for future tourism planning in various plot systems.

In setting this typology within the context of the walled city as a whole, a more complex pattern is evident. The plot typology recognized here draws in part on concepts developed in the Italian typomorphological school, particularly the foundational work of Caniggia on Como itself (Commune di

Como 1970). From this it can be deduced that a slight majority of Como's core city blocks evolved into traditional courtyard areas, either in simple serial aggregations along the street, or composed of large properties with a central, internal focus. These two plot types are well distributed throughout the zone of the Roman grid. Almost as numerous as two other plot types: linear serial aggregations, with or without merchant quarters. Those without merchant quarters are scattered widely, whereas the commercially oriented plots show a distinct ordering, mainly along the key central axial street route, and in parts of what has become the modern Central Business District (CBD). Religious and governmental sites have tended to cluster in relatively peripheral large plots. Not surprisingly, modern redevelopment has occurred near the lake, where growth of the CBD has resulted in major changes to plot boundaries. While evidence of cosmological concerns is scarce in Como, most of the city's intramural churches are in plots that permit, as far as practicable, the altar to be situated at the eastern end of the structure, illustrated by the rounded apse of the cathedral.

In terms of buildings, the architecture of Como's walled city exemplifies its geographic diversity and the long European history of urban construction in stone, combined with the early emergence and general ubiquity of multistory structures, giving a dense, built-up appearance to the typical streetscape. Equally distinctive is the high frequency of windows, doorways, and arched vehicular entranceways, allowing easy access to the interior of plots. Much urban fabric in Europe before the industrial era is shaped by the placement of the main dwelling structure (often including a workplace) of each resident family at the head of the plot, or at the street line. Over time, as households increased in number and size, and the space needed for commerce and crafts grew, rear areas of plots were built upon (cf. the burgage cycle articulated by Conzen 1960). Thus, what began in earlier centuries as simple buildings at the street front evolved into courtyard complexes occupying varying amounts of the plot, usually through the addition of rear wings, and ultimately by joining the wings with a connecting structure at the rear to form an enclosed courtyard. Acquisition of adjoining properties could further complicate the arrangement of buildings and plot boundaries. Such changes often occurred in Como's past as wealthy families bought up neighboring structures.

The three fringe belts of Como

Roman Como's urban fringe was likely a sharp divide between the built-up town and the rural land beyond, demarcated by the city wall (Gioacchini et al. 2008). Over the ensuing centuries, medieval Como slowly filled up within the perimeter ultimately established by the medieval town wall. The earliest and densest core area surrounded the *Piazza San Fedele* in the very center of the town. Expansion proceeded outwards as additional urban blocks were colonized by residential complexes and parish churches serving the new neighborhoods. Concurrent with this was the development of several monasteries and convents, on ground bequeathed by wealthy families seeking to assure their salvation in the afterlife. These institutions, complete with cloisters and living quarters, needed substantial plots of land, most easily found near the wall inside the town, or on donors' property dotted about the rural fringe. Thus, during the Middle Ages, the town developed a distinct urban fringe belt of nonresidential character, with a tight intramural portion inside, and a rather scattered extramural portion outside, the city wall. This wall acted as an emphatic fixation line, influencing later developments in its vicinity by its obstinate presence in the landscape.

Over the last century and a half, Como's unitary fringe belt became embedded within the growing city, with urban extensions leapfrogging well beyond the city wall. Far from disappearing, the somewhat looser texture and institutional land-use character of this zone survived and evolved into an inner fringe belt (IFB). Gardens along the inner edge of the town wall were built upon, and larger structures replaced smaller ones (Figure 6.2a). As the city's civic life expanded, new facilities were needed, such as schools, a market, a theater, law courts, and municipal offices, and many found space along the line of the city wall or the exterior boulevard that replaced the town ditch.

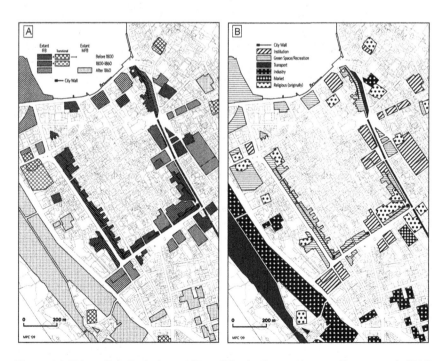

Figure 6.2 Fringe-Belt Evolution and Land Use in Como. (Source: Conzen et al. 2012)

Meanwhile, the railway connection between Como and Milan was being built between 1875 and 1885, which encouraged the development of large factories for the production of silk goods (Cani and Monizza 1994). The first rail line skirted the Old Town to the southwest, hugging the slopes of Monte Olimpio on its way northward towards Switzerland and the St. Gotthard pass. Together with a swift-flowing mountain stream that paralleled it, the railway helped stimulate a linear industrial belt dominated by the *Tintoria Comense* (Ticosa) complex, built in 1872 (Figure 6.2b). This and other weaving and textile printing factories joined the existing monasteries, a large cemetery (1811), a gasworks (1863), and a railway marshalling yard to form a new middle fringe belt (MFB), separated from the IFB by a narrow belt of residential development composed of the medieval arterial *borghi* and newer neighborhoods of generally well-to-do housing. Since these monasteries had comprised distal extramural elements of the original urban fringe belt (now the IFB), their incorporation in the fast-solidifying MFB represents a case of fringe-belt translation.

It is possible that the railway provided a new fixation line for the western part of the MFB, although the southern portion developed with no such strong linear feature and consequently developed a looser character (Figure 6.3). Nevertheless, this portion of the fringe belt gained a clear identity from several classic fringe land uses, including additional textile factories and a large provincial psychiatric hospital campus in 1882. It continued to consolidate this character with the addition of a new military barracks (1909–1914). From the site conditions of the city, topography has inhibited the concentric development of the MFB. With steep mountain slopes on the east leading up to Brunate, institutional, industrial, and recreational development was severely limited, as it was also to the south where morainic hills permit only a narrow gap for communication.

Como's growth was largely directed, spilling into a district containing the ancient village of Camerlata, since from time immemorial routes from Como had fanned out west, south, and east across the Lombardy piedmont. The railway reached from Milan to Camerlata in 1849, and its terminus remained there until it was extended into Como proper (Stazione S. Giovanni) 26 years later. Annexed to Como in 1884, significant growth came to Camerlata only in the twentieth century, particularly during the 1930s, when residential development encircled the village's small retail district with considerable public housing. Away from the village center, several social welfare institutions appeared: an orphanage (1931) and a large hospital campus, *Ospedale Santa Anna*, completed in 1932, which signaled the emergence of Como's southern outer fringe belt (OFB). Surrounding these developments, a large staging area devoted to transport, warehousing, and light industry emerged that amplified the fringe-belt character of the district (Cani and Monizza 1994: 183, 191).

Naturally, Como's long-established IFB has endured the pressures of change. These have included breakthrough streets to improve circulation,

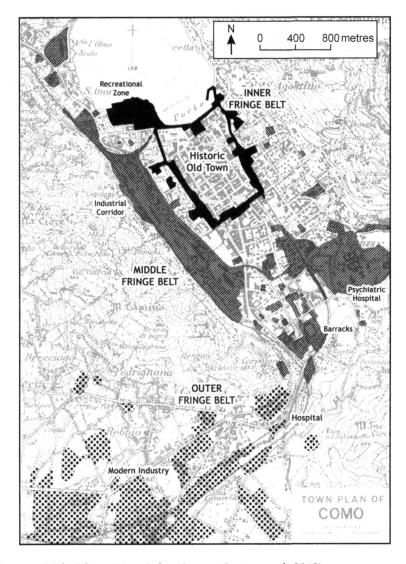

Figure 6.3 The Three Fringe Belts. (Source: Conzen et al. 2012)

expansion of the city's business district outside the old town, and redevelopment of the lakefront to establish parks and other recreational facilities. While the MFB has had a shorter history as an urban land-use zone than the IFB, it also has seen significant change. Since the 1980s, the textile industry has virtually collapsed, and new uses have had to be found for abandoned industrial and institutional buildings (Cani and Monizza 1993: 359–362). Among the largest conversions are a factory complex turned into a gambling casino and the former *Ospedale Psichiatrico* (closed in 1999) becoming the core of a new campus for the Como branch of the University of Insubria, along with bold new buildings in an adjacent portion of the MFB. Meanwhile, as road haulage has replaced rail, and centralization has shifted facilities to centers such as Milan's Malpensa International Airport, Como's OFB today contains many underused or abandoned commercial properties.

Evolving trajectories of tourism development

The archetypal form of Como, largely driven by tourists from Milan and neighboring areas, has rarely been discussed. Its architectural style celebrates heritage, hospitality that delight with good quality in the old town. The fringe-belt development and the morphological change are embedded in the city's physical form representative of a sense of place. Both elements constitute a strong premise for transforming a tourist-historic city. Its naturally developed historic center, along with the concentration of tourism facilities, is the effect of accumulation over the ages. The old town is spatially compact and practically all attractions are accessible on foot; consequently, the dominant economic function and the resulting morphological structure of the old town derive from tourism. Como consists of self-contained tourist precincts characterized by a "spatial thematization" (Pasquinelli and Bellini 2017: 37), where tourism is the main economic and social driver affecting the shape and functioning of the city as a whole.

Rabbiosi (2015), through the extensive study of tourism in Paris, suggests that historic cities in Europe have undergone a process of commercial activity coupled with urban branding, eventually resulting in the following: (1) the society of the spectacle giving rise to "the need to present the tourist with ever more spectacle, exotic and titillating attractions" (Gotham 2002: 1737). The commoditization of leisure, followed by the privatization of public space (Sorkin 1992), has been evident in Europe as the segregation of locals and tourists form a distinct pattern in historic cities. (2) The emergence of the cultural-creative theme, largely due to the popularity of works by theorists such as Florida (2002, 2005) and Landry (2008), who advocate the renaissance of obsolete urban space into buzzing districts. Cultural tourism has started to become associated with local productions, and the notion of history is employed for marketing and branding. Vanolo (2008: 380) pinpoints that the trend in European cities develops "the capabilities both of selling the city and of selling the product, and creating new symbols for both geographical location and the commodity under the aegis of the celebration of culture." (3) The evolution of local streets for tourism and leisure. For example, European countries have successfully implemented Town Center Management and Business Improvement Districts to facilitate downtown regeneration (Coca-Stefaniak et al. 2009, Peel et al. 2009). Vernacular venues like Como have been preserved for tourism, as they tend to attract the most visits. Fringe belts are the dividing lines and socio-spatial prototypes as a part of "urban cultural ecosystem...formed by ordinary city dwellers interacting in vernacular spaces" (Zukin 2012: 282). Ultimately, a new social and cultural identity is created when locality is the valuable asset for tourism.

Economic development, connected with socioeconomic changes in Italy, makes Como an ever-stronger presence on the tourist market. The historic old town has become a *de facto* tourist precinct, characterized by a high percentage of foreign tourists (76% of arrivals and 78% of overnights) (Muti and Salvucci 2014). Como is now a seasonal mecca for tourists seeking waterfront leisure and historic sites during the spring and summer. Judd (1999, 2003) distinguishes "city visitors" and "city users" in the study of urban tourism. While "city visitors" tend to be temporary with limited impact on the destinations, "city users" have become a prominent category whose share in city life steadily growing. They have practically appropriated some areas, pushing residents out of the old town while establishing a pattern of "tourist bubbles" or "amusement enclaves" (Martinotti 1996). On the positive side, tourist activity and changes in the spatial structures of a city are in a coincidence and ever correlation with each other. Kotus et al. (2015) find that more intensive tourist traffic makes selected, usually central parts of the city bloom, but is also associated with the fall of its other precincts. It should be noted that the old town in Como has benefited from a substantial inner-city resident population offering a solid base for entertainment, cultural, and catering facilities. These could be hardly sustained by the demands of tourists alone. Coupled with the Lake Como resort areas, both tourists and residents help maintain a lively scene which is valued by tourism.

Como presents a redefinition of the spatialities of interest for the study of urban tourism. It primarily focuses on the competition for tourists because, unlike other economic sectors where central cities lose out to peripheral areas, the historic old town dominates the "space of flows" of inbound tourism (Castells 2000). Como's history, architectural heritage, inimitable cultural assets and qualities, and clusters of amenities provide the city with built-in advantages as a tourist destination. Cultural establishments, including churches, museums, and theaters, are concentrated in the old town, forming a "honey pot" to attract tourists. This is also a zone where pubs and restaurants tend to concentrate and grow. On the other hand, the spatial pattern of lodgings shows a dispersal in the structure of Como. Although the chain-brand hotels struggle to find new locations in the center, they provide the refurbished buildings for accommodation. The largest number of brand-name resorts are located in the recreational zone concentrating on the lakefront. The resulting "lakefront shift" increases the flow of tourists who use the city as a passage for the Lake Como area. Overall, the morphology of Como exhibits a predominance of tourism resources and facilities in the old town and a tendency of lodgings to disperse along the city's concentric fringe belt, with a shift towards the lakefront.

Como reveals a distinct pattern induced by its IFB, MFB, and OFB. Facing the lakefront of the city, the cluster of facilities evolves into a recreational zone where the city becomes a stepping stone for Lake Como. On the basis of this spatial arrangement, Como is a monocentric city under tourist influence that can be separated into two different segments: an old town for cultural and heritage tourism and the lakeshore for marine recreation. Tourists frequent both clusters while gradually pushing residents to the MFB and OFB. The MFB and OFB are marked by industrial corridors and residential neighborhoods, and the periphery of the walled town, where the residential function in one form or another is likely to play a vital role in the rehabilitation of such areas, and their incorporation into the center. In addition to the imperative of insulating tourists from areas outside tourist enclaves, the MFB and OFB have evolved into supporting areas that finance and manage the various components of tourism.

Kotus et al. (2015: 99–100) propose that the morphology of the tourist-historic city unveils the following spatial arrangements: (1) "induction spots," which lead to the city or allow tourists to plan a network of paths around the city prior to visiting, with the aid of tourist guides and advertisements; (2) "gates to the city," or entrance hubs, such as the railway and coach stations, the airport and promoted lodging; (3) "anchor spots," or attractive places one keeps coming back to during one's stay in the city; and (4) "bridges" between attractions, offering a passage to and a chance of coming out in "non-promoted" places. Como bears all four of these arrangements divided by invisible fringe belts. The old town contains a series of "induction spots" through which tourists move in this compact city. "Gates to the city" are evident where all forms of transportation connect to the old town. However, "anchor spots" and "bridges" are divided by Como's three fringe belts. The inner fringe belt forms an anchor spot connecting the old town with the lakefront recreational zone. The MFB, as a former industrial zone, is used as a residential area to separate tourists from locals. Finally, the OFB remains intact for preserving the historic and heritage sites and hardly for tourism purpose. Como owns a unique bridge to link the Lake Como area to the city. It can be seen as the beginning of the tour to the lakefront, or the end of the tour to be back to the city. Nonetheless, tourist processes in Como have an aggregate rather than a patchwork character. Tourist traffic does not spill into the MFB and OFB, concentrating instead in the old town and the recreational zone. To a certain degree, active tourist movement to the old town is fast becoming overcrowded. This, in turn, can prevent its use by locals. On the other hand, the concentration in both old town and recreational zone protects other spaces for residents, namely, those who live and work inside the MFB and OFB.

Hall and Page (2014) stress the difference between "urbanization tourism" and "tourism urbanization" (Mullins 1991), explicating the embeddedness of tourism in urban form. The notion of urbanization tourism implies that tourism does not predominate in the urban economy, but is one of many dimensions through which to explain the evolutionary trajectory of cities. The latter, tourism urbanization, identifies tourism as a main driver of the physical, social, and economic shaping of the city, playing a primary role in placemaking. Como follows the pattern of the typical lake resort, where tourism is increasingly melted into the territorial cohesion, specifically, the city transitions from fragmentation of MFB and OFB to the surrounding environment. In other words, tourism will eventually radiate out from the old town into the urban fringes; as a result, the demarcations between urban fringes will vanish entirely. Rabbiosi and Giovanardi (2017), through a study of Rimini and Pesaro in Italy, propose a discourse on "networked cities," which link areas of business attractions to cultural spots. By using territorial cohesion and cultural heritage, the morphology of tourism is seen through a more holistic perspective, in which the built environment, land use, and new urban spaces are directly impacted by tourism with the identification of fringe belts. The physical fracture where fringe belts are marked shows the intrusive presence of the railway, splitting the urban fabric into industrial and tourist sections. Fringe belts are largely symbolic and slowly disappearing, as tourist resorts are established to cater to the growing needs of lakefront tourists.

Summary

Over the years, scholars of urban morphology have made a concerted effort to contribute to the integration of the urban tissue, which serves as the fundamental base for bridging an understanding of urban landscapes in different geographical areas (Gu et al. 2008, Conzen et al. 2012). Each urban setting is unique, yet a number of parallels underpin the morphological changes. It is not unusual in many tourist-historic cities that a frequent absence of the recognition of the conservation and redevelopment proposals is existing for the landscape alternation; however, the distinctive architectural and cultural heritage of the urban core has always been regarded as such cities' main attractions. The purpose of tourism is to enhance the character of urban settings and present a platform for tourists to interact with locals. The results can be conflicting, whether a new local identity is born due to the repositioning of tourism, or the vernacular architecture turns into consumption spaces in their entirety, where ancient streets are "malls with no walls" (Gotham 2002).

Recent economic restructuring and intensive tourism development in Como exemplify the problems of traditional urban form conservation. The threat of homogenization of the built environment worldwide is apparent in the era of globalization. At the same time, there is an increasing awareness of the value of preserving regional and local distinctiveness for reinforcing social identity and supporting the synergies of culture and tourism. Theories of urban morphology provide a specific frame of reference for not only understanding how universally the generalizations in one region can be demonstrated in another, but also revealing distinctive urban forms as configurations of characteristics related to particular histories of tourism development. Conzenian (geographical-morphological) and Caniggian (process typological) schools can be used to trace the reconstruction of Como's landscape from a historical perspective, and analyze the expansion of tourism. Both approaches are not only relevant to understanding the morphological structure of the tourist city but also pertinent to tourism planning.

To appreciate their full significance, fringe belts must be seen as agents of change in relation to a wider framework of relationships, including building, plot, street cycles, land values, and the adoption of innovations. They demonstrate variations in the basic characteristics of the environment, such as the density and pattern of roads, the amount of vegetated land, building coverage, tourist patterns, and the sizes and shapes of plots. The study of fringe belts is conducive to reconstructing the physical and cultural character of historic precincts, and then transforming them for tourism purposes. The study of fringe belts provides a method for objectively localizing the process in existing urban spaces and demarcating character areas.

The research resonates with Ashworth's (1989) findings that urban tourism can be studied from a facility approach, an urban ecological approach, a user approach, and a policy approach. Among these four approaches, the relationship between morphology and tourism appears to be intimate, critical, and necessarily complex. Como naturally possesses a well-preserved historic urban environment that is representative of tourism development. Its morphology, defined by three rings of fringe belts, makes it possible to identify a spatial pattern and occurrence. The medieval core of the old town was spared severe pressures for redevelopment by its early extension, which enforced a spatial distinction between institutional and commercial land uses. The physical and functional link between core and extension was divided by the walls and served as a fixation line between the IFB and the MFB. The walled town is thus an historic attraction in itself and the focus for tourist-oriented commercial activity (Ashworth and Tunbridge 2000). The industrial corridor of MFB performs a bridging function between the predominantly tourist-oriented center and residential area. It is also a secondary supporting service or a background environment for tourists engaged in non-tourism activities. The OFB is an extensive discarded area of the medieval city, which is peripheral to both the protected old town and residential areas. The expansions of the OFBs have little of interest to offer tourism-related programs, apart from accommodation.

Fringe belts are sites of urban growth from which active spaces for commercial needs beyond those of the residential and retail sectors radiate. In a city with a long history, the geographical pattern often appears as a series of broadly concentric fringe belts separated by residential integuments. Additionally, there is a contrast between the intramural and extramural parts of a fringe belt, as the latter have a more open-grained character. The patterns and developments of fringe belts are influenced by a city's specific socioeconomic situation, geographical conditions, and cultural traditions; consequently, the impingement of tourism plays a key role in reshaping the city core. Both Herbert Louis (1936) and M. R. G. Conzen (1960) confirm the long-term influence of fringe belts on the form and growth of urban areas. The fringe-belt phenomenon and the characteristics associated with city fortifications are evident in Como, which give rise to a variety of spatial structures ranging from the old town, to residential zones that they separate, and to the physical texture of land use close to Lake Como.

The patterns of the fringe belts in Como result from the dynamics of the city's historico-geographical development, especially after the mid-nineteenth century. The analysis provided in this chapter helps differentiate geographical-historical characteristics that are important for towns and cities. The examination of fringe belts also highlights urban transformation pertinent to tourism. Urban morphologists have long pursued ways to achieve synergies between the "depth of morphological analysis," "qualitative exploration," and "development planning" (Chapman 2006: 24). Particularly, the utility of town plan study garners the interest of urban morphologists when dealing with an historical town. In terms of data collection and handling, elements in topographical maps and town plans may be used to plot in a hierarchical way to show physical fabric and stratification. It appears that the study of tourism morphology contributes to an understanding of urban form through describing temporal-spatial characteristics, as well as linking between historicity and tourism. The growing attention on tourist density and mixed-land use is also applicable in the morphology of tourism.

Conclusions

Unprecedented urban growth and transformation are presenting great challenges for the comprehension and management of landscape. Despite the growing interest in urban morphology, few studies have examined the role of tourism in the context of the development and evolution. Tourism has become integrated, even embedded, in everyday life, as a result of the surge of tourists and ensuing commercial development in virtually every corner of the world. Diverse forms of tourism are reshaping the city as they are responding to structures and stimuli produced by global and local regimes of capital accumulation. Furthermore, tourism process is multifaceted, non-linear, and iterative involving a host of people with constant trade-offs over time. These empirical trends, made for a new fit between morphology and tourism, have profound sociopolitical, economic, and spatial consequences.

The changing urban spatial structure reflects the rise of awareness in quality of life and power play (Peel et al. 2009). When thinking about tourism development and its relationship to the city, one cannot ignore the fact that the geographical space of the city is primarily a lived space, created by the locals (Simmons 1994). Therefore, tourism development is involved with a wide variety of stakeholders and often uses new technologies to map and present the features of the city that are of interest to locals and tourists alike. It is difficult to differentiate tourist sites from "local" spaces because tourism and residential recreation are increasingly intertwined. In reality, residents frequently engage in activities that are indistinguishable from what tourists do, and act like tourists by advocating new urban lifestyles such as *cittaslow*, creative tourism, and waterfront redevelopment. The rise of a new urban culture devoted to aesthetic pursuits has remade cities into places that provide the consumption of travel right at home (Judd 2003). The resulting "localization of leisure" has stimulated, as much as tourism, the conversion of spatial arrangement and changing morphology (Hannigan 1998: 61).

Although recent achievements of the morphology of tourism are made in both research and practice, problems stem from the weak representations between traditional morphological study and the multidisciplinary nature of tourism. In sum, there are four major issues concerning this subject.

First, although the morphology of tourism derives from contemporary recreation geographies and becomes a subdiscipline to the melding and hybridity of geographic binaries, it remains imprecisely defined and vaguely
demarcated. Although there is a reawakening of interest in the exploration
of links between the different disciplines within which urban form is studied (Whitehand et al. 2016), little development of a systematic structure
of understanding was undertaken, especially in the development of more
critical applied geographies of physical change. On the other hand, tourism
geography has been somewhat peripheral in the broader academic field of
geography, which may be due in part to the inertia of academic institutions.
In general, geographers and urban planners do not regard tourism as a
serious subject for study, as well as the difficulty in measuring tourism as
compared to primary and secondary industries.

Second, urban morphology is mainly studied within architectural
schools in many countries. Urban morphologists are predominantly architects, geographers, or urban planners, while archaeologists, anthropologists, and historians are minor contributors to the field. While the number
of attempts at cross-cultural comparison has increased in recent decades,
the approach to morphology tends to be descriptive and physical, even the
growing popularity of space syntax is visual in context. Without a conceptual framework to accommodate and interpret basic data on aspects
of morphology, tourism studies struggle to be associated with urban form.
In contrast to studies on the conservation of heritage sites and buildings of
architectural distinction, research on the morphology of tourism relating to
urban areas is loose. This is especially the case in the planning of tourist-
historic cities, which should play a fundamental role in linking tourism
activities at individual sites and buildings to city-wide perspectives. The
character and significance of individual sites in relation to both adjoining
sites and the wider conservation areas in which they are located is poorly
articulated. Clarity is similarly lacking in relating conservation areas to
their surroundings.

Third, the morphology of tourism is a multidimensional concept that
reinforces physical transformation within the urban environment. It contributes to the emergence of a sphere in which physical transformation is
highly visible guided by a variety of principles. Tourism penetrates and
influences the urban form at all levels: land use, site development, building
regulations, infrastructure, innovation, and social inclusion (Pasquinelli
and Bellini 2017). However, the morphology of tourism has received a disproportionately small amount of attention to linking theoretical research
to case studies more generally. Ashworth and Page (2011: 2) raise the question: why do "those studying tourism neglect cities while those studying
cities neglect tourism"? The changing morphology is relevant to impacts of
tourism theoretically and in matters of empirical research. In recent years,
tourism scholars have advanced strong claims that the understanding of
urban morphology is, in effect, a pragmatic and more appropriate approach

for the study of tourism. For example, the early work of Christaller's (1966) central place theory for tourism proposes that zones located distant from urban and industrial agglomerations were more favorable for tourism development. Hall and Page (2014) identify themes emerging from the research of geographers, including explaining spatialities, tourism planning and places, and development and its critiques, as well as viewing tourism as an "applied" area of research.

Lastly, the morphology of tourism aims to manage change or conserve urban form, then capture cartographically the historical geography of what is being managed or conserved. City maps record the molding of the environment, as humans create the key places in which they interact and seek to determine their development. Maps of landscape units, or character areas, in conjunction with photographs, drawings, and a written explanation for each unit or area, provide those wishing to conserve or make changes to a given space with an important part of the context for preparing management plans. Geographical boundaries are almost invariably given great emphasis by planning authorities. However, the basis of those boundaries has generally been inadequately researched. It is not to be suggested that these issues of morphology of tourism have been resolved in this book. On the contrary, these are subjects alive with challenges to both researchers and practitioners. The morphology of tourism is a nascent broadening of perspective into a more integrated approach by policy makers and practitioners. There is an urgent need for a substantial body of research that has accumulated on morphological and functional duality; of especial relevance is extensive research within the field of tourism and urban morphology. This is germane not only to understanding how history is embodied in urban landscapes, but also to incorporating this knowledge into future landscape planning and management. Much work needs to be done to combine morphology and tourism studies, from where in the vacationscape, physical transformation as well as by whom. In addition, treating the morphology of tourism as if it were merely a function of homogeneity is simplistic. Heterogeneity is not uncommon in very old landscapes; for instance, fringe belts are established through the historico-geographical grain of the cities, and are highly heterogeneous. Typically, the heterogeneity of morphology in many cities is purpose built, largely a by-product of postmodernism.

Summary of the chapters

This book first discusses the concept of urban morphology, modeling and disciplines. Its focus is on practical concerns for those conducting empirical research in urban morphology and tourism planning. Methods for researching the morphology of tourism are dispersed across a broad multidisciplinary community of architects, geographers, and other scholars. One of the early scholarly links between morphology and landscape research in North America was fashioned from Carl Sauer's (1925) seminal study entitled *The Morphology of Landscape*, which discussed the German concept of *landschaft* in geography and serves as a basic template for modern traditions within cultural landscapes. Morphological analysis runs parallel to the existing physical fabric of the city, maps, and city plans, advocated by the Conzenian and Muratorian schools. Not surprisingly, we therefore draw from a wide range of social science disciplines, including traditional urban morphological study, in our consideration of quantitative and qualitative methods, cartography, and mixed-method designs. In so doing, we do not seek to favor one school over another, but rather to offer insights into the selected destinations' temporospatial arrangements and associated issues in terms of tourism impacts.

Chapter 1 documents the forms and functions of places, the relationships between them, and how they change across space and time. Urban form can be described as a series of characteristics, tissues, and a process of historical development. Whitehand (2007) posits the existence of two interrelated challenges within the field of morphology. The first entails the ways in which urban morphology builds upon key works that were already seen to be such a long time ago, for example, in the case of lines of thought pursued by the Conzenian School who set out some of the thinking that is pertinent to finding effective ways forward during recent years. The second challenge may be seen as an extension of the first: to explore the relationships between the different sorts of thinking that the "classics" of twentieth-century urban morphology have pursued. The metaphor of the palimpsest is often used in urban morphology to explain the continuous construction over time. There is an urgent need to form a "philosophical base" (Mugavin 1999) to provide a set of principles for urban morphology and connect with multidiscipline.

In some important respects, Chapter 2 suggests that a conceptual framework for the morphology of tourism helps bring a clearer understanding to the complexity. Following this framework, the selected case studies in this book depict the emergence of morphology and tourism regimes, the processes by which they are supported, and the means by which sites shift from non-tourism purposes to tourist attractions. Case studies from across the world are used to demonstrate the extent to which urban morphology and tourism impacts come together within the realm of various countries, regions, and cities. For instance, the issues raised by forms and functions as well as by impacts on land use are prominent on Denarau Island in Fiji and the redevelopment of the Auckland, New Zealand waterfront. Other chapters compare the ancient cities in Pingyao, China, and Como, Italy, which show the interplay of fringe belts through the various discussions of the role of functional zones and the changing pattern for tourists.

After proposing a theoretical framework that outlines the impacts of tourism on urban form, it systematically analyzes the spatial, political, economic, and historical contexts informing the development of urban tourism over the past years. It depicts how the urban form has been (re)configured through different temporalities, and shows that place identity is evolutionary and contextual in character within a space-time continuum. Through the analysis of morphological changes in various locations, information can be gleaned about who should be involved in, when they should be involved, what their roles should be, and what they need in order to make more informed decisions throughout the process. A difference of degree exists manifested in the selected case studies. One of them lies in the quantity and antiquity of urban tourism resources in a historically varied urban system. The proposed conceptual framework gives a methodological tool for a comparative analysis of phenomena in this field.

Breaking down the framework into several key dimensions, as in Chapter 2, allows us to compare sectors and places, as well as to track similarities and differences to the evolutionary process in multiple cities. This framework identifies three key components that structure relations within tourism and urban morphology: (1) urban forms in natural, street, plot, and building systems; (2) tourism attractions in points, lines, and areas; and (3) a variety of impacts incurred by tourism on urban form including sociocultural, economic, and spatial patterns. The methods described in this book provide a more rigorous basis and enable researchers to address key issues in the morphology of tourism: (1) character, in which the *genius loci* and history coordinately respond to and strengthen distinctive patterns impacted by tourism; (2) continuity and enclosure, in which the clarity of streets, plots, and buildings distinguishes between public and private spaces. In the case of Pingyao, China, the demarcation a *danwei* zone was used to define the walled city; (3) ease of movement, which facilitates tourist travel to and from a space, such as Denarau Island in Fiji; (4) adaptability, in which space can be altered for tourism purposes, such as the case study of waterfronts in Auckland, New Zealand; and (5) diversity, tourist space filled with different traces which allow people to choose from different options, such as the old town in Como, Italy.

Chapter 3 analyzes coastal morphological changes on Denarau Island in Fiji from physical, environmental, and social perspectives. It shows that morphological changes on Denarau Island do not follow the traditional Beach Resort Model due to the influence of the master plan implemented by Territorial Local Authority. After decades of intensive management of coastal tourism, Denarau Island remains Fiji's most valuable attraction. However, despite its high economic importance, an effective coastal governance structure is not in place and residents are excluded from decision-making processes. This results in coastal development where beaches are set aside for exclusive use, and the capacity of many coastal stakeholders to make and influence decisions remains small in Fiji. The study observes a need for legislative reform to require a comprehensive spatial plan suitable for sustainable tourism.

Chapter 4 presents a case study of spatial morphology in Pingyao, China, to illustrate the significance of architectural heritage, via a study of

Pingyao's city wall. This chapter provides a historical overview of urban conservation in the Chinese historic city, and assesses its current tourism condition and the benefits of a much more systematic morphological approach. It traces three stages of intramural and extramural changes under governmental policies, as tourism has become a means of economic growth. It has profound impact on the transformation of the *danwei* units and preservation of historic buildings. Pingyao's walls place betwixt and between *danwei*-heritage boundaries of identity, the marginality and ambiguous geographies of its physical landscape developed over decades.

Unlike urban expansion, restructuring, and economic development in China, which have been the subject of considerable research in the past years, the conservation of Chinese towns and cities like Pingyao received little attention until the 1980s. Insofar as any urban conservation existed during the first half of the twentieth century, it was almost entirely concerned with identifying a wide range of ancient archaeological and architectural objects considered worthy of protection. During the Cultural Revolution in China, historical features were destroyed on a massive scale. The volte-face in the early 1980s, given momentum by the passing of the Heritage Conservation Act and the creation of a List of Precious Chinese Historic Cities, occurred at much the same time as a major increase in redevelopment and concomitant pressure on the traditional cores of cities. Recognition by the late 1980s of the major gap between, on the one hand, the traditional concern with the excavation of individual historic sites and restoration and protection of special structures and, on the other hand, the "listing" of entire Precious Cities for special treatment gave rise to an intermediate level of concern: the designation of historico-cultural conservation areas for tourism. However, largely influenced by urban conservation in Western countries and suffering from some of the same defects, the lack of a theoretical basis has limited the effectiveness of plans for Pingyao.

The study of Pingyao is a test of the empirical usefulness of morphological research on tourism in a non-Western society. It sheds light on concepts and methods in cultural areas markedly different from those in which Western cities were formulated. Simultaneously, a timely contribution can be made to the search for solutions to the acute problems of urban landscape management faced by Chinese towns and cities. The study of the morphology of tourism in Pingyao inspires two reflections. First, there is an urgent need in China and other industrializing countries to put this field on a sound footing. In a rapidly changing country like China, which contains large areas of culturally valuable landscapes, it is important that such investigations are undertaken before serious further loss of those assets is suffered. Second, and arguably more importantly, there are wider cross-cultural implications. Though honed in the West, the morphology of tourism has been shown to be applicable to China.

Chapter 5 details the redevelopment of Auckland's and Wellington's waterfronts in New Zealand over the past decades, and charts its socioeconomic consequences. The trend of waterfront redevelopment has attracted a great deal of scholarly attention. Extant research includes, but is not limited to, changing political-economic frameworks, urban revitalization, planning and design, spatial and land-use transformation in waterfront districts, the role of history and heritage in regeneration, and ecological and environmental issues concerning waterfronts. From a tourism planning perspective, there are generally two types of waterfront renewal projects. One entails a complete transformation, in which tourism and leisure functions are imagined to be the prime objective of waterfront development. Such projects in Auckland aim to generate a marketable aesthetic, promote historic interest, and cultivate cultural attractions through hosting urban festivities. In the second type of renewal project, in the case of Wellington, waterfronts maintain their original uses but incorporate leisure and tourism, because the working port remains a draw factor. As a result, different models of waterfront regeneration emerge: some of which create bland standardization and gentrification, and others focus more on heritage renaissance, community development, or contemporary culture.

Specifically, in Auckland, the largest commercial center in New Zealand, the process of Central Business District colonization has come to dominate waterfront redevelopment. The waterfront zones are more susceptible than ever to pressures for change, and in most cases, they have succumbed to inadequately coordinated high-density commercial and residential developments. The waterfront landscape in Auckland is therefore fragmented and lacks integration. Like many port cities around the world, the agents of change on the waterfronts of Auckland include a mixture of government agencies, port authorities, the development industry, professional groups, and the general public. It is appropriate now to take a closer look at the interplay of these actors in the drama of waterfront redevelopment. In particular, special events, such as the Rugby World Cup and America's Cup, play a key role in precipitating and shaping waterfront redevelopment in Auckland. The hosting of hallmark events provides an impetus for the redevelopment of unattractive and poorly utilized waterfront areas the world over. The success of these events also exerts profound influence on urban tourist space. Waterfront represents its spatial, social, and historical transformation over time, set in architectural morphology, building typology, and, more importantly, neighborhood evolution. The revitalization of waterfront illustrates the synergy between two seemingly contradictory strands: the preservation and marketing of local culture and architecture, versus the construction of new tourist areas and of a modernized accessible infrastructure.

Comparative urban research has been used in Chapter 5 to better understand waterfront transformation. It has helped to overcome the problem of idiographic studies in which particular findings fail to yield useful generalizations. Comparative urban morphology in the context of tourism makes it possible to identify urban landscapes common to different geographical regions; it also helps to distinguish unique historical characteristics and developments that are important for cities in seeking place identity. The morphological process provides a frame of reference for depicting, explaining, and comparing the physical structure and change of urban landscapes and the dynamics of morphological agencies. More empirical investigation from other geographical regions will be needed, but it should prove highly beneficial in the longer term.

Chapter 6 introduces the concept of the fringe belt, a key element of cities from which one can observe processes and patterns of urban morphology, and examines its role as a boundary for tourism development. By observing and recording the features of Como, Italy, we examine the streets, plots, and buildings as urban tissues that form a narrative about tourist attractions in the old town and the recreational zone facing Lake Como. Caniggian and Conzenian concepts offer a promising start to learn the morphological structures in Como. In tandem, they also provide a route through which the longer term need for comparison and integration of ideas with markedly different disciplines is satisfied. In this sense, Como provides the basis for a conceptual exploration, and what is suggested here is just a step towards fulfilling the much larger task of creating morphology of tourism for future development. The integration of spatial morphology with tourism planning will foster a better understanding of the complex interplay of urban form and function.

In addition, there has been an increasing attempt to move conservation policy away from the current pattern of *ad hoc* approaches to heritage conservation at the citywide scale. The case study of Como can be used as a template for many different European cities. The fringe belts serve as a spatial distinction between the old town and tourism facilities, and between concentrations of tourist-historic and other central commercial functions. The recognition of three fringe belts produced by the process of urban growth is crucial in maintaining and reconstructing traditional urban characteristics for tourism as a whole. The morphological approach spreads to various European cities based on the study of Como. For example, English Heritage, the Government's statutory adviser on the historic environment in the UK, has engaged in a long-term program of character area surveys (Thomas 2006). The idea of historic urban landscapes, which is being promoted by UNESCO and supported by the International Council on Monuments and Sites, is an attempt to develop an overarching tool that protects historic cities without inhibiting their tourism development (Landorf 2009). Though classifying extant urban landscapes has been important for the management of the built environment in those efforts, the identification and appreciation of character areas that consist of a spatial mixture of different period types and styles as a result of the dynamics of historico-geographical development is highly recommended.

In total, these case studies reveal that tourism is a force for diversification as much as for uniformity. They provide directions for a systematic comparative study, while pointing to a more progressive urban morphology. By using the paradigm of urban morphology as a unifying theme, these case studies illustrate the constraints on the interaction between tourism and evolving urban form, the forces that reshape the operations of tourism and tourism-related industries, and the effect of a tourism-oriented economy on urban form.

Conjoining habitus, parallax, and the *longue durée*

The morphology of tourism always carries out social context. The French sociologist, Pierre Bourdieu, uses the word "habitus" to describe the complex of social space, process, power, and capital produced by a contemporary society. Habitus, according to Bourdieu (1977), is a historically constituted, shared generative schema of perception, appreciation, and categorization, mediating between structure and agency (Nash 1999). Habitus is a useful concept for thinking through the relationship between urban form and changing society, as it is produced from the acquisitions related to particular forms of social belonging and consists of dispositions acquired through life (Amaro 2016). It is learned and inculcated to the point where one's cultural and class tastes are felt as an irrefutable bodily reality. Habitus is also created and reproduced by dispositions, forces that are shaped by past events and structures. It embodies a set of individualized perceptions and is viewed as both idiosyncratic and objective aesthetic judgments by individuals. There is an important concept for understanding contextually determined habitus, for example, notions of "the field," referring to various social and institutional arenas reflected in morphological changes (Gaventa 2003). According to Bourdieu (1990), a cultural field can be understood as both imaginary and material sociocultural spaces, composed of a network of relationships, in which people reproduce dispositions and compete for different kinds of capital. A subject's habitus is usually either congruent with or subject to a strong influence from the logics, discourses, and values of that field. Very often, therefore, tensions and contradictions arise when people encounter different contexts and experience power differently, depending on which field they are in at a given moment; therefore, context and environment are key influences on habitus. Physical changes, spatial arrangements, and urban structures are thus not derived from calculations or plans, but are the results of the relations between habitus and the environment (Webb et al. 2002).

The study of urban morphology and tourism revolves around the notion of habitus, where the spatial development has become fluid by taking everybody together from facilities, roads, health, and leadership. DeJean (2014: 102) traces the transformation of Paris from an urban ghetto to a tourist setting by tracing the use of the term *quai*, a seventeenth-century word to designate the embankments along the Seine. In 1636, municipal authorities responsible for transforming the Right Bank shore faced the new island, when they announced their intention of adding a paved river walk that would both be functional (particularly for loading merchandise that had reached Paris by boat) and give locals a space where they could "walk with great ease" while admiring the river. The creation of the term *quai* indicates an emerging consciousness about the importance of leisure space and its potential role in developing an eventual tourist destination changing the landscape of Paris.

Searle and Byrne (2002) stress that habitus is not a natural space, but is rather a social space that is apprehended through a set of social practices. It is also a domain of contestation since the field encompasses "the socially structured space within which actors struggle" to achieve their objectives (Hillier 2001: 4). Most importantly, habitus implies *genius loci* (re)created by a variety of stakeholders. Cosgrove (2000) proposes that habitus eventually results in the formation of place attachment, derived from intrinsic characters, feelings, and sentiments of attachment that people experience in a given place. It goes beyond the physical qualities, but is full of meanings, conflict, and memories. Morphology eventually represents the experience of "home" where one feels "in one's place." In a contemporary society, *genius loci* have become necessary to turn social space into "invented space" (Edensor 2001) or a communal space conducive to communication based on social exchange theory. As Harvey (2000: 209) notes, the tradition and custom, space, and sense of place through which people perceive their common identity provide "the recourse to a familiar landscape of experience that allows the unchallenged transmission of social memory."

Bourdieu's theory of habitus offers an excellent tool for conceptualizing the morphology of tourism. Primarily, space used for tourism is a certain amount of land acquired at a reasonable cost and situated in an appropriate location (Tiesdell et al. 1996). In the case study of Pingyao, China, in Chapter 4, the metamorphic, hypometamorphic, and orthomorphic processes of development outcomes mixed with *feng shui* ideology have become important attractions for tourists to get off the beaten track. The problem is that physical differentials that manifest as power differentials, like class, race, and gender, can affect the extent to which people have access to tourism resources. These differentials play a role in deciding who has the power to transform cultural spaces in their own image, and which version of history promoted by those sites will constitute the "official" version. In the context of tourism, tourists have power to demand a new set of morphology. Various dimensions of the tourist space are used to reflect the sociocultural identity of the city, which Stratton (2000: 22) refers to as "environmental capital." Timms (2008) further argues that tourist space is not a physical area of land, but the ideal representation perceived from a particular viewpoint. By using the term "parallax," the apparent change in appearance of an object when viewed from different positions in the context of photogrammetry, it shows the significance of creating a complementary parallax of perspectives to address shifting morphology of tourism.

Morphology yields the insight that is essential for urban landscape managers to consider individual city features in context. Rather than focusing on isolated buildings that are deemed worthy of preservation, the overriding consideration must be the identity of the city as a whole and its constituent parts. Contemporary society should not just pay attention to how we perceive landscapes, but how the purposes of social formation brought on by forces of capitalism and globalization are reflected in landscape representation. Wallace (1956), employing an anthropological approach, proposes a processual model of revitalization movements in which an initial steady state is followed by various external changes that trigger a period of revitalization, eventually returning to a new form of steady state. A tourism landscape does not arise overnight, but is the end result of a process of social construction that plays out over a number of decades and perhaps centuries (Knudsen et al. 2008).

In a similar vein, Giddens' structuration theory (1984) addresses what Wallace's mazeway resynthesis and Willis's (1994) paradigm means in sociological research. His underlying assumption is that social structure and action are evolving and constantly influenced by individual agents. A social structure including the elements of tradition, heritage, and culture can be transformed when people start to ignore, replace, or reproduce them. The transformation is gradual and incremental, taking place at a micro level according to a traceable and identifiable cycle. Giddens (1984), following French historian Fernand Braudel's terminology, refers to the goal of bringing social change to existing landscapes as a *longue durée*. Although Giddens has not used tourism as a case study to substantiate his theory of structuration, it is a typical social force impacting the everyday world and changing the way people think. Debate on the morphology of tourism are incomplete without an embodiment of social forces, both internal and external, which could be random, ephemeral, contradictory, and fluid. The *longue durée* is essential to understanding the morphology of tourism, which has gone through multiple dynamic stages of cultural and historical evolution. Since tourism is hybrid and liminal, there is not any stable referent upon which changes are based. The meaning of morphology is not merely history; rather, it is a process realized in material objects, such as commercial activities, sites, special places, and even whole landscapes. Through the collective impact of tourists and other stakeholders on the urban landscape, the present touches the past and the modern glorifies the ancient, all reflected in the changing landscape of streets, buildings, spaces, and other features.

Critical considerations for the morphology of tourism

The conservation of cultural heritage has until recently been concerned with individual structures: notable buildings, landmarks, and monuments.

Researchers tend to view historic features in geographical isolation, but to realize the full potential of a given landscape; they must understand it as a cultural, educational, intellectual, and economic resource connected historically and geographically. Few stakeholders appreciate the necessity and benefits of preserving and maintaining the integrity of the historic landscape as a whole, rather than treating individual sites as isolated parcels. Greater recognition of the significance of tourism is belatedly and sporadically beginning to be evident.

Major cities around the world are fast becoming destinations for tourist consumption, transforming from "historic cities" to "tourist-historic cities" or "hospitable cities." Concepts such as the "playable city" provide the basis for concrete projects in different cities across the world facing the challenge of reconciling the needs of residents and tourists. Playfulness elicits active engagement from different stakeholders to examine the manner in which historicity over identity have reshaped landscapes that have subsequently become foci for tourism. The interpretation and practices of a "playable city" encourage residents and tourists alike to interact with, compete in, and ultimately cocreate urban space. The playfulness of the city is increasingly connected to the "smart tourism city" concept, which involves a relationship to technology that becomes the reification of identity (Marques and Borba 2017).

This book, focusing on the issue of morphology in the historic landscapes of contemporary and ancient cities, explores the transformation of tourism development from both contextual and evolutionary perspectives. The case studies demonstrate that morphological change can be both temporary and permanent. Temporary spaces for tourism include social practices and a capacity to stimulate flexibility, innovation, and imagination in urban settings (Pasquinelli and Bellini 2017). Although temporary tourist spaces do not entail direct modifications of the built and physical environment, they host new activities and practices that may have enduring effects on urban tissue, such as streets, plots, and buildings. Tourists and the cities tend to develop around a number of distinct nodes linked by corridors of tourist movement. A critical mass of tourist clusters, visits, and consequent development of supporting services produce polycentricity in a tourist city.

Spatial integration is also evidenced through an extensive clustering of the inner city's economic activities which, as identified by Gospodini (2006: 311), formulate "signifying epicenters." These clusters can be further classified into four subcategories: (1) entrepreneurial, in which high-level financial services, creative islands, technology-intensive, and knowledge-based institutions are concentrated; (2) high-culture, encompassing museums and arts centers; (3) popular leisure, which may include revitalized residential and commercial areas; and (4) culture and leisure waterfronts, or maritime sites (ibid.: 324). In order for an epicenter to maintain its viability, it needs to undergo a constant restructuring cycle, both socially and spatially. Its configuration should therefore be approached as a process-based morphology (Hanson 2000, Psarra 2012) through which changes in its spatial, social, and historical structure and meaning are studied over time. Temporary tourist spaces eventually become permanent when tourism becomes a mainstay business, as in the case of "eventification" (Jacob 2012), where the promotion of annual festivals and events is deployed as an economic development strategy. Ultimately, new spatialities emerge and impact long-term space representation.

Though there is little likelihood of the morphology of tourism developing into an exact science, there is considerable potential for investigations of the type illustrated here. The morphology of tourism is deemed to be diverse, a great deal of its practice is concerned essentially with the manipulation of and control over the three interrelated urban form elements, for example, ground plan, building fabric, and land and building utilization. The morphological study of the characteristics of the urban form elements as the product of tourism development is essential to support the formation of design control policy and development plans that contribute to urban spatial continuity and integrity. In terms of scale, tourism morphological research ranges from the examination of individual plots and buildings to the configuration of entire urban areas. To effectively serve the purposes of tourism planning, the adaptive use of morphological tools to investigate study areas of different scales and development contexts needs to be clearly communicated among different stakeholders. In the process of identifying morphological units for tourism, it is possible to divide an urban area, based on one, a combination of two, or all of these urban form elements, into landscape divisions that each has a unity distinguishing them from adjoining areas. The physical geographical and natural landscape elements (e.g., topographical features and green spaces) and building materials can also be taken into consideration for possible tourism impacts.

Research in urban morphology generally, and on the aspects outlined in this book in particular, benefits from collaborations between various schools of thought within architectural urban morphology. For instance, the idea of the morphological region is benefiting from research on the architectural concept of urban tissue. It has become evident, over the last decades, that the work of M. R. G. Conzen carried out during the middle decades of the twentieth century shares major common ground with work undertaken by the Italian architects Saverio Muratori and Gianfranco Caniggia. Recognition of this has been one of the stimuli for the formalization of an international movement in urban morphology that follows and incorporates observations about tourism development. The burgeoning literature associated with the coming together of these schools of thought has significant implications for the management of morphology of tourism.

Several recommendations are made to conclude this book. The first relates to the use of tourism to the historicity of the urban landscape, whose historical expressiveness derives from the *longue durée*, parallax, and the notion of habitus. The city should always be viewed as a long-term asset whose importance extends far beyond its contemporary functional value. The urban landscape is an invaluable source of experience, especially because it constitutes the predominant environment of resident-tourist interaction. The fact that the tourism landscape is a visual and, for many people, practically omnipresent experience gives it an advantage over many other sources of knowledge. However, realizing its potential requires appreciating societal activities and processes in what can be observed on the ground, and an important part of this appreciation is the uncovering of historical and geographical order. Fundamental to this is the intellectual activity of regionalization and fully understanding the impacts of tourism.

Second, the morphology of tourism falls into the context of Hillier's (2016) fourth sustainability of the city, for example, creativity, where he proposes that apart from energy, society, and economics. All are the consequences of their spatial form; however, creativity allows the evolution of both social stability and morphogenesis via social networks. In this respect, future study ought to aim to analyze those tangible elements manifest in the spatial form of tourist cities and distinguish those intangible attributes which constitute living expressions of their legacy. Particularly, the mobilities reflect processes of traveler movement. The ways things move and are moved, modes of transport, their control and usage, and the technologies of modern travel and communication utilized, albeit for different purposes, by different categories of travelers, all contribute to the underlying processes of traveling (Hannam et al. 2014). The mobilities are widely seen phenomenologically that embody social interaction between tourists and social actors (Harrison 2017). They generate highly social dynamics that eventually impact on urban morphology.

Lastly, the morphology of tourism is an analytical domain that, more than increasing the number of urban morphology and geography approaches, is widening the research arena and providing an ongoing shift of perspective in this field. It is a truism that urban form is spatially "structured" to serve particular human needs and purposes. Tourism is both a means of functional efficiency and, through its embodiment of the endeavors of past societies, a sociocultural resource of inestimable value. Relying on the existing physical fabric of the city, maps, and city plans, ranging from two-dimensional to three-dimensional objects, tourism morphology provides a more systematic and dynamic approach to the spatial structure of the physical urban fabric. The central purpose of morphological analysis is to interpret urban manifestations and decipher the inherent information about local authority for planning control purposes and tourism developers', planners', and users' responsibilities for urban changes. This book emphasizes tourism beyond simply outlining postmodern phenomena of the tourist city, draws attention to the ways in which tourism shapes the complexity of urban settings, and is conversely shaped by the spatial arrangements and socioeconomic dynamics occurring within them. This analytical domain, combining the identification of fringe belts and other tools, provides new directions and methodological challenge for future research.

References

Aas, D. (1975). Observing environmental behavior: the behavior setting. In M. Michelson (Ed.), *Behaviour Research Methods in Environmental Design* (pp. 280–300). Stroudsburg, PA: Dowden, Hutchinson & Ross.

Adamietz, J. (2012). Urban tourism and waterfronts: exploring the case of the Auckland Waterfront Development (Master of Tourism Studies), Auckland University of Technology.

Agarwal, S. (1997). The resort cycle and seaside tourism: an assessment of its applicability and validity. *Tourism Management*, 18(2), 65–73.

Agarwal, S. (2002). Restructuring seaside tourism: the resort life-cycle. *Annals of Tourism Research*, 29(1), 25–55.

Agarwal, S. (2012). Relational spatiality and resort restructuring. *Annals of Tourism Research*, 39(1), 134–154.

Aiesha, R., & Evans, G. (2007). VivaCity: Mixed-use and urban tourism. In M. Smith (Ed.), *Tourism, Culture & Regeneration* (pp. 35–48). Cambridge, MA: CABI.

Alexander, C. (1964). *Notes on the Synthesis of Form*. Cambridge, MA: Harvard University Press.

Allain, R. (2004). *Morphologie urbaine: géographie, aménagement et architecture de la ville*. Paris: Armand Colin.

Allen, J., Lu, K., & Potts, T. (1999). *A GIS-based analysis and prediction of parcel land-use change in coastal tourism destination area*. Paper presented at the The World Congress on Coastal and Marine Tourism, Vancouver, Canada.

Alsayyad, N. (2001). *Consuming Tradition, Manufacturing Heritage*. New York: Routledge.

Amaro, V. (2016). Linguistic practice, power and imagined worlds: the case of the Portuguese in Postcolonial Macau. *Journal of Intercultural Studies*, 37(1), 33–50.

Anderson, G. (1984). *Fresh about Cook Strait: An Appreciation of Wellington Harbour*. Auckland: Methuen Publication NZ Ltd.

Andersson, T., & Getz, D. (2008). Stakeholder management strategies of festivals. *Journal of Convention and Event Tourism*, 9(3), 199–220.

Andrews, H., & Roberts, L. (2012). *Liminal Landscapes: Travel, Experience and Spaces In-Between*. New York: Routledge.

Andriotis, K. (2003). Coastal resorts morphology: the Cretan experience. *Tourism Recreation Research*, 28(1), 67–76.

Andriotis, K. (2006). Hosts, guests and politics: coastal resorts morphological change. *Annals of Tourism Research*, 33(4), 1079–1098.

Anfuso, G., Williams, A., Cabrera Hernandez, J., & Pranzini, E. (2014). Coastal scenic assessment and tourism management in Western Cuba. *Tourism Management*, 42, 307–320.

Anfuso, G., Williams, A., Casas Martinez, G., Botero, C., Cabrera Hernandez, J., & Pranzini, E. (2017). Evaluation of the scenic value of 100 beaches in Cuba: implications for coastal tourism management. *Ocean and Coastal Management*, 142(15), 173–185.

Appleyard, D., Lynch, K., & Myer, J. (1965). *The View from the Road*. Cambridge, MA: The MIT Press.

Ascher, K. (2007). *The Works: Anatomy of a City*. New York: The Penguin Press.

Ashworth, G. (1989). Accommodation and the historic city. *Built Environment*, 15(2), 92–100.

Ashworth, G., & Page, S. (2011). Urban tourism research: recent progress and current paradoxes. *Tourism Management*, 32(1), 1–15.

Ashworth, G., & Tunbridge, J. (1990). *The Tourist-Historic City*. London: Belhaven.

Ashworth, G., & Tunbridge, J. (2000). *The Tourist-Historic City: Retrospect and Prospect of Managing the Heritage City*. London: Elsevier.

Auckland City Council (2006). *Draft Wynyard Point Concept Vision*. Auckland: Auckland City Council.

Auckland Regional Council and Auckland City Council (2005). *Auckland Waterfront 2040*. Auckland: Auckland Regional Council and Auckland City Council.

Auckland Waterfront Development Agency (2010). *Our Role in Auckland's Waterfront*. Auckland: Auckland Waterfront Development Agency.

Augé, M. (2009). *Non-Places: An Introduction to Supermodernity*. London: Verso.

Baker, N., & Slater, T. (1992). Morphological regions in English Medieval towns. In J. Whitehand & P. Larkham (Eds.), *Urban Landscapes: International Perspectives* (pp. 43–68). London: Routledge.

Ball, M. (1986). The built environment and the urban question. *Environment and Planning D*, 4, 447–464.

Barnes, T. (2001). Retheorizing economic geography: from the quantitative revolution to the "cultural turn". *Annals of the Association of American Geographers*, 91(3), 546–565.

Barrett, J. (1958). *The seaside resort towns of England and Wales* (Ph.D.), University of London, London.

Bégin, S. (2000). The geography of a tourist business: hotel distribution and urban development in Xiamen, China. *Tourism Geographies*, 2(4), 448–471.

Bender, O., Boehmer, H., Jens, D., & Schumacher, K. (2005). Using GIS to analyse long-term cultural landscape change in Southern Germany. *Landscape and Urban Planning*, 70, 111–125.

Berdet, M. (2013). *Fantasmagories du capital: L'invention de la ville-marchandise*. Paris: Zones.

Beriatos, E., & Gospodini, A. (2004). Glocalising urban landscapes—Athens and the 2004 Olympics. *Cities*, 21(3), 187–202.

Bidesi, R., Lal, P., & Conner, N. (2011). *Economics of Coastal Zone Management in the Pacific*. Suva: Quality Print.

Billinge, M. (1996). A time and place for everything: an essay on recreation, recreation and the Victorians. *Journal of Historical Geography*, 22, 443–459.

Birchfield, R. (2004). *Business Travel Fiji's Denarau Island*. Auckland: Profile Publishing Limited.

Board, A. H. (1973). *Waitemata Harbour Study: Preliminary Report on Fill*. Auckland: Auckland Harbour Board.

Bobek, H., & Lichtenberger, E. (1966). Wien. Paper presented at the Jahrhunderts Schriften der Kommission für Raumsforschung der Österreichischen Akademie der Wissenschaften 1.

Boerwinkel, H. (1995). Management of recreation and tourist behaviour at different spatial levels. In G. Ashworth & A. Dietvorst (Eds.), *Tourism and Spatial Transformations: Implications for Policy and Planning* (pp. 241–263). Wallingford: CABI.

Borsay, P. (2006). *A History of Leisure: The British Experience since 1500*. Basingstoke: Palgrave.

Botz-Bornstein, T. (2015). *Transcultural Architecture: The Limits and Opportunities of Critical Regionalism*. London: Routledge.

Bourdieu, P. (1977). *Outline of a Theory of Practice*. Cambridge: Cambridge University Press.

Bourdieu, P. (1990). *The Logic of Practice*. Stanford, CA: Stanford University Press.

Bowen, M. (1981). *Empiricism and Geographical Thought: from Francis Bacon to Alexander von Humboldt*. Cambridge: Cambridge University Press.

Boyer, J. (1980). Residences secondaires et rurbanisation en region Parisienne. *Tijdschrift voor Economische en Sociale Geografie*, 71(2), 78–87.

Bray, D. (2005). *Social Space and Governance in Urban China: The Danwei System from Origins to Reform*. Palo Alto, CA: Stanford University Press.

Breitung, W., & Lu, J. (2016). Suzhou's water grid as urban heritage and tourism resource: an urban morphology approach to a Chinese city. *Journal of Heritage Tourism*, 12, 251–266.

Brent, M. (1997). *Coastal Resort Morphology as a Response to Transportation Technology* (Ph.D. thesis), University of Waterloo.

Burak, S., Dogan, E., & Gazioglu, C. (2004). Impact of urbanization and tourism on coastal environment. *Ocean and Coastal Management*, 47(9–10), 515–527.

Burgers, J. (2000). Urban landscapes on public space in the post-industrial city. *Journal of Housing and the Built Environment*, 15(2), 145–164.

Burgess, E. (1925). The growth of the city. In R. Park, E. Burgess, & R. McKenzie (Eds.), *The City* (pp. 47–62). Chicago: University of Chicago.

Butler, R. (1980). The concept of a tourist area cycle of evolution: implications for management of resources. *Canadian Geographer*, 24(1), 5–12.

Butler, R. (1993). Tourism: an evolutionary perspective. In J. Nelson, R. Butler, & G. Wall (Eds.), *Tourism and Sustainable Development: Monitoring, Planning, Managing*. Waterloo, ON: University of Waterloo.

Butler, R. (2004). The tourism area life cycle in the twenty-first century. In A. Lew, C. M. Hall, & A. Williams (Eds.), *A Companion to Tourism* (pp. 159–170). Oxford: Blackwell Publishing.

Butler, R. (2011). Tourism area life cycle. In C. Cooper (Ed.), *Contemporary Tourism Reviews* (pp. 1–33). Oxford: Goodfellow Publishers.

Caglioni, M., & Rabino, G. (2007). Theoretical approach to urban ontology: a contribution from urban system analysis. *Studies in Computational Intelligence*, 61, 109–119.

Calvino, I. (1978). *Invisible Cities*. San Diego, CA: Helen and Kurt Wolff Book.

Camacho-Hubner, E., & Golay, F. (2007). Preliminary insights on continuity and evolution of concepts for the development of an urban morphological process ontology. In J. Teller, J. Lee, & C. Roussey (Eds.), *Ontologies for Urban Development* (pp. 95–108). New York: Springer.

Cani, F., & Monizza, G. (1994). *Como e la sua storia: La citta murata vol. 3*. Como. Rome: Nodo Libri.

Caniggia, G. (1963). *Lettura di una Citta: Como*. Rome: Centro Studi di Storia Urbanistica.

Caniggia, G., & Maffei, G. (2001). *Architectural Composition and Building Typology: Interpreting Basic Building*. Firenze: Alinea.

Carsjens, G., & van Lier, H. (2002). Fragmentation and land-use planning: an introduction. *Landscape and Urban Planning*, 58(2–4), 79–82.

Cartwright, T. (1991). Planning and chaos theory. *APA Journal*, 57(1), 44–56.

Castagnoli, F. (1971). *Orthogonal Town Planning in Antiquity*. Cambridge, MA: MIT Press.

Castello, L. (2010). *Rethinking the Meaning of Place, Conceiving Place in Architecture-Urbanism*. Surrey: Ashgate.

Castells, M. (1989). *Informational City*. Oxford: Blackwell.

Castells, M. (2000). *The Rise of Network Society*. Oxford: Blackwell.

Certeau, M. (2011). *The Practice of Everyday Life* (3rd edition). Berkeley: University of California Press.

Chan, S. (2005). Temple-building and heritage in China. *Ethnology*, 44(1), 65–79.

Chang, K. (1987). *The Archaeology of Ancient China*. New Haven, CT: Yale University Press.

Chang, T., & Huang, S. (2011). Reclaiming the city: waterfront development in Singapore. *Urban Studies*, 48(10), 2085–2100.

Chapman, D. (2006). Applying macro urban morphology to urban design and development planning: Valletta and Floriana. *Urban Morphology*, 10(1), 23–40.

Chatley, H. (1917). Feng-Shui. In P. Couling (Ed.), *Encyclopaedia Sinica*. Shanghai: Kelly and Walsh.

Chen, M., Lu, D., & Zha, L. (2010). The comprehensive evaluation of China's urbanization and effects on resources and environment. *Journal of Geographical Sciences*, 20(1), 17–30.

Cheng, S., Yu, Y., & Li, K. (2017). Historic conservation in rapid urbanization: a case study of the Hankow historic concession area. *Journal of Urban Design*, 22, 433–454.

Christaller, W. (1964). Some considerations of tourism location in Europe. *Regional Science Association Papers*, 12, 95–105.

Christaller, W. (1966). *Central Places in Southern Germany*. Englewood Cliffs: Prentice Hall.

Cicin-Sain, B., & Knecht, R. (1998). *Integrated Coastal and Ocean Management: Concepts and Practices*. Washington, DC: Island Press.

Clark, G., & Crichter, C. (1985). *The Devil Makes Work: Leisure in Capitalist Britain*. Basingstoke: MacMillan.

Clark, T. (2004). Introduction: taking entertainment seriously. In T. Clark (Ed.), *The City as an Entertainment Machine* (Vol. 9, pp. 1–18). New York: Elsevier.

Clave, S., & Wilson, J. (2017). The evolution of coastal tourism destinations: a path plasticity perspective on tourism urbanisation. *Journal of Sustainable Tourism*, 25(1), 96–112.

Coca-Stefaniak, J., Parker, C., Quin, S., Rinaldi, R., & Byrom, J. (2009). Town centre management models: a European perspective. *Cities*, 26(2), 74–80.

Collins, D., & Kearns, R. (2010). It's a Gestalt experience: landscape values and development pressure in Hawke's Bay, New Zealand. *Geoforum*, 41, 433–446.

Como, C. d. (1970). La Città Murata di Como: Atti della Ricerca promossa dall'Amministrazione comunale negli Anni 1968 e 1969: Relazioni e Tavole (The walled city of Como: Proceedings of research sponsored by the local administration in 1968 and 1969: Reports and Tables), Como, Italy: Commune di Como.

Company, T. N. Z. (2008). Fiji. Retrieved from https://protect-us.mimecast.com/s/XxMfCmZ2EotjkNxLkiNXRl8?domain=nz.travel.yahoo.com

Compiling Committee for Pingyao Gazetteer (1999). *Pingyao Xianzhi (Pingyao Gazetteer)*. Beijing: Zhonghua Shuju Press.

Conzen, M. (1958). The growth and character of Whitby. In G. Daysh (Ed.), *A Survey of Whitby and the Surrounding Area* (pp. 49–89). Eton: Shakespeare Head Press.

Conzen, M. (1969). *Alnwick, Northumberland: A Study in Town-Plan Analysis*. London: Institute of British Geographers, Publication No. 27.

Conzen, M. (1932). *Die Havelstadte*. University of Berlin.

Conzen, M. (1949). The Scandinavian approach to urban geography. *Norsk Geografisk Tidskrift*, 12, 86–91.

Conzen, M. (1960). *Alnwick, Northumberland: A Study in Town-Plan Analysis*. London: George Philip.

Conzen, M. (1962). *The plan analysis of an English city centre*. Paper presented at the The IGU symposium in urban geography Lund 1960, Gleerup, Lund.

Conzen, M. (1966). Historical townscapes in Britain: a problem in applied geography. In J. House (Ed.), *Northern Geographical Essays in Honour of G.H.J. Daysh* (pp. 56–78). Newcastle upon Tyne: Oriel Press.

Conzen, M. (1988). Morphogenesis, morphological regions and secular human agency in the historic townscape, as exemplified by Ludlow. In D. Denecke & G. Shaw (Eds.), *Urban Historical Geography*. Cambridge: Cambridge University Press.

Conzen, M. (2004). *Thinking about Urban Form: Papers on Urban Morphology, 1932–1998*. Oxford: Peter Lang.

Conzen, M., Gu, K., & Whitehand, J. (2012). Comparing traditional urban form in China and Europe: a fringe-belt approach. *Urban Geography*, 33(1), 22–45.

Cooper, M. (1993). Access to the waterfront: transformation of meaning on the Toronto lakeshore. In R. Rotenburg & G. McDonogh (Eds.), *The Cultural Meaning of Urban Space* (pp. 157–171). Westport, CT: Bergin & Garvey.

Cormack, G. (2009). *The Auckland Waterfront Case Study*. Auckland: Committee for Auckland. Retrieved from Auckland: http://www.aucklanddesignmanual.co.nz/resources/case-studies

Cosgrove, D. (2000). Sense of place. In R. Johnston, D. Gregory, G. Pratt, & M. Watts (Eds.), *The Directionary of Human Geography*. Oxford: Blackwell.

Craig-Smith, S. (1995). The role of tourism in inner-harbor redevelopment: a multinational perspective. In S. Craig-Smith & M. Fagence (Eds.), *Recreation and*

Tourism as A Catalyst for Urban Waterfront Redevelopment: An International Survey (pp. 16–35). Westport, CT: Praeger.

Crompton, J. (2015). Clare Gunn: pioneer, maverick and "founding father" of academic tourism in the USA. *Anatolia, 26*(1).

Cullen, G. (1961). *Townscape*. London: The Architectural Press.

Daly, M., & Malone, P. (1996). Sydney: the economic and political roots of Darling Harbour. In P. Malone (Ed.), *City, Capital and Water* (pp. 90–109). New York: Routledge.

Davis, J. (2001). Commentary: tourism research and social theory—expanding the focus. *Tourism Geographies, 3*(2), 125–134.

DeJean, J. (2014). *How Paris Became Paris: the Invention of Modern City*. New York City: Bloomsbury USA.

Delaney, S. (2009). Lazy lakeside frolicking: an insider's guide to Lake Como. *Guardian*.

DePaule, J. (1995). L'Anthropologies de l'Espace. In J. Castex (Ed.), *Histoire Urbaine, Anthropologie de l'Espace* (pp. 15–74). Paris: CNRS-Editions.

Desfor, G., & Jorgensen, J. (2004). Flexible urban governance: the case of Copenhagen's recent waterfront development. *European Planning Studies, 12*(4), 479–496.

Ding, C., & Gerrit, K. (2003). Urban land policy reform in China. *Land Lines, 15*(2), 1–3.

Dong, G. (2006). *A 50-Year Evolutionary Record of the Ancient City of Beijing*. Nanjing: Southeast University Press.

Dong, J. (1982). *Zhongguo chengshi jiansheshi* (History of Chinese urban construction). Beijing: Zhongguo Jianzhu Gongye Press.

Dong, J., & Li, D. (1999). Chengshi guihua zhuanye 45 nian de zuji (Development of urban planning in the past 45 years). In J. Dong (Ed.), *Chengshi guihua lishi yu lilun yanjiu* (Historical and theoretical research on urban planning). Shanghai: Tongji University Press.

Doorne, S. (1998). Power, participation and perception: an insider's perspective on the politics of the Wellington waterfront redevelopment. *Current Issues in Tourism, 1*(2), 129–166.

Dredge, D., & Jenkins, J. (2003). Destination place identity and regional tourism policy. *Tourism Geographies, 5*(4), 383–407.

Du, L. (2002). *History of the Old Town of Pingyao*. Beijing: Zhonghua Shuju Press.

Duffy, M. (2009). Festivals and spectacle. In R. Kitchin & N. Thrift (Eds.), *International Encyclopedia of Human Geography*. Oxford: Elsevier.

Dupont, V., Jordhus-Lier, D., Sutherland, C., & Braathen, E. (2016). *The Politics of Slums in the Global South*. New York: Routledge.

Dwyer, L., Forsyth, P., & Spurr, R. (2005). Estimating the impacts of special events on an economy. *Journal of Travel Research, 43*(4), 351–359.

Edensor, T. (2001). Performing tourism, staging tourism. *Tourist Studies, 1*(1), 59–81.

Edwards, D., & Griffin, T. (2013). Urban tourism research: developing an agenda. *Annals of Tourism Research, 35*(4), 1032–1052.

Edwards, D., Griffin, T., & Hayllar, B. (2008). Urban tourism research: developing an agenda. *Annals of Tourism Research, 35*(4), 1032–1052.

Eisenhut, K. (2008). *A critical evaluation of local government influence on waterfront development: a case study of Auckland and Melbourne* (Master thesis), University of Auckland.

Evans, G. (2002). Living in a world heritage city: stakeholders in the dialectic of universal and particular. *International Journal of Heritage Studies*, 8(2), 117–135.

Exline, C., Peters, G., & Larkin, R. (1982). *The City, Patterns and Processes in the Urban Ecosystem*. Boulder: Westview Press.

Fagence, M. (1995). City waterfront redevelopment for leisure, recreation and tourism: some common themes. In S. Craig-Smith & M. Fagence (Eds.), *Recreation and Tourism as A Catalyst for Urban Waterfront Redevelopment: An International Survey* (pp. 135–156). Westport, CT: Praeger.

Fainstein, S., Hoffman, L., & Judd, D. (2003). Making theoretical sense of tourism. In L. Hoffman, S. Fainstein & D. Judd (Eds.), *Cities and Visitors: Regulating People, Markets, and City Space* (pp. 239–253). Oxford: Blackwell.

Fainstein, S., & Judd, D. (1999). Cities as places to play. In D. Judd & S. Fainstein (Eds.), *The Tourist City* (pp. 261–272). New Haven: Yale University Press.

Faludi, A. (1973). *Planning Theory*. Oxford: Pergamon.

Fang, Y., & Yao, L. (2006). Study on the synthetic measurement of urbanization level in Shandong Province. *Urban Studies*, 13(4), 19–24.

Faulkner, B. (2002). Rejuvenation of maturing tourist destination: the case of the Gold Coast. *Current Issues in Tourism*, 5, 472–520.

Feliciotti, A., Romice, O., & Porta, S. (2017). Urban regeneration, masterplans and resilience: the case of Gorbals, Glasgow. *Urban Morphology*, 21(1), 53–58.

Fischler, R. (1995). Strategy and history in professional practices: planning as world making. In H. Liggett & D. Perry (Eds.), *Spatial Practices: Critical Explorations in Social/Spatial Theory* (pp. 13–58). London: Sage.

Florida, R. (2002). *The Rise of the Creative Class*. New York: Basic Books.

Florida, R. (2005). *Cities and the Creative Class*. New York: Routledge.

Foucault, M. (1977). *Discipline and Punish: The Birth of the Prison*. London: The Penguin Books.

Foucault, M. (1982). The subject and power. In H. Dreyfus & P. Rabinow (Eds.), *Michel Foucault: Beyond Structuralism and Hermeneutics*. Chicago, IL: Chicago University Press.

Foucault, M. (1986). Of other spaces. *Diacritics*, 16, 22–27.

Frampton, K. (1983). Toward a critical regionalism: six points for an architecture of resistance. In H. Foster (Ed.), *The Anti-Aesthetic: Essays on Postmodern Culture* (pp. 16–30). Seattle, WA: Bay Press.

Franklin, A. (2016). Journeys to the Guggenheim Museum Bilbao: towards a revised Bilbao effect. *Annals of Tourism Research*, 59, 79–92.

Franklin, A., & Crang, M. (2001). The trouble with tourism and travel theory? *Tourist Studies*, 1, 5–22.

Fritz, J. (1894). *Deutsche Stadtanlagen*. Strassburg: Heitz & Mündel.

Fuller, R., & Gaston, K. (2009). The scaling of green space coverage in European cities. *Biology Letters*, 5(3), 352–355.

Galland, D., & Hansen, C. (2012). The roles of planning in waterfront redevelopment: from plan-led and market-driven styles to hybrid planning? *Planning Practice & Research*, 27(2), 203–225.

Gant, R., Robinson, G., & Fazal, S. (2011). Land-use change in the edgelands: policies and pressures in London's rural-urban fringe. *Land Use Policy*, 28, 266–279.

Gauthier, P., & Gilliland, J. (2006). Mapping urban morphology: a classification scheme for interpreting contributions to the study of urban form. *Urban Morphology*, 10(1), 41–50.

Gaventa, J. (2003). *Power after Lukes: A Review of Literature.* Brighton: Institute of Development Studies.

Gehl, J. (2011). *Life between Buildings: Using Public Space.* Washington, DC: Island Press.

Geisler, W. (1918). *Danzig: ein Siedlungsgeographischer Versuch.* Danzig: Kafemann.

Getz, D. (1993). Planning for tourism business district. *Annals of Tourism Research*, 26(4), 772–791.

Getz, D. (2012). *Event Studies: Theory, Research and Policy for Planned Events.* London: Routledge.

Gianoncelli, M., & Della Torre, S. (1984). *Microanalisi di una Citta: Proprieta e Uso delle Case della Murata di Como dal Cinquecento all'Ottocento.* Como: New Press.

Giddens, A. (1984). *The Constitution of Society: Outline of the Theory of Structuration.* Berkeley, CA: University of California Press.

Gilbert, E. (1939). The growth of inland and seaside health resorts in England. *Scottish Geographical Magazine*, 55(1), 16–35.

Gilbert, E. (1949). The growth of Brighton. *The Geographical Journal*, 114(1/3), 30–52.

Gioacchini, P., Farina, P., Ravaglia, M., Verga, L., Butti, F., & Rovi, A. (2008). *Como nell' Antichita.* Como: Societa Archeologica Comense.

Gleick, J. (1987). *Chaos: Making a New Science.* New York: Viking.

Goldblatt, J. (2005). *Special Events: Event Leadership for a New World.* Hoboken, NJ: John Wiley & Sons.

Gosling, D., & Maitland, B. (1984). *Concepts of Urban Design.* London: St Martin's Press.

Gospodini, A. (2001). Urban design, urban space morphology, urban tourism: an emerging new paradigm concerning their relationship. *European Planning Studies*, 9(7), 925–934.

Gospodini, A. (2004). Urban morphology and place identity in European cities: built heritage and innovative design. *Journal of Urban Design*, 9(2), 225–248.

Gospodini, A. (2006). Portraying, classifying and understanding the emerging landscapes in the post-industrial city. *Cities*, 23(5), 311–330.

Gotham, K. (2002). Marketing Mardi Gras: commodification, spectacle and the political economy of tourism in New Orleans. *Urban Studies*, 39(10), 1735–1756.

Gotham, K. (2005). Tourism gentrification: the case of New Orleans' Vieux Carre (French Quarter). *Urban Studies*, 42(7), 1099–1121.

Graham, W. (2017). *Dream Cities: Seven Urban Ideas that Shape the World.* New York: HarperCollins.

Grainger, A. (1995). National land use morphology: patterns and possibilities. *Geography*, 80(3), 235–245.

Griffin, T., & Hayllar, B. (2006). Historic waterfronts as tourism precincts: an experiential perspective. *Tourism and Hospitality Research*, 7(1), 3–16.

Griffiths, S., Jones, C., Vaughan, L., & Haklay, M. (2010). The persistence of suburban centres in Greater London: Combining Conzenian and space syntax approaches. *Urban Morphology*, 14(2), 85–99.

Grosz, E. (2001). *Architecture from the Outside: Essay on the Virtual and Real Space.* London: MIT Press.

Grosz, E. (2008). *Chaos, Territory, Art: Deleuze and the Framing of the Earth*. London: Columbia University Press.

Group, G. (2006). Westin's first resort in the South Pacific Opens in Fiji: Sheration Royal Denarau Resort Transformed to the Westin Denarau Island Resort & Spa Following Extensive Rennovation. *Business Wire*, 1–2.

Group, W. L. (2001). *The Wellington Waterfront Framework*. Wellington: Wellington City Council.

Gu, H., & Ryan, C. (2012). Tourism destination evolution: a comparative study of Shi Cha Hai Beijing Hutong businesses' and residents' attitudes. *Journal of Sustainable Tourism*, 20(1), 23–40.

Gu, K. (2001). Urban morphology of China in the post-socialist age: toward a framework for analysis. *Urban Design International*, 6, 125–142.

Gu, K. (2010). Exploring the fringe-belt concept in Auckland: an urban morphological idea and planning practice. *New Zealand Geographer*, 66, 44–60.

Gu, K. (2014). Morphological processes, planning and market realities: Reshaping the urban waterfront in Auckland and Wellington. In P. Larkham & M. Conzen (Eds.), *Shapers of Urban Form: Exploration in Morphological Agency* (pp. 268–284). London: Routledge.

Gu, K. (2018). The teaching of urban design: a morphological approach. *Journal of Planning Education and Research*, 38(3), 1–10.

Gu, K., & Ryan, C. (2008). Place attachment, identity and community impacts of tourism: the case of a Beijing Hutong. *Tourism Management*, 29, 637–647.

Gu, K., Tian, Y., Whitehand, J., & Whitehand, S. (2008). Residential building types as an evolutionary process: the Guangzhou area, China. *Urban Morphology*, 12(2), 97–115.

Gunn, C. (1972). *Vacationscape: Designing Tourist Regions*. Austin: University of Texas.

Gunn, C. (1979). *Tourism Planning*. New York: Crane Russak.

Hadid, Z. (2016) *Zaha Hadid: Virtual Reality Experience*, Leicester Square 1990. Google, Google Arts & Culture.

Hall, C. M. (2004). Reflexivity and tourism research: situating myself and/with others. In J. Phillimore & L. Goodson (Eds.), *Quantitative Research in Tourism: Ontologies, Epistemologies and Methodologies* (pp. 137–155). London: Routledge.

Hall, C. M., & Selwood, J. (1995). Event tourism and the creation of a postindustrial portscape: the case of Fermantle and the 1987 America's Cup. In S. Craig-Smith & M. Fagence (Eds.), *Recreation and Tourism as A Catalyst for Urban Waterfront Redevelopment: An International Survey* (pp. 105–114). Westport, CT: Praeger.

Hall, M., & Page, S. (2014). *The Geography of Tourism and Recreation: Environment, Place and Space*. London: Routledge.

Hall, P. (2000). Creative cities and economic development. *Urban Studies*, 37(4), 639–649.

Hamm, E. (1932). Die Stadtegrundungen der Herzoge von Zahringen in Sudwestdeutschland: Freiburg, i.B.

Hannam, K., Butler, G., & Paris, C. (2014). Development and key issues in tourism mobilities. *Annals of Tourism Research*, 44(1), 171–185.

Hannigan, J. (1998). *Fantasy City: Pleasure and Profit in the Postmodern Metropolis*. New York: Routledge.

Hannigan, J. (2007). Casino cities. *Geography Compass*, 1(4), 959–975.

Hanson, J. (2000). Urban transformations: a history of design ideas. *Urban Design International*, 5(2), 97–122.

Hanson, J., & Hillier, B. (1987). The architecture of community: some new proposals on the social consequence of architectural and planning decisions. *Architecture and Behaviour*, 3(3), 251–273.

Harris, C., & Ullman, E. (1945). The nature of cities. *Annals of the American Academy of Political and Social Science*, 242, 7–17.

Harris, J., & Williams, R. (2011). Re: "Regenerate": the art and architecture of a mixed metaphor. In J. Harris & R. Williams (Eds.), *Regenerating Culture and Society: Architecture, Art and Urban Style within the Global Politics of City-Branding* (pp. 11–30). Liverpool: Liverpool University Press.

Harrison, D. (2017). Tourists, mobilities and paradigms. *Tourism Management*, 63, 329–337.

Harvey, D. (1978). The urban process under capitalism: a framework for analysis. *International Journal of Urban and Regional Research*, 2(1–3), 101–131.

Harvey, D. (1985). *The Urbanization of Capital: Studies in the History and Theory Capitalist Urbanization*. Baltimore, MD: The John Hopkins University Press.

Harvey, D. (1989). *The Condition of Postmodernity*. Oxford: Basil Blackwell.

Harvey, D. (2000). Landscape organization, identity and change: territoriality and hagiography in medieval west Cornwall. *Landscape Research*, 25, 201–212.

Hassinger, H. (1916a). *Kunsthistorischer Atlas und verzeichnis der erhaltenswerten historischen Kunst und Naturdenkmale des Wiener Ortsbildes*. Wien: Schroll.

Hassinger, H. (1916b). Kunsthistorischer Atlas von Wien Osterreichische Kunsttopographie 15. Vienna.

Hayllar, B., Griffin, T., & Edwards, D. (2008). *City Spaces-Tourist Places: Urban Tourism Precincts*. Oxford: Butterworth-Heinemann.

Herr, C. (1996). *Critical Regionlism and Cultural Studies*. Gainesville: University of Florida Press.

Hillier, B., Hanson, J., & Graham, H. (1987). Ideas are in things: An application of the space syntax method to discovering house genotypes. *Environment and Planning B*, 14(4), 363–385.

Hillier, B. (1996). *Space is the Machine: A Configurational Theory of Architecture*. Cambridge: Cambridge University Press.

Hillier, B. (2009). Explaining space syntax. In R. Cooper, G. Evans, & C. Boyko (Eds.), *Designing Sustainable Cities* (pp. 300–310). Oxford: Wiley-Blackwell.

Hillier, B. (2016). The fourth sustainability, creativity: statistical association and credible mechanisms. In J. Portugali & E. Stolk (Eds.), *Complexity, Cognition, Urban Planning and Design* (pp. 75–92). Cham: Springer.

Hillier, B., & Hanson, J. (1984). *The Social Logic of Space*. Cambridge: Cambridge University Press.

Hillier, B., Turner, A., Yang, T., & Park, H. (2007). *Metric and topo-geometric properties of urban street networks: some convergences, divergences and new results*. Paper presented at the the 6th International Space Syntax Symposium, Istanbul.

Hillier, B., Yang, T., & Turner, A. (2012). Normalising least angle choice in depthmap and how it opens up new perspectives on the global and local analysis of city space. *The Journal of Space Syntax*, 3(2), 155–193.

Hillier, J. (2001). Mind the gap. In J. Hillier & E. Booksby (Eds.), *Habitus: A Sense of Place*. Aldershot: Ashgate.

Hodge, G. (1998). *Planning Canadian Communities: An Introduction to the Principles, Practice and Participants*. Toronto, ON: ITP Nelson.

Hoffman, L., Fainstein, S., & Judd, D. (2003). *Cities and Visitors: Regulating People, Markets and City Space*. Oxford: Blackwell.

Hollinshead, K. (1999). Tourism as public culture: Horne's ideological commentary on the legerdemain of tourism. *International Journal of Tourism Research*, 1, 267–292.

Honey, M., & Krantz, M. (2007). Global Trends in Coastal Tourism. Retrieved from https://protect-us.mimecast.com/s/79e_ClYvpnu26Nrq6iYmRR9?domain=responsibletravel.org _Tourism_by_CESD_Jan_08_LR.pdf.

Hough, M. (1989). *City Form and Natural Process: Towards a New Urban Vernacular*. London: Routledge.

Hoyle, B., Pinder, D., & Husain, M. (1988). *Revitalizing the Waterfront: International Dimensions of Dockland Redevelopment*. London: Belhaven Press.

Hoyt, H. (1939). The pattern of movement of residential rental neighborhoods. In H. Mayer & C. Kohn (Eds.), *Readings in Urban Geography* (pp. 499–510). Chicago, IL: University of Chicago.

Huffadine, M. (2000). *Resort Design: Planning, Architecture and Interiors*. New York: McGraw-Hill Companies.

Hussain, M., & Ismail, H. (2015). Understanding the morphology in the form of business expansion: perspective of small tourism firm in coastal resort destination. *International Journal of Built Environment and Sustainability*, 2(4), 269–277.

Hutton, T. (2009). Trajectories of the new economy: regeneration and dislocation in the inner city. *Urban Studies*, 45(5/6), 987–1001.

Inskeep, E. (1988). Tourism planning: an emerging specialization. *Journal of the American Association*, 54(3), 360–372.

Jacob, D. (2012). The eventification of place: urban development and experience consumption in Berlin and New York City. *European Urban Regional Studies*, 20(4), 447–459.

Jacobs, A., & Appleyard, D. (1987). Toward an urban design manifesto. *APA Journal*, 53(1), 113–120.

Jacobs, J. (1961). *The Death and Life of Great American Cities*. New York: Random House.

Jakle, J. (1987). *The Visual Elements of Landscape*. Amherst, MA: University of Massachusetts Press.

Jansen-Verbeke, M., & Ashworth, G. (1990). Environmental integration of recreation and tourism. *Annals of Tourism Research*, 17(4), 618–622.

Jansen-Verbeke, M., & Lievois, E. (1999). Analysing heritage resources for urban tourism in European cities. In R. Butler & D. Pearce (Eds.), *Contemporary Issues in Tourism Development* (pp. 81–107). London: Routledge.

Jauhiainen, J. (1995). Waterfront redevelopment and urban policy: The case of Barcelona, Cardiff and Genoa. *European Planning Studies*, 3(1), 3–23.

Jayne, M. (2006). *Cities and Consumption*. New York: Routledge.

Jeans, D. (1990). Beach resort morpholoy in England and Australia: a review and extension. In P. Fabbri (Ed.), *Recreational Uses of Coastal Areas*. Dordrecht: Springer.

Jenkins, J., & Walmsley, D. (1993). Mental maps of tourists: a study of Coffs Harbour, New South Wales. *GeoJournal*, 29(3), 233–241.

Jiang, B., & Claramunt, C. (2002). Integration of space syntax into GIS: new perspectives for urban morpholgy. *Transactions in GIS*, 6(3), 295–309.

Jim, C. (2000). Environmental changes associated with mass urban tourism and nature tourism development in Hong Kong. *The Environmentalist*, 20, 233–247.

Jiven, G., & Larkham, P. (2003). Sense of place, authenticity and character: a commentary. *Journal of Urban Design*, 8, 67–81.

Jones, A. (2007). On the water's edge: developing cultural regeneration paradigms for urban waterfronts. In M. Smith (Ed.), *Tourism, Culture & Regeneration* (pp. 143–150). Wallingford: CABI.

Judd, D. (1993). Promoting tourism in US cities. *Tourism Management*, 16(3), 175–187.

Judd, D. (1999). Constructing the tourist bubble. In D. Judd & S. Fainstein (Eds.), *The Tourist City* (pp. 35–53). New Haven, CT: Yale University Press.

Judd, D. (2003). Visitors and spatial ecology of the city. In L. Hoffman, S. Fainstein, & D. Judd (Eds.), *Cities and Visitors* (pp. 23–39). Oxford: Blackwell.

Judd, D., & Fainstein, S. (1999). Cities as places to play. In D. Judd & S. Fainstein (Eds.), *The Tourist City* (pp. 261–272). New Haven, CT: Yale University Press.

Kadar, B. (2013). *A morphological approach in defining the causes of tourist-local conflicts in tourist-historic cities*. Paper presented at the International RC21 Conference, Berlin, Germany.

Kalivas, D., Kollias, V., & Karantounias, G. (2003). A GIS for the assessment of the spatio-temporal changes of the Kotychi Lagoon, Western Peloponnese, Greece. *Water Resources Management*, 17(1), 19–36.

Karimi, K. (2000). Urban conservation and spatial transformation: preserving the fragments or maintaining the "spatial spirit". *Urban Design International*, 5(3–4), 3–4.

Karimi, K. (2012). A configurational approach to analytical urban design: space syntax methodology. *Urban Design International*, 17(4), 297–318.

Kashef, M. (2008). Architects and planners approaches to urban form and design in the Toronto region: a comparative analysis. *Geoforum*, 39(1), 414–437.

Kay, R., & Alder, J. (2005). *Coastal Planning and Management*. London: Taylor & Francis.

Keeble, L. (1952). *Principles and Practice of Town and Country Planning*. London: Estates Gazette.

Kelsey, J. (1995). *The New Zealand Experiment: A World Model for Structural Adjustment*. Auckland: Auckland University Press.

Kipfer, S., & Keil, R. (2002). Planning Inc.? Planning the competitive city in the new Toronto. *Antipode*, 34(2), 227–264.

Kitolelei, J., & Sato, T. (2016). Analysis of perceptions and knowledge in managing coastal resources: a case study of Fiji. *Frontiers in Marine Science*, 28, 76–79.

Knapp, R. (2000). *China's Walled Cities*. Oxford: Oxford University Press.

Kneafsey, M. (2001). Rural cultural economy: tourism and social relations. *Annals of Tourism Research*, 28(3), 762–783.

Knox, P. (1991). The restless urban landscape: economic and sociocultural change and the transformation of Metropolitan Washington, DC. *Annals of the Association of American Geographers*, 81(2), 181–209.

Knox, P. (1992). Facing up to urban change. *Environment and Planning A*, 24, 1217–1220.

Knudsen, D., Soper, A., & Metro-Roland, M. (2008). Landscape, tourism, and meaning: an introduction. In D. Knudsen, M. Metro-Roland, A. Soper, & C. Greer (Eds.), *Landscape, Tourism, and Meaning*. Aldershot: Ashgate.

Kostof, S. (1991). *The City Shaped: Urban Patterns and Meanings through History*. London: Thames and Hudson.

Kotus, J., Rzeszewski, M., & Ewertowski, W. (2015). Tourists in the spatial structures of a big Polish city: development of an uncontrolled patchwork or concentric spheres? *Tourism Management*, 50, 98–110.

Krier, L., & Vidler, A. (1978). *Rational Architecture*. London: George Wittenborn Incorporated.

Krier, R. (1993). *Urban Space*. New York: Rizzoli.

Krolikowski, C., & Brown, G. (2008). The structure and form of urban tourism precincts: setting the stage for tourist performances. In B. Hayllar, T. Griffin, & D. Edwards (Eds.), *City Spaces—Tourist Places: Urban Tourism Precincts* (pp. 127–149). Oxford: Butterworth-Heinemann.

Kropf, K. (2009). Aspects of urban form. *Urban Morphology*, 13, 105–120.

Kropf, K. (2011). Morphological investigations: cutting into the substance of urban form. *Built Environment*, 37, 393–408.

Kropf, K. (2017). *The Handbook of Urban Morphology*. Chichester: Wiley.

Lafrenz, J. (1988). The metrological analysis of early modern planned towns. In D. Denecke & G. Shaw (Eds.), *Urban Historical Geography: Recent Progress in Britain and Germany* (pp. 273–284). Cambridge: Cambridge University Press.

Lamb, R. (1983). The extent and form of exurban sprawl. *Growth and Change*, 14(1), 40–47.

Landorf, C. (2009). Managing for sustainable tourism: a review of six cultural World Heritage Sites. *Journal of Sustainable Tourism*, 17(1), 53–70.

Landry, C. (2008). *The Creative City: A Toolkit for Urban Innovators*. London: Earthscan.

Lane, A. (1993). Urban morphology and urban design: a review. Occasional Paper 35, Department of Planning and Landscape. Manchester: University of Manchester.

Lane, B., Kastenholz, E., Lima, J., & Majewsjki, J. (2013). *Industrial Heritage and Agri/Rural Tourism in Europe*. Brussels: Europe Parliament.

Lane, M. (2006). *The governance of coastal resources in Fiji—an analysis of the strategic issues*. Retrieved from https://www.sprep.org/att/publication/000524_IWP_PTR20.pdf

Larkham, P. (1996). *Conservation and the City*. London: Routledge.

Larkham, P., & Conzen, M. (2014). *Shapers of Urban Form: Explorations in Morphological Agency*. London: Routledge.

Larner, W., & Craig, D. (2005). After neoliberalism? community activism and local partnerships in Aotearoa New Zealand. *Antipode*, 37(3), 402–424.

Lasansky, M., & McLaren, B. (2004). *Architecture and Tourism: Perception, Performance and Place*. New York: Berg Publishers.

Lavery, P. (1971). Resorts and recreation. In P. Lavery (Ed.), *Recreation Geography* (pp. 167–195). New York: Wiley.

Law, C. (1996). *Tourism in Major Cities*. London: International Thomson Business Press.

Le, J. (2005). *History of Chinese Architecture*. Beijing: Tuanjie Press.

Lee, M., & Rii, H. (2016). An application of the vicious circle schema to the World Heritage Site of Macau. *Journal of Heritage Tourism*, 11, 126–142.

Lee, Y., Lee, C., Choi, J., Yoon, S., & Hart, R. (2014). Tourism's role in urban regeneration: examining the impact of environmental cues on emotion, satisfaction, loyalty, and support for Seoul's revitalized Cheonggyecheon stream district. *Journal of Sustainable Tourism*, 22, 726–749.

Lefebvre, H. (1992). *The Production of Space* (D. Nicholson-Smith, Trans.). Oxford: Blackwell.

Levy, J. (2017). *Contemporary Urban Planning*. New York: Taylor & Francis.

Lew, A. (1987). A framework of tourist attraction research. *Annals of Tourism Research*, 14(4), 553–575.

Lew, A. (2007). Pedestrian shopping streets and urban tourism in the restructuring of the Chinese city. In A. Church & T. Coles (Eds.), *Tourism, Power and Space* (pp. 150–170). New York: Routledge.

Lew, A. (2017). Tourism planning and place making: place-making or placemaking? *Tourism Geographies*, 19(3), 448–466.

Lew, A., & McKercher, B. (2006). Modeling tourist movements: a local destination analysis. *Annals of Tourism Research*, 33(2), 403–423.

Lewis, N., Larner, W., & Le Heron, R. (2008). The New Zealand designer fashion industry: Making industries and co-constituting political projects. *Transactions for the Institute of British Geographers*, 33, 42–59.

Li, M., Fang, L., Huang, X., & Goh, C. (2015). A spatial-temporal analysis of hotels in urban tourism destination. *International Journal of Hospitality Management*, 45, 34–43.

Li, X., & Yeh, A. (2004). Analyzing spatial restructuring of land use patterns in a fast growing region using remote sensing and GIS. *Landscape and Urban Planning*, 69, 335–354.

Li, Y., Xiao, L., Ye, Y., Xu, W., & Law, A. (2016). Understanding tourist space at a historic site through space syntax analysis: the case of Gulangyu, China. *Tourism Management*, 52, 30–43.

Lilley, K., Lloyd, C., Trick, S., & Graham, C. (2005). Mapping and analysing medieval built form using GPS and GIS. *Urban Morphology*, 9(1), 5–15.

Liu, J. (2008). *Resort morphology: Chinese applications* (Ph.D.), University of Waterloo.

Liu, J., & Wall, G. (2009). Resort morphology research: history and future perspectives. *Asia Pacific Journal of Tourism Research*, 14(4), 339–350.

Liu, J., Zhan, J., & Deng, X. (2005). Spatial-temporal patterns and driving forces of urban land expansion in China during economic reform era. *Journal of Human Environment*, 34(6), 450–455.

Logan, J., & Molotch, H. (1987). *Urban Fortunes*. Berkeley: University of California Press.

Lohmann, G., & Duval, D. (2014). Destination morphology: a new framework to understand tourism-transport issues? *Journal of Destination Marketing and Management*, 3(3), 133–136.

Long, H., & Li, T. (2012). The coupling characteristics and mechanism of farmland and rural housing land transition in China. *Journal of Geographical Sciences*, 22(3), 548–562.

Louis, H. (1936). Die geographische Gliederung von Gross-Berlin. In H. Louis & W. Panzer (Eds.), *Landerkundliche Forschung: Festschrift zur Vollendung des sechzigsen Lebensjahres Nobert Krebs* (pp. 146–171). Stuttgart: J. Engelhorns Nachf.

Low, N. (1996). Urban planning, regulation theory and institutionalism: the planner's role in the global economy after Fordism. *Scandinavian Housing and Planning Research*, 13, 59–78.

Lowenthal, D., & Prince, H. (1972). English landscape tastes. In P. English & R. Mayfield (Eds.), *Man, Space and Environment*. Oxford: Oxford University Press.

Lu, D. (2006). *Remaking Chinese Urban Form*. New York: Routledge.

Lundgren, J. (1974). On access to recreational lands in dynamic metropolitan hinterlands. *Tourist Review*, 29, 124–131.

Luo, J., Qiu, H., & Lam, C. (2016). Urbanization impacts on regional tourism development: a case study in China. *Current Issues in Tourism*, 19(3), 282–295.

Lynch, K. (1960). *The Image of the City*. Cambridge, MA: The MIT Press.

Lynch, K. (1972). *What Time is This Place?* Cambridge, MA: The MIT Press.

Lynch, K. (1981). *A Theory of Good City Form*. Cambridge, MA: The MIT Press.

Macleod, D. (2004). *Tourism, Globalization and Cultural Change: An Island Community Perspective*. Clevedon: Channel View Publications.

Makowska-Iskierka, M. (2013). Spatial and morphological effects of tourism urbanisation in the Lodz metropolitan area. *Tourism*, 23(2), 33–42.

Malfroy, S. (1995). *Urban tissue and the idea of urban morphogenesis*. Paper presented at the Typological process and design theory, Cambridge, MA.

Malone, P. (1996). Introduction. In P. Malone (Ed.), *City, Capital and Water* (pp. 1–14). New York: Routledge.

Marcus, L., & Colding, J. (2011). *Towards a spatial morphology of urban social-ecological systems*. Paper presented at The 18th International Conference on Urban Form, ISUF 2011, Montreal, Quebec.

Marcus, L., Giusti, M., & Barthel, S. (2016). Cognitive affordances in sustainable urbanism: contributions of space syntax and spatial cognition. *Journal of Urban Design*, 21(4), 439–452.

Marques, L., & Borba, C. (2017). Co-creating the city: digital technology and creative tourism. *Tourism Management Perspectives*, 24, 86–93.

Martin, L., & March, L. (1972). *Urban Space and Structures*. Cambridge: Cambridge University Press.

Martinotti, G. (1996). Four population: human settlements and social morphology in contemporary metropolis. *European Review*, 4(1), 1–21.

Massey, D. (1993). Power geometry and a progressive sense of place. In J. Bird, B. Curtis, T. Putnam, G. Robertson, & L. Tickner (Eds.), *Mapping the Futures: Local Cultures, Global Change* (pp. 59–69). London: Routledge.

Mathieson, A., & Wall, G. (1982). *Tourism: Economic Physical and Social Impacts*. London: Longman.

Maxwell, R. (1976). An eye for an I: the failure of the townscape tradition. *Architecture Design*, 46(9), 534–536.

Mbaiwa, J. (2005). The problems and prospects of sustainable tourism development in the Okavango Delta, Botswana. *Journal of Sustainable Tourism*, 13(3), 203–227.

McClean, R. (1997). *Te Whanganui-A-Tara Foreshores Reclamations Report*. Retrieved from https://forms.justice.govt.nz/search/Documents/WT/wt_DOC_93486402/Wai%20215%2C%20B004.pdf

McGlynn, S., & Samuels, I. (2000). The funnel, the sieve and the template: towards an operational urban morphology. *Urban Morphology*, 4(2), 79–89.

McHarg, I. (1995). *Design with Nature.* New York: Wiley.

McKenzie, F. (1997). Growth management or encouragement? a critical review of land use policies affecting Australia's major exurban regions. *Urban Policy and Research*, 15(2), 83–101.

McKercher, B., & Lew, A. (2004). Tourist flows and the spatial distribution of tourists. In A. Lew, C. M. Hall, & A. Williams (Eds.), *A Companion to Tourism* (pp. 36–48). Malden, MA: Blackwell Publishing.

McKercher, B., Ho, P., & Du Cros, H. (2005). Relationship between tourism and cultural heritage management: evidence from Hong Kong. *Tourism Management*, 26(4), 539–548.

McLoughlin, J. (1969). *Urban and Regional Planning: A System Approach.* London: Faber.

McLoughlin, J. (1994). Core or periphery: town planning and spatial political economy. *Environment and Planning A*, 26, 1111–1122.

Meyer-Arendt, K. (1990). Recreational business districts in Gulf of Mexico seaside resorts. *Journal of Cultural Geography*, 11(1), 39–55.

Meyer-Arendt, K. (1993). Morphologic patterns of resort evolution along the Gulf of Mexico. *Geoscience and Man*, 32, 311–323.

Michelson, M. (1970). *Man and His Urban Environment: A Sociological Approach.* Reading, MA: Addison Wesley.

Michelson, M. (1975). *Behaviour Research Methods in Environmental Design.* Stroudsburg, PA: Dowden, Hutchinson & Ross.

Minca, C., & Oakes, T. (2006). *Travel in Paradox.* Lanham, MD: Rowman & Littlefield Publishers.

Minhat, H., & Amin, R. (2012). Socio-demographic determinants of leisure participation among elderly in Malaysia. *Journal of Community Health*, 30, 840–847.

Miossec, A. (1977). The physical consequences of touristic development on the coastal zone as exemplified by the Atlantic coast of France between Gironde and Finistere. *Ocean and Shoreline Management*, 11, 303–318.

Mitchell, C. (1998). Entrepreneurialism, commodification and creative destruction: a model of post-modern community development. *Journal of Rural Studies*, 14(3), 273–286.

Mitchell, C. (2013). Creative destruction or creative enhancement? Understanding the transformation of rural spaces. *Journal of Rural Studies*, 32, 375–387.

Montgomery, C. (2014). *Happy City: Transforming Our Lives.* New York: Farrar, Straus and Giroux.

Moudon, A. (1994). Getting to know the built landscape: typomorphology. In K. Franck & L. Schneekloth (Eds.), *Ordering Space: Types in Architecture and Design* (pp. 289–311). New York: Nostrand Reinhold.

Moudon, A. (1997). Urban morphology as an emerging interdisciplinary field. *Urban Morphology*, 1, 3–10.

Moughtin, C. (2003). *Urban Design: Street and Square.* London: Routledge.

Moulaert, F., Rodriguez, A., & Swyngedouw, E. (2005). *The Globalized City: Economic Restructuring and Social Polarization in European Cities.* Oxford: Oxford University Press.

Movono, A., Dahles, H., & Becken, S. (2017). Fijian culture and the environment: a focus on the ecological and social interconnectedness of tourism development. *Journal of Sustainable Tourism*, 26(3), 451–469.

Mugavin, D. (1999). A philosophical base for urban morphology. *Urban Morphology*, 3, 95–99.

Mullins, P. (1991). Tourism urbanization. *International Journal of Urban and Regional Research*, 15(3), 326–342.

Murayama, M., & Parker, G. (2007). Sustainable leisure and tourism space development in post-industrial cities: the case of Odaiba, Tokyo, Japan. In M. Smith (Ed.), *Tourism, Culture & Regeneration* (pp. 69–84). Cambridge, MA: CABI.

Murphy, L. (2008). Third-wave gentrification in New Zealand: The case of Auckland. *Urban Studies*, 45(12), 2521–2540.

Muti, G., & Salvucci, G. (2014, September 1–5, 2014). *Como lake and tourism imbalance: the limits to sustainable development*. Paper presented at the Fifteenth World Lake Conference, Perugia, Italy.

Nahm, K. (1999). Downtown office location dynamics and transformation of central Seoul, Korea. *GeoJournal*, 49(3), 289–299.

Nash, R. (1999). Bourdieu, 'Habitus' and educational research: is it all worth the candle? *British Journal of Sociology of Education*, 20(2), 175–187.

Nepal, S. (2009). Traditions and trends: a review of geographical scholarship in tourism. *Tourism Geographies*, 11(1), 2–22.

New Zealand Herald (2018). New Zealand Maritime Museum celebrates 25th anniversary. See https://www.nzherald.co.nz/nz/news/article.cfm?c_id=1&objectid=12111065 (accessed August 2018).

Newman, O. (1972). *Defensible Space: Crime Prevention through Urban Design*. New York: MacMillan.

Noizet, H. (2009). Fabrique urbaine: a new concept in urban history and morphology. *Journal of Urban Morphology*, 13(1), 55–76.

Nordstrom, K. (2000). *Beaches and Dunes of Developed Coasts*. Cambridge: Cambridge University Press.

Oldenburg, R. (1989). *The Great Good Place*. New York: Paragon House.

Oliveira, V. (2016). *Urban Morphology: An Introduction to the Study of Physical Form of Cities*. Basel: Springer.

Oliveira, V., Monteiro, C., & Partanen, J. (2015). A comparative study of urban form. *Urban Morphology*, 19(1), 73–92.

Oppermann, M. (1993). Tourism space in developing countries. *Annals of Tourism Research*, 20(3), 535–556.

Oppermann, M., Din, K., & Amri, S. (1996). Urban hotel location and evolution in a developing country: the case of Kuala Lumpur, Malaysia. *Tourism Recreation Research*, 21(1), 53–63.

Oram, R. (2007). *The Resource Management Act: Now and in the future*. Paper presented at the Beyong the RMA: An In-depth Exploration of the Resource Management Act 1991, Auckland, NZ.

Orbasli, A. (2000). *Tourism in Historic Towns: Urban Conservation and Heritage Management*. London: E & FN Spon.

Ouf, A. (2001). Authenticity and the sense of place in urban design. *Journal of Urban Design*, 6(1), 73–86.

Pacione, M. (2009). *Urban Geography: A Global Perspective*. New York: Routledge.

Page, S. (1996a). Wellington. *Cities*, 13, 125–134.

Page, S. (1996b). Wellington waterfront. In R. Le Heron & E. Pawson (Eds.), *Changing Places: New Zealand in the Nineties* (pp. 341–343). Auckland: Longman Paul Limited.

Page, S. (2002). Visitor safety in urban tourism environments: The case study of Auckland, New Zealand. *Cities*, 19(4), 273–282.

Page, S. (2011). *Tourism Management: An Introduction*. Oxford: Elsevier.

Papadakis, A. (1984). *Architectural Design Profile: Leon Krier.* London: London Architectural Design AD Editions.

Parkinson, A., Scott, M., & Redmond, D. (2017). Revalorizing colonial era architecture and townscape legacies: memory, identity and place-making in Irish towns. *Journal of Urban Design*, 22, 502–519.

Pasquinelli, C., & Bellini, N. (2017). Global context, policies and practices in urban tourism: an introduction. In N. Bellini & C. Pasquinelli (Eds.), *Tourism in the City* (pp. 1–28). Cham: Springer.

Pearce, D. (1978). Form and function in French resorts. *Annals of Tourism Research*, 5(1), 142–156.

Pearce, D. (1979). Towards a geography of tourism. *Annals of Tourism Research*, 6(3), 245–272.

Pearce, D. (1998). Tourist districts in Paris: structure and functions. *Tourism Management*, 19(1), 49–65.

Peel, D., Lloyd, G., & Lord, A. (2009). Business improvement districts and the discourse of contractualism. *European Planning Studies*, 17(3), 401–422.

Penn, A. (2009). The generation of diversity. In R. Cooper, G. Evans, & C. Boyko (Eds.), *Designing Sustainable Cities* (pp. 218–237). Chichester: Blackwell.

Pickett, S., Cadenasso, M., & McGrath, B. (2013). *Resilience in Ecology and Urban Design.* New York: Springer.

Pigram, J. (1977). Beach resort morphology. *Habitat International*, 2(5/6), 525–541.

Pinho, P., & Oliveira, V. (2009). Cartographic analysis in urban morphology. *Environment and Planning B*, 36(1), 107–127.

Planning, D. o. T. a. C. (2007). *Planning and developing in Fiji.* Retrieved from https://protect-us.mimecast.com/s/hrk8CjRvnlfnZQr1ZH7PqAZ?domain=townplanning.gov.fj.

Polyak, L. (2015). Recycling the industrial between West and East: heritage and the politics of urban memory in New York and Budapest. In O. Heike & A. Harald (Eds.), *Industrial Heritage Sites in Transformation* (pp. 167–184). New York: Taylor and Francis Group.

Powell, D. (2007). *Critical Regionalism.* Chapel Hill: The University of North Carolina Press.

Preteceille, E. (1976). Urban planning: the contradiction of capitalist urbanisation. *Antipode*, 8, 69–76.

Prideaux, B. (2000). The resort development spectrum: a new approach to modeling resort development. *Tourism Management*, 21, 225–240.

Prideaux, B. (2009). *Resort Destinations: Evolution, Management and Development.* Oxford: Elsevier.

Prideaux, B., & Singer, P. (2005). Space tourism - a future dream or a cyber-tourism reality. *Journal of Tourism Recreation Research*, 30(3), 27–35.

Proshansky, H., & Altman, I. (1979). Overview of the field. In W. White (Ed.), *Resources in Environment and Behavior* (pp. 3–36). Washington, DC: American Psychological Association.

Psarra, S. (2012). Spatial morphology, urban history and design in Julienne Hanson's 'Urban transformations: a history of design ideas'. *Journal of Space Syntax*, 3(1), 7–19.

Rabbiosi, C. (2015). Renewing a historical legacy: tourism, leisure shopping and urban branding in Paris. *Cities*, 42, 195–203.

Rabbiosi, C., & Giovanardi, M. (2017). Rediscovering the "urban" in two Italian tourist coastal cities. In N. Bellini & C. Pasquinelli (Eds.), *Tourism in the City* (pp. 247–258). Cham: Springer.

Rapoport, A. (2008). Theme issue: environmental design research: the field of study and guide to the literature. *Journal of Architectural and Planning Research*, 25(4), 276–281.

Rifkin, J. (2011). *The Third Industrial Revolution: How Lateral Power Is Transforming Energy, the Economy and the World*. New York: Palgrave MacMillan.

Ringer, G. (1998). *Destinations: Cultural Landscapes of Tourism*. New York: Routledge.

Ritchie, J., & Crouch, G. (2003). *The Competitive Destination: A Sustainable Tourism Perspective*. Oxon: CABI.

Roberts, P., Roberts, P., & Sykes, H. (2000). *Urban Regeneration: A Handbook*. London: Sage Publications.

Robinson, P., Luck, M., & Smith, S. (2013). *Tourism*. Cambridge, MA: CABI.

Rossi, A. (1975). Tipologia, manualistica, architetture. In R. Bonicalzi (Ed.), *Scritti Scelti sull'Architettura e la Citta 1956–1972* (pp. 13–52). Milan: CLUP.

Rossi, A. (1984). *The Architecture of the City*. Cambridge, MA: The MIT Press.

Rothman, H. (1998). *Devil's Bargains: Tourism in the Twentieth-Century American West*. Kansas City, MO: University Press of Kansas

Rowe, C., & Koetter, F. (1978). *Collage City*. Cambridge, MA: The MIT Press.

Roweis, S. (1981). Urban planning in early and late Capitalist societies: outline of a theoretical perspective. In M. Dear & A. Scoot (Eds.), *Urbanisation and Urban Planning in Capitalist Society* (pp. 159–177). London: Methuen.

Roweis, S. (1983). Urban planning as a professional mediation of territorial politics. *Environment and Planning D*, 1, 139–162.

Royal Commission on Auckland Governance (2009). Report of the Royal Commission Auckland. Royal Commission on Auckland Governance.

Ruan, Y. (2003). *Documenting Urban Conservation*. Beijing: Zhongguo Jianzhu Gongye Press.

Russo, A. (2002). The "vicious circle" of tourism development in heritage cities. *Annals of Tourism Research*, 29(1), 165–182.

Sailer, K., & Penn, A. (2009). *Spatiality and transpatiality in workplace environments*. Paper presented at the The 7th International Space Syntax Symposium, Stockholm, Sweden.

Sairinen, R., & Kumpulainen, S. (2006). Assessing social impacts in urban waterfront regeneration. *Environmental Impact Assessment Review*, 26, 120–135.

Samuel, R. (1994). *Theatres of Memories*. London: Verso.

Samuels, I. (1990). Architectural practice and urban morphology. In T. Slater (Ed.), *The Built Form of Western Cities: Essays for M.R.G. Conzen on the Occasion of His Eightieth Birthday* (pp. 415–435). Leicester: Leicester University Press.

Sarri, S. (2016). *Palimpsest Industry: Industrial Heritage and Intangible Cultural Heritage in the Creative City* (Master of Science Built Environment), University College London, London.

Sarrion-Gavilan, M., Benitez-Marquez, M., & Mora-Rangel, E. (2015). Spatial distribution of tourism supply in Andalusia. *Tourism Management Perspectives*, 15, 29–45.

Sauer, C. (1925). *The Morphology of Landscape*. Berkeley: University of California Press.

Scheidel, W. (2009). *Rome and China: Comparative Perspectives on Ancient World Empires*. New York: Oxford University Press.

Schluter, O. (1899). Bemerkungen zur Siedlungsgeographie. *Geographische Zeitschrift*, 5, 65–84.

Schurch, T. (1999). Reconsidering urban design: thoughts about its definition and status as a field or profession. *Journal of Urban Design*, 4(1), 5–28.

Searle, G., & Byrne, J. (2002). Selective memories, sanitized futures: constructing vision of future place in Sydney. *Urban Policy and Research*, 20(1), 7–25.

Settis, S. (2016). *If Venice Dies*. Venice: New Vessel Press.

Sheller, M., & Urry, J. (2006). The new mobilities paradigm. *Environment and Planning A*, 38, 207–226.

Sheng, N., Tang, U., & Grydehoj, A. (2017). Urban morphology and urban fragmentation in Macau, China: island city development in the Pearl River Delta megacity region. *Island Studies Journal*, 12(1), 3–16.

Siedler, E. (1914). *Markischer Stadtebau im Mittelalter*. Berlin: Julius Springer.

Simmons, D. (1994). Community participation in tourism planning. *Tourism Management*, 15(2), 98–108.

Slater, T. (1990). English Medieval new towns with composite plans: evidence from the Midlands. In T. Slater (Ed.), *The Built Form of Western Cities: Essays for M.R.G. Conzen on the Occasion of his Eightieth Birthday* (pp. 60–82). Leicester: Leicester University Press.

Smith, M. (2002). A critical evaluation of the global accolade: the significance of world heritage site status for Maritime Greenwich. *International Journal of Heritage Studies*, 8(2), 137–151.

Smith, M. (2009). *Issues in Cultural Tourism Studies*. London: Routledge.

Smith, N. (2002). New globalism, new urbanism: gentrification as global urban strategy. In N. Brenner & N. Theodore (Eds.), *Spaces of Neoliberalism: Urban Restructuring in North America and Western Europe* (pp. 80–103). Oxford: Blackwell.

Smith, R. (1991). Beach resorts: a model of development evolution. *Landscape and Urban Planning*, 21, 189–210.

Smith, R. (1992a). Beach resort evolution: implications for planning. *Annals of Tourism Research*, 19(2), 304–322.

Smith, R. (1992b). Review of integrated beach resort development in Southeast Asia. *Land Use Policy*, 9, 209–217.

Smith, S. (1983). Restaurants and dining out: geography of a tourism business. *Annals of Tourism Research*, 10(4), 515–549.

Smith, S. (1987). Regional analysis of tourism resources. *Annals of Tourism Research*, 14, 254–272.

Soja, E. (1980). The socio-spatial dialectic. *Annals of the Association of American Geographers*, 70(2), 207–225.

Song, K. (2000). *Pingyao Gucheng Yu Mingu (The Ancient City and Local Style Houses in Pingyao)*. Tianjin: Tianjin Press.

Sorkin, M. (1992). *Variations on a Theme Park: the New American City and the End of Public Space*. New York: Hill & Wang.

Southworth, M. (1990). *City Sense and City Design: Writings and Projects of Kevin Lynch*. Cambridge, MA: The MIT Press.

Spector, J. (2010). *From Dockyard to Esplanade: Leveraging Industrial Heritage in Waterfront Regeneration* (Masters thesis), University of Pennsylvania.

Spirou, C. (2011). *Urban Tourism and Urban Change: Cities in a Global Economy*. New York: Routledge.

Stanilov, K. (2010). Briding the gap between urban morphology and urban modelling. *Journal of Urban Morphology*, 14(2), 67–77.

Stansfield, C. (1969). Recreational land use patterns within an American seaside resort. *Tourist Review*, 24, 128–136.

Stansfield, C. (1972). The development of modern seaside resorts. *Parks and Recreation*, 5(10), 14–46.

Stansfield, C., & Rickert, J. (1970). The recreational business district. *Journal of Leisure Research*, 2(4), 213–225.

Statistics, F. I. B. o. (2011). *Tourism and Migration: Key Statistics March 2011*. Retrieved from https://protect-us.mimecast.com/s/FBFzCgJxkgiA4Z354I2eJ1b?domain=statsfiji.gov.fj.

Steadman, P. (1983). *Architectural Map: An Introduction to the Geometry of Building Plans*. London: Pion.

Stratton, M. (2000). Reviving industrial building. In M. Stratton (Ed.), *Industrial Buildings: Conservation and Regeneration* (pp. 8–29). New York: E & FN Spon.

Studer, R. (1966). On environmental programming. *Architectural Associate Journal*, 81, 290–296.

Sudradjat, I. (2012). Foucault, the other spaces, and human behavior. *Procedia-Social and Behavioral Science*, 36, 28–34.

Syamwil, I. (2012). Social construction view in environment behaviour studies: the potential for Asian context in environment behaviour knowledge in architecture and urban design. *Procedia- Social and Behavioral Science*, 42, 27–33.

Tabua Investments Limited (2010). *History-Denarau Island Resort*. Retrieved August 23, 2008 https://protect-us.mimecast.com/s/cYksCkRwomfOozE3oFJepjV?domain=denarau.com.

Tang, W. (2000). Chinese urban planning at fifty: an assessment of the planning theory literature. *Journal of Planning Literature*, 14(3), 347–366.

Taylor, L., & Hochuli, D. (2017). Defining greenspace: multiple uses across multiple disciplines. *Landscape and Urban Planning*, 158, 25–38.

Teller, J., Lee, J., & Roussey, C. (2007). *Ontologies for Urban Development*. London: Springer.

Tewdwr-Jones, M., & Allmendinger, P. (1998). Deconstructing communicative rationality: a critical of Habermasian collaborative planning. *Environment and Planning A*, 30(11), 1975–1989.

Thomas, R. (2006). Mapping the towns: English heritage's urban survey and characterisation programme. *Landcapes*, 7(1), 68–92.

Thompson, E., Horne, M., & Fleming, D. (2006, August 3–4, 2006). *Virtual reality urban modelling—An overview*. Paper presented at the CONVR2006: the 6th conference of construction applications of virtual reality, Florida, USA.

Thrift, N. (2003). Space: the fundamental stuff of human geography. In S. Hollaway, S. Rice, & G. Valentine (Eds.), *Key Concept in Geography* (pp. 95–107). London: Sage.

Throgmorton, J. (1992). Planning as a persuasive storytelling of the future: the case of electric power rate settlement in Illinois. *Journal of Planning Education and Research*, 10, 17–31.

Tiesdell, S., Oc, T., & Heath, T. (1996). *Revitalizing Historic Urban Quarters*. New York: Hartnolls

Timms, B. (2008). The parallax of landscape: situating Celaque National Park, Honduras. In D. Knudsen, M. Metro-Roland, A. Soper, & C. Greer (Eds.), *Landcape, Tourism, and Meaning* (pp. 95–106). Aldershot: Ashgate.

Timothy, D., & Boyd, S. (2014). *Tourism and Trails: Cultural, Ecological and Management Issues*. Bristol: Channel View Publications.

Trancik, R. (1986). *Finding Lost Space: Theories of Urban Design*. New York: John Wiley & Sons.

Tremblay, P. (2005). GIS techniques in tourism and recreation planning: application to wildlife tourism. In B. Richie, P. Burns, & C. Palmer (Eds.), *Tourism Research Methods: Integrating Theory with Practice* (pp. 163–178). Oxfordshire: CABI Publishing.

Trigueiro, E. (2005). *Reaching Your Destination: Safe and Easy Movement in Stockwell*. London: Space Syntax Ltd.

Troughton, M. (1981). The rural-urban fringe: a challenge to resource management. In K. Beesley & L. Russwurm (Eds.), *The Rural-Urban Fringe: Canadian Perspectives* (pp. 218–243). Toronto, ON: York University Geographical Monographs.

Tuan, Y. (1977). *Space and Place*. London: Edward Arnold.

Tzonis, A., & Lefaivre, L. (1990). Why critical regionalism today. *A & U Architecture and Urbanism*, 234, 19–33.

Uniquest Party Limited (2010). RETA 6471: Strengthening Coastal and Marine Resource Management in the Coral Triangle of the Pacific -Phase 1. Retrieved from https://www.devex.com/organizations/uniquest-22266

Urry, J. (2007). *Mobilities*. Cambridge: Polity Press.

Urry, J., & Larsen, J. (2011). *The Tourist Gaze 3.0*. London: Sage.

Vale, L. (1992). *Architecture, Power and National Identity*. London: Routledge.

Vallega, A. (2001). Urban waterfront facing integrated coastal management. *Ocean and Coastal Management*, 44(5/6), 379–410.

Valls, J., Rucabado, J., Sarda, R., & Parera, A. (2017). The beach as a strategic element of governance for Spanish coastal towns. *Journal of Sustainable Tourism*, 25(9), 1338–1352.

Vance, J. (1990). *The Continuing City: Urban Morphology in Western Civilization*. Baltimore, MD: John Hopkins University Press.

Vanolo, A. (2008). The image of the creative city: some reflections on urban branding in Turin. *Cities*, 25(6), 370–382.

Varoudis, T. (2012). *DepthmapX Multi-platform Spatial Network Analysis Software*. Retrieved from https://protect-us.mimecast.com/s/Eg6_C0R296fGYwx0YIDxMDY?domain=varoudis.github.io.

Vedenin, U. (1982). *Changes of Territorial Recreational System*. Moscow: Science Press.

Veldpaus, L., Roders, A., & Colendrander, J. (2013). Urban heritage: putting the past into the future. *The Historic Environment: Policy & Practice*, 4(1), 3–18.

Visitdenarau. (2009). *Buying and selling real estate on Denarau Island*. Retrieved May 20, 2009 https://protect-us.mimecast.com/s/SLVlC9rp25HkrE0VrIolpP7?domain=visitdenarau.com.

Waldheim, C. (2016). *Landscape as Urbanism*. Princeton, NJ: Princeton University Press.

Wall, G. (1997). Tourism Attractions: Points, lines and areas. *Annals of Tourism Research*, 24(1), 240–243.

Wall, G., & Mathieson, A. (2006). *Tourism: Change, Impacts and Opportunities*. New York: Pearson.

Wall, G., & Sinnott, J. (1980). Urban recreational and cultural facilities as tourist attractions. *The Canadian Geographer*, 24(1), 50–59.

Wall, G., Dudycha, D., & Hutchinson, J. (1985). Point pattern analyses of accommodation in Toronto. *Annals of Tourism Research*, 12(4), 603–618.

Wallace, A. (1956). Revitalisation movements. *American Anthropologist*, 58, 265–272.

Walter, E. (1988). *Placeways: A Theory of the Human Environment*. Chapel Hill: University of North Carolina Press.

Wang, J., Ruan, Y., & Wang, L. (1999). *The Theories of Historical Urban Preservation*. Shanghai: Tongji University Press.

Wang, S. (2008). A mirror with two sides: heritage development and urban conservation in the ancient city of Pingyao, China. *Historic Environment*, 21(3), 22–26.

Wang, S. (2010). *In search of authenticity in historic cities in transformation: the case of Pingyao, China*. Paper presented at the Asia Research Institute Working Paper Series (#133), Singapore.

Weaver, D. (1993). Model of urban tourism for small Caribbean islands. *Geographical Review*, 83(2), 134–140.

Weaver, D., & Lawton, L. (2001). Resident perceptions in the urban-rural fringe. *Annals of Tourism Research*, 28(2), 439–458.

Webb, J., Schirato, T., & Danaher, G. (2002). *Understanding Bourdieu*. London: Sage.

Wei, Y., & Zhang, Z. (2012). Assessing the fragmentation of construction land in urban areas: an index method and case study in Shunde, China. *Land Use Policy*, 29(2), 417–428.

Wellington City Council. (2005). *Old Shoreline Heritage Trail* (2nd ed.). Wellington: Wellington City Council.

Whitehand, J. (1977). The basis for an historico-geographical theory of urban form. *Transactions of the Institute of British Geographers*, 2(3), 400–416.

Whitehand, J. (1981). Background to the urban morphogenetic tradition. In J. Whitehand (Ed.), *The Urban Landscape: Historical Development and Management* (pp. 1–24). London: 13 Academic Press.

Whitehand, J. (1987). *The Changing Face of Cities: A Study of Development Cycles and Urban Growth*. Oxford: Blackwell.

Whitehand, J. (1988). Urban fringe belts: development of an idea. *Planning Perspectives*, 3, 47–58.

Whitehand, J. (1992). Recent advances in urban morphology. *Urban Studies*, 29(3&4), 619–636.

Whitehand, J. (2007). *Conzenian urban morphology and urban landscapes*. Paper presented at the 6th International Space Syntax Symposium, Istanbul, Turkey.

Whitehand, J. (2014a). The changing face of urban morphology: achievements and challenges. *Urban Morphology*, 18(2), 95–96.

Whitehand, J. (2014b). *Conzenian research and urban landscape management*. Paper presented at the ISUF conference keynote presentation, Porto, Portugal.

Whitehand, J. (2015). Conservation, heritage and urban morphology. *Urban Morphology*, 19, 115–116.

Whitehand, J., & Gu, K. (2003). Chinese urban form: a European perspective. In A. Petruccioli, M. Stella, & G. Strappa (Eds.), *The Planned City* (pp. 731–736). Bari: Uniongrafica Corcelli Editrice.

Whitehand, J., & Gu, K. (2006). Research on Chinese urban form: retrospect and prospect. *Progress in Human Geography*, 30(3), 337–355.

Whitehand, J., & Gu, K. (2007). Extending the compass of plan analysis: a Chinese exploration. *Urban Morphology*, 11, 91–109.

Whitehand, J., & Larkham, P. (1992). *Urban Landscapes: International Perspectives*. London: Routledge.

Whitehand, J., & Whitehand, S. (1984). The physical fabric of town centres: the agents of change. *Transactions for the Institute of British Geographers*, 9(2), 231–247.

Whitehand, J., Conzen, M., & Gu, K. (2016). Plan analysis of historical cities: a Sino-European comparison. *Urban Morphology*, 20(2), 139–158.

Whitehand, J., Gu, K., & Whitehand, S. (2011). Fringe belts and socioeconomic change in China. *Environment and Planning B*, 38(1), 41–60.

Williams, A., & Shaw, G. (1998). Tourism and the environment: sustainability and economic restructuring. In C. M. Hall & A. Lew (Eds.), *Sustainable Tourism Development: Geographical Perspectives* (pp. 49–59). Harlow: Addison Wesley Longman.

Willis, S. (1994). Memory and mass culture. In G. Fabre & R. O'Meally (Eds.), *History and Memory in African-American Culture* (pp. 178–188). New York: Oxford University Press.

Wolfe, R. (1952). Wasaga beach: the divorce from the geographic environment. *Canadian Geographer*, 2, 57–66.

Wolfe, R. (1982). Recreational travel: the new migration, revisited. *Ontario Geography*, 19, 103–122.

Wong, P. (1998). Coastal tourism development in Southeast Asia: relevance and lessons for coastal management. *Ocean and Shoreline Management*, 38(2), 89–109.

Wood, R., & Handley, J. (1999). Urban waterfront regeneration in the Mersey Basin, North West England. *Journal of Environmental Planning and Management*, 42(4), 565–580.

Worskett, R. (1969). *The Character of Towns*. London: Architectural Press.

Wu, B., & Cai, L. (2006). Spatial modeling: suburban leisure in Shanghai. *Annals of Tourism Research*, 33(1), 179–198.

Wu, D., & Wang, S. (1883). *Guangxu Pingyao Xian Zhi (Gazetteer of Pingyao)*. Henan: Tianzhen Bi.

Wu, F. (1998). The new structure of building provision and the transformation of the urban landscape in Metropolitan Guangzhou, China. *Urban Studies*, 35(2), 259–283.

Wu, F. (2015). *Planning for Growth: Urban and Reginal Planning in China*. New York: Routledge.

Wu, L. (1986). *A Brief History of Ancient Chinese City Planning*. Kassel: Gesamthochschulbibliothek.

Xi, J., Wang, X., Kong, Q., & Zhang, N. (2015). Spatial morphology evolution of rural settlements induced by tourism: a comparative study of three villages in Yesanpo tourism area, China. *Journal of Geographical Sciences*, 25(4), 497–511.

Xiao, J., Shen, Y., Ge, J., Tateishi, R., Tang, C., Liang, Y., & Huang, Z. (2006). Evaluating urban expansion and land use change in Shijiazhuang, China by using GIS and remote sensing. *Landscape and Urban Planning*, 75(1–2), 69–80.

Xie, F., & Gu, K. (2011). Urban morphology and tourism planning: exploring the city wall in Pingyao, China. *Journal of China Tourism Research*, 7, 229–242.

Xie, J., & Heath, T. (2017). Conservation and revitalization of historic streets in China: Pingjiang Street, Suzhou. *Journal of Urban Design*, 22, 455–476.

Xie, P. (2003). Managing aboriginal tourism in Hainan, China. *Annals of Leisure Research*, 3, 279–302.

Xie, P., & Sohoni, A. (2010). The search for vernacular identity: Maratha temples in Maharashtra, India. *Journal of Heritage Tourism*, 5(3), 175–188.

Xie, Y., & Costa, F. (1991). Urban design practice in socialist China. *Third World Planning Review*, 13, 277–296.

Xiong, W. (2003). *Pingyao: the Living Ancient City* (Master thesis), Texas Tech University.

Xu, Y. (2000). *The Chinese City in Space and Time: The Development of Urban Form in Suzhou*. Honululu: University of Hawaii Press.

Yan, X. (1995). Chinese urban geography since the late 1970s. *Urban Geography*, 16(6), 469–492.

Yang, K. (2003). *Zhongguo gudai ducheng zhidushi yanjiu (An institutional history of ancient Chinese cities)*. Shanghai: Renmin Press.

Yang, Z., Hao, P., & Cai, J. (2015). Economic clusters: a bridge between economic and spatial policies in the case of Beijing. *Cities*, 42, 171–185.

Ye, Y., & Van Nes, A. (2014). Quantitative tools in urban morphology: combining space syntax, spacematrix and mixed-use index in a GIS framework. *Urban Morphology*, 18(2), 97–118.

Yigitcanlar, T., & Dizdaroglu, D. (2015). Ecological approaches in planning for sustainable cities: a review of the literature. *Global Journal of Environmental Science Management*, 1(2), 159–188.

Zhang, H., Chong, K., & Ap, J. (1999). An analysis of tourism policy development in modern China. *Tourism Management*, 20, 471–485.

Zhang, H., Luo, J., Xiao, Q., & Guillet, B. (2013). The impact of urbanization on hotel development: evidence from Guangdong Province in China. *International Journal of Hospitality Management*, 34, 92–98.

Zhang, Y. (2008). Steering towards growth: symbolic preservation in Beijing, 1990–2005. *Town Planning Review*, 79, 187–208.

Zhangh, Y., & Song, K. (1996). Shanxi De Bao Yu Lifang Zhidu Tanxi (Analysis of Bao in Shanxi and An Exploration of Lifang Regulation). *Jianzhu Xuebao (Architectural Journal)*, 4, 50–54.

Zukin, S. (2012). The social production of urban cultural heritage: identity and ecosystem on an Amsterdam shopping street. *City, Culture and Society*, 3(4), 281–291.

Index

Accessibility 24, 53, 56, 135
Actor-network theory 3
Aestheticization 115, 136
Adaptation 30, 34–35, 60, 64, 74, 122, 131, 140
Agents 6, 11, 60
Agents of change 40, 117, 130, 138, 156, 164
Agriculture 96, 112
Airbnb 141
Alleys 98, 147
Alnwick 21, 23
Alteration 79, 140, 143
Amenity 9, 43, 80, 129
America's Cup 118, 125, 132–134
Amusement 140, 153
Anchor spots 109, 154
Architects 4, 13, 19, 26, 28, 31, 38, 40, 45, 106, 160, 170
Architecture i, 1–2, 5, 10–11, 18, 28, 30, 32–34, 44, 47–48, 72, 93, 110, 132, 143, 148; city 48; geometry 35; landscape xi, 36, 58; vernacular 67, 105, 107
Architectural: approaches 19, 29–31, 163, 170; aesthetic 126; element 93, 105; heritage 14, 91–92, 94, 109, 111, 113, 116, 153, 155, 162; morphology 7, 10, 164, 170; pollution 82; school 37, 159; style 20, 61, 90, 152
Areas 11, 13–15, 19, 23–24, 34, 46, 49, 54, 62–63, 68, 150, 152–155, 160, 162, 164; built-up 24, 42; character 127, 165; coastal 70–71, 81; courtyard 102, 148; residential 7–8, 61, 72, 74, 76, 80, 85, 145, 156, 169; urban xi, 9, 19–20, 25, 35–36, 84, 92, 96, 117, 157, 159, 170; waterfront 119–122, 130–132

Auckland 119–124, 125–138
Augé, M. 45–46
Authenticity 14, 45, 50, 92, 93, 105, 111–113, 119

Beach Resort Model (BRM) 13, 70, 74–75, 77, 84, 86, 88, 162
Berkeley School 20, 25, 37
Berlin 11, 21, 141
Birmingham xiii
Blocks 2, 17, 21, 34, 50, 60, 64, 90, 98, 102–103, 110, 143, 146, 148
Breakthrough streets 143, 147, 150
Bridges 2, 43, 76, 135, 154
Buildings 71–72, 76–77, 82, 86, 90–94, 102–110, 113, 125–131, 139–143, 145–156, 162, 168–170
Built environment 3, 5, 7, 11–12, 18, 25–26, 28–30, 40–41, 48, 51–52, 89, 94, 112, 120, 129, 137, 155, 165; fabric 1, 43, 51
Burgage cycle 23, 60, 148

Canals 55, 63, 77, 81
Caniggia, G. 4, 29–30, 37, 90, 143, 147, 156, 165, 170
Caniggian School 90, 156, 165
Capital: accumulation 26, 158; circuits 25; environmental 167; mobility 116; social 62
Capitalism 25, 44, 168
Cartography 36, 161
Central Business District (CBD) 8, 51, 71, 73, 82, 92, 110, 112, 119–121, 148, 164
Central place theory 4, 25, 160
Chaos theory 2, 27–28
Character 44–45, 47, 49–51, 62, 68, 85, 92, 102, 112, 117, 119

Characteristics 3, 8–11, 15, 18–24, 28, 30–31, 33–34, 36, 38, 48, 54, 57, 61, 64–67, 70–73, 76–87, 90, 93, 99–100, 124–125, 127, 129–134, 140–142, 146, 149–150, 152–159, 170
Cheonggyecheon stream 58–59
Chicago School 3, 8
China xii, 8–9, 14, 35, 55, 58, 61–62, 91, 109, 113, 161–163, 167
Cittaslow 158
City Beautiful 2; image 18, 49; sails 122; square 11, 147; wall 14, 92, 94–96, 98, 100, 104, 104–106, 112–114, 144, 148–149, 163
Civilization 17, 20
Closeness 62, 143
Coastal tourism i, xii, 12–14, 69–70, 73, 84, 87–88, 162
Coastal Zone Management 89
Commercialization 2, 40, 42, 67, 93, 110
Commodification 6, 54, 85, 115, 136
Communities xii, 34, 41, 43, 63, 72, 76, 85, 88, 106, 118, 128, 134, 136–137, 146, 160, 164
Como 15, 96, 141, 142–145, 146–152, 153–157, 162, 165
Comparative study 58, 64, 77, 162, 164, 166
Concentric pattern 7, 71, 150, 153, 156
Configuration 11, 18, 35, 37, 42–43, 56, 61, 65, 68, 88, 117, 139, 147, 156, 170
Congruence 28
Connectivity 116, 135
Consequent streets 96, 98, 100, 143
Conservation 3, 14–15, 33, 40, 42, 53, 55–56, 61, 68, 89–90, 92–93, 108–109, 112, 118, 139, 155, 159, 163, 165, 168
Conzen, M.R.G. 4, 20–21, 23, 24, 37, 50, 90–91, 98, 112, 139, 157, 170
Conzenian School 21, 24, 35, 38–39, 90, 156, 161, 165
Core-periphery pattern 8, 17, 25
Courtyard 100, 102–107, 110–111, 113, 143, 147–148
Creative class 7, 72; destruction 62, 85; tourism 158
Critical consciousness 21, 57, 61; regionalism 91, 93, 113–114
Culs-de-sac 98, 100, 147

Cultural-creative city 5, 152
Cultural: authenticity 92, 105, 111–112; degradation 5, 72; disruption 74; geography 3, 12, 20, 25, 37, 47, 90; heritage 5, 91, 93, 108–109, 132, 136, 155, 168; identity 96, 113, 140, 153; landscape 1, 19, 21, 36, 47, 50, 161, 163; marker 105; resource 36, 89, 171; strategies 118; tourism i, 105, 142, 152, 154; tradition 4, 85, 157; turn 44, 57
Cup Village 134

Danzig 20
Danwei 14, 105–113, 162–163
Degradation 62, 69, 72, 84, 88
Denarau Island 13–14, 70, 75–89
Density 62, 64, 107, 129, 133, 145, 156, 164
DepthmapX 64
Destructive creation 62
Developers 8, 72, 75, 77, 89, 108, 110, 125, 135–136, 138, 172
Discipline ii, xi, 10, 12–13, 18, 20, 25, 33, 35, 37–38, 40, 47, 67, 90, 160–161, 165
Disneyfied 111
Distinctiveness 6–7, 42, 155
Districts 32, 38, 43, 49, 52, 87, 91–92, 104, 110, 117, 124–126, 132, 140, 143, 150, 152, 164

Economy 3, 19, 25–26, 28, 32, 39, 41, 44, 46, 54, 84–85, 89, 104, 106, 108, 114, 117–118, 128, 130, 132, 134, 136–137, 154, 166
Ecosystem 19, 31–32, 39, 41, 69–70, 84, 153
Edge 7, 48–49, 81, 96, 111, 119, 123–124, 126, 131, 143, 149
Elements 5, 17–18, 22, 24, 30, 32, 34–36, 44, 46–47, 49, 53, 61, 63–67, 74, 78, 87, 91, 93, 112, 114, 116, 143, 145, 150, 152; anchor 109; built 3, 12, 76; physical 4, 20, 41, 157; structural 17, urban form 17, 20, 33, 56–60, 170
Ellis curve 52
Elongation 8, 98
Engazement 94
Entertainment 2–4, 6, 11, 15, 43, 45, 69, 83, 115, 132, 153
Environment-behavior studies 27–29

Environmental: capital 167; characteristics 28, 82–84; impacts 2, 9, 29, 40, 65, 73, 83; justice 29; movement 31; problem 32, 48, 51
Environmentalism 31
Environment psychology 27
Epicenter 169
Eventification 170
Events 14, 33, 45, 57, 59, 64, 118, 125, 132–135, 138, 164, 166
Event tourism 118, 132–137
Evolutionary analysis 14, 111, 117; growth 27, 88, 115; model 7–8, 71–73, 86; process i, xii, 11, 21, 24, 38, 46, 50, 75, 91, 139–140, 146, 155, 162, 169
Ex Situ 61
Exogenous forces 57, 60, 67, 139
Expressive intelligibility 45

Fabrique urbaine 2
Fatehpur Sikri (the City of Victory) 60
Feng Shui 98, 99–100, 105, 107, 167
Field xi, 2, 4–5, 10, 15, 144–145, 159, 166
Fiji 13–14, 68–89, 161–162
Fixation line 24, 96–97, 149–150, 156
Florence 30
Foucault 1, 43
Fortification 1–2, 14, 94, 98, 100, 141, 143, 157
Fringe belt 15, 21, 23–24, 42, 96, 102, 113, 139, 141–145, 148–157, 160–161, 165, 172; inner 149–150, 154; middle 150; outer 150
Fritz, J. 19–20
Frontier 137, 142

Garden 2, 76, 142, 149
Gates 95, 98–100, 143, 154
Genius loci 42, 44–45, 93, 113, 139, 162, 167
Gentrification 1, 15, 26, 118–119, 125, 136, 164
Geography i, xi, 3–7, 10–11, 17, 19–20, 25, 37, 39, 44, 47, 49, 54, 65, 67, 88, 91, 159–161, 171
Geographers xii, 4, 12–13, 19–20, 46–47, 90, 159–160
Geographic information systems (GIS) 18, 37, 56–57
Geomorphology 42
Globalization 5, 43–44, 63, 155, 168

Greek 4, 17
Green belt 47–48, 110; space 3, 11, 42–43, 170
Greenwich Village 50
Grid 55, 60, 97–98, 130–131, 141, 143, 145, 147–148
Ground plan 19, 21–22, 40, 90–91, 146, 170

Habitus 166–167, 171
Hassinger, H. 20
Heritage 5, 14, 26, 39–40, 50, 55, 58, 61, 68, 87–88, 90–94, 104–105, 107–116, 119, 129, 132–134, 136–137, 141–142, 146, 152–155, 159, 162–165, 168
Hinterland 32, 51, 142
Historical development xii, 10, 15, 17–41, 45–47, 91–92, 161; events 57; expressiveness 20–21, 50, 91, 139, 146, 171
Historicity 21, 50, 66, 90, 139–140, 157, 169, 171
Historico-geographical approach xii, 10, 15, 18, 21, 37, 57, 65, 68, 112, 157, 160, 165
Homogeneity 23, 125, 160
Homologous 47
Hong Kong xii, 9, 36, 61, 94
Hybridization 6, 38, 137, 159, 168
Hypometamorphic plots 100, 147, 167

In Situ 9, 61
Induction spots 154
Image 3, 18, 29, 36, 44–45, 49, 64, 76, 92, 109–110, 115, 118, 132, 137, 167
Industrialization 1, 3, 11, 14–15, 34, 54, 92, 105–107, 109, 115–119, 121, 125–126, 128–130, 134–137, 144–145, 148, 150–156, 160, 163
Inheritance 50
Inner city 53, 108–109, 128–129, 153, 169
Interconnectedness 65
International Seminar on Urban Form (ISUF) xi, 37
Intra-urban scale 20, 140–141
Isomorphic form 1, 44

Jersey City 7, 49

Kropf, K. 1, 18, 20, 146

Lake Como 15, 142–143, 146, 153–154, 157, 165
Lakefront 144, 146, 151, 153–155
Land use 3, 5–6, 8, 24–25, 35–36, 40, 42, 47–48, 51–53, 56–57, 64, 69–73, 75–76, 81, 83, 87, 90, 115, 119, 122, 124, 129, 131, 135–136, 141, 144–145, 149–151, 155–159, 161, 164
Landmark 9, 14, 40, 49, 61–62, 92, 109, 134, 168
Landscape i, xi, 1, 4, 6, 8–9, 19, 25, 28, 32, 35, 37–38, 43–44, 47, 50, 53, 55, 60, 62, 72, 75, 82, 89, 94, 115–118, 129, 135–136, 138–139, 145, 149, 156, 158, 160–161, 167, 169–170; alternation 35, 155; architecture xi, 2, 5, 36; cultural 1, 19, 21, 36, 47, 50, 161; natural 5, 71, 76, 79, 84, 170; tourism 6–7, 15, 45, 65–67, 113, 128, 168, 171; urban 3–4, 6, 10, 18–20, 26, 28, 40, 44, 49, 67, 90–91, 105, 108, 112–113, 137, 139, 141–142, 155, 160, 163–165, 168, 171
Legibility 49
Legislation 14, 70, 75, 77, 83, 87, 89, 162
Legerdemain of tourism 93
Leicester Square 43
Leisure 1, 3, 14–15, 34, 41, 42–43, 45, 48, 50–51, 55, 59, 69, 81, 109, 116, 122, 124, 128–129, 133, 135–137, 152–153, 158, 164, 167, 169
Lines 10–11, 15, 46, 58, 61–63, 64–68, 96–98, 104, 143, 152, 161–162
Localities 16, 137
Locational interdependence school 8, 25
Localization of leisure 158
London 35, 64, 115
Longue durée 166, 168, 171
Lynch, K. 49

Macau xii, 55, 62
Medieval 1, 23, 93, 96, 142–143, 147–148, 150, 156
Mapping 20, 29, 36, 56, 65, 75–76, 112, 119
Master plan 13, 74–76, 79–81, 84, 86–87, 162
Memory 3, 33, 45, 63, 94, 96, 109, 167
Mental map 35
Metamorphic plots 99, 147, 167
Metrological analysis 23

Mobility 3, 4, 12, 43, 63, 65, 67, 73, 116, 171
Modernist movement 33–34
Monoculture 63, 136
Monuments 2, 33–34, 40, 61, 67, 134, 165, 169
Morph 4, 57
Morphogenesis 1, 44, 47, 90, 171
Morphogenetic method xii, 4, 19–20, 91
Morphological: analysis 3, 5, 11, 24, 26, 28, 38, 41, 52–53, 57, 64, 70, 75, 76–86, 117, 135, 157, 161, 171; process i, 10, 57, 116, 119, 145, 165; regionalization 19; research i, xii, 12, 40, 163, 170; structure 9, 121, 152, 156; transformation i, xiii, 13, 75
Movement economy 42
Muratori, S. 4, 29, 37, 48, 170
Muratorian School 30, 38–39, 49, 90, 161

Neighborhoods 1, 12, 26, 50, 58, 108, 149–150, 154
Neo-rationalism 32–34
Neo-Ricardian school 26
Networked cities 155
Nodes 49, 62–63, 83, 169
Non-lieux 42, 45

Objectivation 50, 139
Organism 47–48
Originality 23, 30, 33, 45, 52, 61, 67, 79, 88, 95, 98, 109–110, 113, 122, 129, 131, 140, 144–145, 150, 164
Orthomorphic plots 100, 147, 167
Otherness 85
Overtourism 54, 63

Palimpsest 2, 161
Parallax 166–167, 171
Paris 2, 11, 62–63, 140, 152, 166–167
Paths 49, 56, 62, 146, 154
Personnalité 50
Phantasmagorias 6
Piecemeal approach 69, 98
Pilgrimage 8, 94
Pingyao 14, 92, 95–113, 161, 163, 167
Placelessness xii, 137
Placemaking 11–12, 66, 113, 155
Planners xii, 12–13, 26–27, 29, 40, 45, 50, 67, 87, 94, 105, 109, 111, 118, 137, 159, 172
Plan analysis 8, 19–24, 41, 72, 90; units 21, 23, 122–123, 125, 129–131

Playfulness 169
Plots xii, 2, 4, 17, 21, 23–24, 59–60, 65, 90, 96, 99–100, 125, 129–131, 141–142, 145–148, 156, 162, 165, 169–170
Points 1, 21, 26, 33, 46, 49, 61–66, 68, 147, 162
Political economy 19, 24–27, 28, 39, 41, 130
Polycentricity 62, 169
Porto 23, 35
Postindustrial 3, 91, 115–116
Postmodernism 6, 26, 42, 45, 160, 172
Power geometry 117
Precinct 1, 77, 87, 112, 119, 124, 152–153, 156

Quai 166–167

Recreational activities 1, 3, 42, 51, 76–77, 136
Recreational Belts Around Metropolis (ReBAM) 55
Recreational Business District (RBD) 7–8, 51, 53, 71, 73, 82, 86, 92
Refurbishment 136, 143
Regionalization 5, 91, 171
Remote sensing 36
Resort morphology 7, 47, 71–73
Resource Management Act (RMA) 135
Revitalization 5, 60, 92, 115, 117, 124, 135, 137, 164, 168
Roman 142–143, 146, 148
Rugby 14, 79, 80–81, 86, 125, 132–133, 164

Sauer, C. 19–20, 37, 47, 145, 160
Schlüter, O. 4, 19, 20
Seaside resort 7–8, 47, 50, 68, 69
Shoreline 70, 116, 143
Smart city 11
Social ecology 18, 51; fabric 50
Sociocultural i, xi, 9, 11, 18, 24–25, 41, 44, 46, 54–55, 65, 68, 84–86, 93, 112, 124, 127, 139, 145, 162, 166–167, 171
Space: defensible 50; flows 153; morphology studies 34–37; open 20, 23, 29–30, 40, 45, 48–49, 52, 56, 58, 60, 76, 81, 96, 127, 132, 135, 147; public 14, 31, 58, 64, 112, 114, 127, 132, 134–135, 137, 152; production 117, 136; syntax 35, 37, 56–57, 159; urban 1–2, 5–6, 12, 33–34, 115, 118, 152, 155–156, 169

Spatial: analytical approach 18, 56, 65; configuration 11, 18, 35, 56, 61, 88; integration 169; structure 2, 4, 14, 67, 74, 90, 117, 140, 142, 153, 157–158, 171; spirit 44, 111; thematization 152
Spatial-structure-resident triad 141
Spatial-temporal development 3
Spontaneous consciousness 57, 60
Squares 4, 11, 34, 147
Strategic alliance 62
Stratification 71, 117, 157
Streets xii, 2, 4–5, 9, 17, 20–21, 23, 34, 40, 50, 58–59, 90–92, 95–100, 104, 109, 125, 129–131, 141–145, 146–150, 152, 155, 162, 165, 168–169
Supermodernity 45–46
Surveillance 50, 82
Sustainability 88–89, 116, 119, 171
Synchronic cuts 10
Synergy 62, 164

Territorial Local Authority (TLA) 13, 72, 162
Theatres of memory 94
Themed backgrounds 115
Time-space compression 43
Tokyo 115
Tortoise city 95
Topological attributes 18, 33, 56
Tourism Area Life Cycle(TALC) 52, 72
Tourism Business District (TBD) 52–54, 73, 125
Tourism zone 110
Tourist bubbles 153
Tourist consumption ii, 3, 6, 9, 42, 45, 52, 92, 117, 135, 155, 158, 169
Tourist Cultural District 92
Tourist-historic city 5, 53, 92, 139–141, 152, 154–155, 159, 165, 169
Touristification 8–11
Town plan analysis 19–24
Townscape 18, 21, 30, 42, 44, 48, 50
Transnationalism 65
Transport 1, 8, 28–29, 35–36, 53, 55–56, 62, 69, 73, 81, 83, 88, 106, 115, 120–121, 126–131, 140, 150, 154, 171
Tripartite division 21
Typological process 10, 29–30, 33, 35, 37, 156
Typo-morphological analysis 18, 65

Urban: core 92–96, 102, 104, 106–110, 113, 119, 144, 145,

147–148, 155–157, 163; fabric 2,
17, 30, 34, 39, 54, 56, 61, 65, 67,
116, 129, 148, 155, 171; fallow 60,
23; form xi, xii, 1, 6, 8, 10, 12–21,
24–30, 33–37, 41, 45–46, 48–49,
51–59, 60, 62, 65–68, 91–92, 112,
125, 141, 154–162, 165–166,
170–171; fortunes 3; fragmentation
6, 55; morphology xi–xiii, 1–2, 4–5,
8–10, 12, 17–20, 31, 33, 36, 37–38,
40–41, 46, 55–56, 64–67, 90–93,
111, 113, 116–117, 140, 146,
155, 158–162, 164–166, 170–171;
planning xi, 1–2, 5, 21, 26, 31,
36, 40, 48–49, 67, 75, 104–105,
108–109, 113, 115, 117, 125–127,
136; regeneration 45, 65, 94, 117;
sprawl 48, 51; tissue 18, 20, 43, 46,
48, 50, 56–58, 65, 67, 140, 155,
165, 169–170; tourism i, xii, 12, 14,
63, 91–92, 94, 104, 110–114, 125,
153, 156, 161–162
Urbanism 2, 18, 32, 48
Urbanization 9, 14–15, 28, 32, 51–52,
55, 57, 59, 63, 70, 72, 87–88, 92,
112, 117, 141, 154–155

Vacationscape xi, 6, 44, 48, 50–51, 160
Venice 9, 48, 63, 81, 140
Vienna 9, 20
Virtual reality 37

Walled city 14, 92, 95–96, 98–100, 102,
105–107, 110–113, 146–148, 162
Waterfront xii, 1, 11–12, 14–15, 61,
79, 83, 115–138, 143, 153, 158,
161–164, 169
Wellington 14, 116, 119–138, 163–164
Wholeness 17, 23, 49
World Heritage Sites 90, 108–109

Zócalo 59
Zonation 7, 71, 73, 87
Zone 7, 33, 36, 42, 48, 71, 77, 91, 94,
96, 99, 113, 145, 153, 160; boundary
14; buffer 124; carousal 43;
coastal 89; concentric 11, 25, 68;
fortification 98; functional 37, 140,
161; intramural 111, 114; peri-
urban 48; recreational 153–154,
165; residential 72, 85, 110, 157;
trading 8; transition 92, 105
Zoning 53, 69, 76–77, 87

Printed in the United States
by Baker & Taylor Publisher Services